Limiting Exchange Rate Flexibility

Limiting Exchange Rate Flexibility

The European Monetary System

Francesco Giavazzi and
Alberto Giovannini

The MIT Press
Cambridge, Massachusetts
London, England

Library of Congress Cataloging-in-Publication Data

Giavazzi, Francesco.
  Limiting exchange rate flexibility.

  Includes bibliographies and index.
  1. Foreign exchange administration—Europe.
2. Money—Europe. 3. International finance.
I. Giovannini, Alberto. II. Title.
HG3942.G53 1989   332.4'56904   88-13682
ISBN 0-262-07116-9

Contents

Preface

In this book we bring together the results from a joint research project on the European Monetary System which began in the spring of 1984. Chapters 4, 5, and 6 contain material that has appeared in earlier versions in a number of journals, including *Economica*, *Economic Policy*, *Giornale degli Economisti*, and *Weltwirtschaftliches Archiv*, and in conference volumes, including a special issue of *Thema* (Torino: Istituto Bancario San Paolo, 1985), *Global Macroeconomics* (New York: Macmillan, 1987), and *The European Monetary System*) Cambridge, UK: Cambridge University Press, 1988). The balance of these chapters, and the remaining five chapters, contain previously unpublished work.

Over the years this project has been financed by a number of institutions whose support we wish to acknowledge: the Centre for Economic Policy Research; the Consiglio Nazionale delle Ricerche; the Commission of the European Communities; the Istituto Bancario San Paolo di Torino; and the Olin Foundation. The National Bureau of Economic Research has provided a congenial and efficient research environment in the last stages of the project.

Among the people who offered comments and advice, we would like to thank, without implicating, Giorgio Basevi, Susan Collins, Rudiger Dornbusch (who encouraged us to begin this project), Jeffrey Frankel, Maurice Obstfeld, and Marco Pagano. We also obtained helpful criticism from discussants at various conferences where we presented our work in progress, including David Begg, William Branson, Louka Katseli, Richard Marston, Luigi Spaventa, David Vines, and Charles Wyplosz.

Sabine Miltner and Alberto Antonini provided us with tireless and competent research assistance. Donna Zerwitz and Patrizia Cavazzini helped us with the editorial work.

—Cambridge, Mass., June 1988

Introduction

In this book we examine the European Monetary System, an arrangement among European central banks to limit fluctuations of their respective currency values. We have made an effort to integrate the empirical analysis with a rather detailed account of the relevant institutions and historical experience. In our opinion this experiment has paid off. We were able to identify some important empirical regularities that can be the basis for further theoretical and empirical research.[1] Furthermore, our work may help those wishing to assess the European Monetary System as an experiment that could be copied outside of Europe.

In its first few years the European Monetary System was regarded by many observers as an example of international monetary cooperation at the European level. An alternative view, probably best represented by the work of Rogoff (1985a), stressed the crucial role of capital controls imposed by "weak currency" countries for the sake of gaining limited monetary autonomy between parity realignments. In our research we have argued—despite initial skepticism from some of our colleagues—that the most useful model of the European Monetary System has West Germany in the "driver's seat" and the other countries simply pegging their currencies to the Deutsche mark. Indeed, the main conclusion of this book is the basic similarity between the European Monetary System and previous experiences of limited exchange rate flexibility, like the Bretton Woods regime. We explore

---

1 Comparisons of alternative exchange rate regimes, a major area of research in the late 1960s and early 1970s, have almost disappeared from the literature during the second half of the 1970s. Theoretical interest in exchange rate regimes has been recently revived. See for example Helpman and Razin (1979, 1982, 1984), Helpman (1981), and Hsieh (1984). For a survey of the issues, see Obstfeld (1985) and Krugman (1989).

the various aspects of this asymmetric arrangement and the reasons why member countries might desire to belong to it.

In chapter 1 we discuss the motivations of European nations to limit intra-European exchange rate fluctuations, from the perspective of both the interwar and the second postwar experience. The effects of intra-European exchange rate fluctuations on Europe's agricultural markets are a good example of the costs attached to such fluctuations. The most glaring exception to the principle of free trade within the European Economic Community, the system of Monetary Compensatory Amounts in agriculture, was directly motivated by the effects of intra-European exchange rate changes on the prices of agricultural products.

In chapter 2 we describe the institutional features of the EMS; we concentrate on the rules for foreign exchange market intervention and balance of payments financing, and compare them with the IMF rules. We also ask to what extent foreign exchange market intervention rules can induce a symmetric monetary system. In chapter 3 we study the evidence on exchange rates. We first ask whether the European Monetary System has had any impact on bilateral European exchange rates, both nominal and real. Next we try to determine whether, given the fluctuations of the dollar and the yen, the decision to join the European Monetary System has indeed resulted in a stabilization of external competitiveness for all member countries. We argue that one motivation for West Germany to join the European Monetary System could have been its desire to stabilize its overall competitiveness by limiting the effects of dollar fluctuations on the competitiveness of the mark relative to other European currencies.

In chapter 4 we analyze some direct empirical evidence on the question of asymmetry of European monetary policies. We find strong indications that the European Monetary System resembles a "greater Deutsche mark area," although the use of capital controls by countries such as Italy and France complicates the interpretation of the data. In chapter 5 we study the disinflation of the 1980s. In particular, we analyze the motivation that countries other than West Germany might have had to join the system: "importing" the antinflationary reputation of the Bundesbank and inducing a downward adjustment of inflationary expectations at home, thus easing the disinflationary process. Chapters 6 and 7 are devoted to an analysis of the effects of capital controls. Chapter 6 attempts to quantify the effects of capital controls on international portfolio diversification and on the observed asymmetric fluctuations of European exchange rates vis-à-vis the dollar. Chapter 7 describes the structure of capital controls in European countries, empirically analyzes the effects of controls on interest rates, and offers an equilibrium model of the effects of existing trade credits regulations on interest rate differentials and capital flows.

Finally, in chapter 8 we try to use our findings to address a number of policy questions and focus in particular on the relevance of the experience of the European Monetary System for the rest of the world.

Limiting Exchange Rate Flexibility

1   The Quest for Exchange Stability in Europe

1.1 Introduction

The European Monetary System (EMS) is simply a recent step in the historical quest for exchange rate stability in Europe. Europeans dislike exchange rate fluctuations for three reasons. First, they all live in relatively open countries. Second, many of them hold the floating rates of the 1920s and 1930s responsible for the ensuing collapse of national economies and of the international trading and monetary systems. Third, postwar European institutions—particularly the common agricultural market—depend for their survival on exchange rate stability.

Analyzing the EMS without considering why Europeans are averse to exchange rate fluctuations would not give a clear picture of the system. The EMS is just one element of a much richer set of agreements among European countries in the trade, industrial, and agricultural areas. These agreements rest on exchange rate stability, and thus lend credibility to intra-European exchange rate targets. Leaving the EMS is perceived in Europe as a move that would endanger other spheres of cooperation as well.

In the next section we illustrate why Europeans are averse to exchange rate fluctuations. Section 1.2.1 discusses openness and the effects of the interwar experience on international monetary institutions in the second postwar period. Section 1.2.2 describes the Treaty of Rome and the consequences of the decision to create the European Economic Community (EEC). Section 1.2.3 illustrates the working of the Europe's common agricultural market: We show the effects of intra-European exchange rate fluctuations on food prices and on the EEC budget, and we explain why intra-European parity realignments resulted in the suspension of free trade in agricultural products across Europe.

In order to understand the motivations that brought European policy makers to set up the EMS, it is also necessary to note the political and intellectual climate in which such a decision took shape, characterized by the controversy over the collapse of Bretton Woods and the disappointing experiments of the mid-1970s aimed at narrowing intraEuropean exchange rate margins. Thus in section 1.3 we first look back at the European experience during Bretton Woods, explaining why the expectation of the collapse of the system prompted a sequence of initiatives aimed at monetary unification. We then review the European exchange rate initiatives of the 1970s up to the creation of the EMS.

1.2 Why Are Europeans Averse to Exchange Rate Fluctuations?

1.2.1 Openness and the Legacy of the Interwar Experience

When Belgium, France, Germany, Italy, Luxembourg, and the Netherlands formed the European Economic Community in the late 1950s, the output of the Community was half that of the United States (see table 1.1a). By 1988 the Community had grown from 6 to 12 members and was almost identical in total output to the United States and twice as large as Japan. The EEC is also about as open as the United States and Japan: In 1985 the share of imports in GDP was 12 percent in the EEC, 10 percent in the U.S., and 11 percent in Japan. These data suggest that fluctuations of the ECU[1] relative to the dollar and the yen should not be a particular source of concern in Europe, at least no more so than fluctuations of the dollar for the U.S. economy. Europe, though, is not a common currency area.

While the EEC is a relatively closed economy, its individual countries are all very open. As shown in table 1.1b, imports as a share of GDP are as high as 75 percent in Belgium, 60 percent in the Netherlands, and 25 percent on average in the four largest countries—France, Germany, Italy, and the United Kingdom. The difference between the

---

1 The (European Currency Unit) is a currency basket that serves as the numeraire in the EEC. One ECU is equal to the sum of fixed amounts of nine Community currencies. We discuss the properties of the ECU in chapter 2.

Table 1.1a
The relative size of Europe

	Population (million) (1987)	Gross domestic product (billion of current U.S. $)	
		(1960)	(1987)
EC6	–	270.0	–
EC12	323	–	4,400
United States	244	513.5	4,500
Japan	122	44.0	2,300

Source: *European Economy*, no. 34, November 1987.

Table 1.1b
Openness: imports as a share of GDP

	(1960)	(1987)
Belgium	39.3	75.6
Ireland	37.2	60.0
Netherlands	45.9	59.3
Denmark	33.4	36.7
Germany	16.2	28.5
United Kingdom	22.4	28.2
France	12.9	25.0
Italy	12.5	23.4
EC12	10.4	12.3
United States	4.4	10.1
Japan	11.0	11.4

Source: *European Economy*, no. 34, November 1987.

degree of openness of individual countries and that of the Community as a whole is explained by intra-Community trade: EEC countries are highly integrated, and over half of their total trade is with each other. As can be seen in table , trade integration is much higher now than it was in the 1950s, partly because of the customs' union.[2] Thus if Europeans are concerned about exchange rate fluctuations, they should worry most about fluctuations in *intra-Community* exchange rates.

---

2 For a review of empirical estimates of the trade-creation effects of the European customs' union see Balassa (1974), Mayes (1978), Winters (1986), and Jaquemin and Sapir (1987).

Table 1.1c
Trade with the 12 EC countries as a share of total trade

	Exports			Imports		
	1958	1970	1986	1958	1970	1986
Denmark	59.4	44.2	46.8	60.0	48.7	47.2
Be-Lux	55.4	75.2	72.9	55.5	66.3	69.9
Netherlands	58.3	72.6	75.7	50.7	63.4	61.0
France	30.9	58.1	57.8	28.3	56.0	64.4
Germany	37.9	49.8	50.9	36.3	51.7	54.2
Italy	34.5	51.7	53.5	30.2	47.5	55.4
UK	21.8	32.7	47.9	21.8	29.4	50.4
EC12	37.2	53.4	57.2	35.2	50.3	57.8

Source: *European Economy*, no. 34, November 1987.

The empirical evidence on the effects of exchange rate fluctuations on economic activity—and thus on whether Europeans *should* worry about intra-Community exchange rate fluctuations—is ambiguous. Fluctuating exchange rates pose problems for an economy, but the problems vary widely depending on the nature of the fluctuations. It is useful to distinguish between short-term exchange rate uncertainty and the persistence of exchange rate fluctuations.

The day-to-day or month-to-month variability of exchange rates may have no trend; empirically it is very hard to reject the hypothesis that such fluctuations have no effect on economic activity. For example, statistical analysis has been unable to establish that the higher volatility experienced under flexible rates has negatively affected international trade.[3]

There is more evidence that long run trends of competitiveness do affect economic activity.[4] (These issues are discussed in chapter 3.) However, one piece of evidence suggests why Europeans may be concerned about fluctuations of intra-Community exchange rates. Estimates of cross-country exchange rate multipliers, reported in table 1.2, show the response, after three quarters, of GDP to a 10 percent depreciation of the nominal exchange rate relative to the EMS countries and to all OECD countries respectively. The responses are obtained from the simulation of large econometric models, holding all other

---

3 For a recent survey of this evidence see Marston (1988).

4 See for example the evidence reported for the U.S. in Branson and Love (1986, 1987).

Table 1.2
Cross-country exchange rate multipliers: impact on GDP of a 10 percent nominal exchange rate depreciation relative to the currencies of:[a]

	All OECD countries	Only OECD countries that are EMS members[b]
Denmark	0.5	0.4
Belgium	0.7	0.6
Netherlands	0.8	0.7
France	0.5	0.4
Germany	0.5	0.4
Italy	0.6	0.5
United Kingdom	0.5	0.4

a. The numbers in the table are percent changes in real GDP after 3 quarters.
b. Belgium, Denmark, France, Germany, Ireland, and Italy.
Sources: for Denmark, Belgium, and Netherlands: EEC, COMET model; for France, Germany, Italy and the U.K.: Brookings model.

policy variables constant. Like all multipliers from large macro models, these numbers should be viewed with caution: The effects of a change in the exchange rate are not independent of the source of the shock that has induced the change in the first place. These multipliers can be interpreted as an average of the correlation between changes in GDP and changes in the exchange rate associated with the shocks during the estimation period. Table 1.2 shows the relative magnitude of the two multipliers for each country. Their similarity tells us that most of the effect of an exchange rate change relative to all OECD countries is accounted for by the exchange rate change relative to the subset of countries also members of the EMS. This is consistent with the view that fluctuations of intra-Community exchange rates have a much larger effect on domestic GDP in member countries than fluctuations vis-à-vis the dollar and the yen.

The quest for exchange rate stability is also deeply rooted in Europe's history. The experience of the 1920s and 1930s, as described by the influential work of Ragnar Nurske, was vivid in European memory after the war:

The post-war history of the French franc up to the end of 1926 affords an instructive example of completely free and uncontrolled exchange rate variations. The dangers of cumulative and self-aggravating movements under a regime of freely fluctuating exchanges are clearly demonstrated by the French experience of 1922–26. Self-aggravating movements [of exchange rates], instead of promoting adjustment in the balance of payments, are apt to intensify any initial disequilibrium, and to produce what may be termed "explosive" conditions of instability. We may recall in particular the example of the French franc in 1924–26.[5]

In the immediate postwar period the wide exchange rate fluctuations of the 1920s were seen as partly responsible for the ensuing collapse of national economies and of the international trading and monetary systems. In the 1920s and 1930s some countries had sought to defend themselves against external shocks through competitive exchange rate depreciations, to the detriment of other countries. They had hoped to export their own unemployment by cheapening the international price of their currencies. The results were chaotic financial conditions, massive unemployment, protectionism, and trade wars that contributed to the rise of fascism. Because of this experience there was a quest for exchange rate stability after the war which led to the Bretton Woods system.

Under the rules of Bretton Woods, member countries agreed to maintain market exchange rates for their currencies within one percent of the declared par value. Until the mid-1950s, however, European currencies were not freely convertible. In the years immediately after the war payments were settled bilaterally. Between 1950 and 1958, settlements were arranged through the European Payments Union. In 1958 most European currencies became convertible.

Convertibility meant that countries allowed nonresidents who earned their currencies as a result of current transactions to convert them into any other currency at exchange rates within the official margins. For transactions involving two European currencies these margins were narrower than those implied by the rules of Bretton Woods: 0.75 percent rather than 1 percent, around each currency's dollar parity. Still, they implied that the maximum excursion of the bilateral exchange rate of any two European currencies could be as large as 3 percent.

1.2.2 The Treaty of Rome

Historical experience and the high degree of integration of European countries lie behind the pronounced European distaste for exchange rate volatility. But in 1957 the Treaty of Rome and the creation of the European Economic Community added two additional motives to the

---

5 Nurske (1944), pp. 117, 118, 211.

list. First, the aim of the Treaty was to set up a common market, free of trade barriers, in which goods, services, labor, and capital would move without hindrance across national boundaries. The Treaty recognized that the customs union required exchange rate stability: "Exchange rates between member countries shall be considered a matter of common concern."[6]

The other important institutional change was the decision to set up a common market for cereals. The common market started working in 1964 and soon became the main activity of the EEC. Ultimately the very survival of the new institution was viewed as dependent on the success of its agricultural policy. But as Europeans soon realized, the common market could only function if intra-Community exchange rates remained stable. The fluctuations allowed under the rules of Bretton Woods, permitting excursions of up to 3 percent between any two currencies, were large enough to create serious problems for the functioning of the common market.

The existence of the EEC was important in shaping Europeans' distaste for exchange rate fluctuations. As time went by, the new institution became further and further entangled with the problems associated with running its common agricultural market. By the mid-1970s, with two-thirds of its total financial resources absorbed by agriculture, the EEC was left with very little room for action in other areas. The problem of how to control expenditure in agriculture became its vital issue.

As we discuss in detail in the next section, the mechanisms of the common market make exchange rate fluctuations exert an independent upward pressure on agricultural prices in Europe. This contributes to the overproduction of food, thus adding to the drain of resources from the EEC budget. For that reason the EEC became a natural advocate of exchange rate stability.

Political scientists describe this phenomenon as an example of the "functional" approach to integration. According to it, the way to control international conflicts and to force cooperation among sovereign nations is to set up international agencies to deal with technical issues extending beyond national borders. The common market for cereals is one example. Once such agencies are created, and cooperation on some specific issue has started, there will be a need to extend that

---

6 "Traité Instituant la Communauté Economique Europeenne," hereafter referred to as the "Treaty of Rome," article 107, par. 1.

cooperation to other related areas of economic policy. The process will continue until the individual states are virtually deprived of their autonomy.[7]

The Treaty of Rome also contains the seeds of a much more ambitious economic integration of Europe. Articles 103 through 108 lay down a set of principles for the conduct of macroeconomic policy in the Community: (1) short-term macroeconomic policy should be considered a matter of common interest and form the subject of mutual consultations; (2) member States should follow policies that will ensure the equilibrium of their balance of payments and maintain confidence in the value of the currency; (3) economic policies should be coordinated to attain the objectives of high employment and price stability; (4) exchange controls should be lifted, along with the liberalization of trade; (5) the exchange rate of each member country should be considered a matter of common interest. Finally, article 108 introduces the possibility of mutual assistance in case of serious balance of payments difficulties. To pursue these obectives, article 105 establishes a permanent body, the Monetary Committee of the European Communities, whose role is to promote the coordination of monetary policy.[8]

Except for the establishment of the Monetary Committee, however, the stated objective of greater coordination in the field of macroeconomic and monetary policy was not accompanied by concrete steps. Until the early 1970s the rules of Bretton Woods constituted the cornerstone of monetary arrangements in Europe: "It was nearly unthinkable to set up in the EEC an independent monetary system that would have left out the dollar and sterling. If the need for monetary cooperation arose, the type of cooperation one naturally thought of was 'Atlantic'—thus including the United States and the United Kingdom—rather than European."[9] The behavior of the Italian government in 1964 is an example of Atlantic cooperation. Faced with a serious balance of payments crisis, Italy avoided a devaluation by

---

7 On the functionalist approach to integration see Haas (1964), and Lindberg (1963). Tsoukalis (1977) offers a review of alternative integration theories and strategies, and of the debate that developed in Europe in the late 1950s.

8 The committee includes two representatives from each country, one appointed by the central bank, the other by the Treasury.

9 van Ypersele (1985). An early voice in favour of closer monetary integration in Europe was Robert Triffin's, whose 1961 book *Gold and the Dollar Crisis* foreshadows the difficulties of the Bretton Woods system and calls for the creation, by stages, of a European monetary union with a common currency.

turning to the United States and the IMF for a loan, without even consulting its European partners.[10]

The 5 percent revaluations of the Deutsche mark and the Dutch guilder in March 1961—the first intra-European parity changes after the signing of the Treaty of Rome—brought the exchange rate question to center stage. The EECs reacted to the parity realignment with a proposal ("The Commission's Action Program for the Second Stage") of concrete steps for the establishment of a monetary union. The Commission made two points. The first, rather general, stated that "the coordination of national economic policies envisaged by the Treaty of Rome would be incomplete, and thus could not work, if similar action was not extended to the monetary domain." In this area, as we have seen, the Treaty previously had been rather vague.

The second point expressed a more immediate preoccupation: the common market for cereals was supposed to become fully operational in 1964, and the rules for setting prices in the common market had just been established. Prices were to be set once a year in a common unit, the "European Unit of Account" (EUA), whose value was expressed in grams of gold and thus was fixed in terms of dollars. From then on, whenever the currency of a member country was revalued or devalued under the rules of Bretton Woods—and thus its gold parity changed—the price of one EUA in terms of that currency would also change. As a result, the price of cereals on agricultural markets in the revaluing and in the devaluing country also would change abruptly. The EEC feared that such disturbances to agricultural markets could jeopardize the working and the very existence of the common market. In its annual report the Monetary Committee wrote, "Progressive integration within the EEC will make devaluations and revaluations increasingly difficult and unlikely. The establishment of a single agricultural market will strengthen this trend." The Commission added: "the task of the Community institutions is now to render internal devaluations or revaluations impossible or unnecessary, instead of merely difficult or unlikely."[11]

---

10 See De Cecco (1969) and Modigliani and La Malfa (1967) for an analysis of the Italian crisis of 1963–64.

11 EEC, *Seventh Report of the Activities of the Monetary Committee*, Brussels (1965), and EEC Commission, *General Report*, (1965), respectively.

The official steps taken by member countries in response to the Commission's report went in the direction of strengthening the Community institutions. The role of the Monetary Committee was extended requiring that "consultations shall take place within the Monetary Committee in respect of any important decision taken by member States in the field of international monetary relations."[12] Three new permanent committees were also created, including the Committee of Governors of the Central Banks of the Member States.

After the revaluations of 1961 intra-Community exchange rates were stable until the end of the decade. Europeans believed that exchange rate stability was no longer in question. They focused on the Bretton Woods margins and how to narrow them. Preoccupation with the width of the margins was justified by the view, held outside the Community, that the working of the Bretton Woods system could be improved by widening the permissible fluctuations of bilateral exchange rates. In its 1964 report on the balance of payments the Joint Economic Committee of the U.S. Congress had recommended that "the United States, in consultation with other countries, should give consideration to broadening the limits of permissible exchange rate variations," and in its 1965 report it had added that "broadening the limits of exchange rate variations could discourage short-term capital outflows, permit greater freedom for monetary policy to promote domestic objectives, and discourage speculation against currencies by increasing risk."[13]

The 1967 devaluation of sterling, which took place only shortly after the United Kingdom had asked to join the EEC, again raised the question of the ability of the common market to survive a realignment of intra-Community exchange rates.[14] General De Gaulle used the devaluation of sterling as an argument to justify his veto of United Kingdom membership. In his press conference of November 1967 he declared that the weak state of sterling "would not allow the country to be part of the solid, interdependent, and assured society in

---

12 Council Decision of May 8, 1964 on "Cooperation Between Member States in the Field of International Monetary Relations."

13 As quoted in Halm (1969) who provides a review of the proposals advanced to improve the working of the Bretton Woods system.

14 Until then, there had been no direct experience with realignments, since the 1961 revaluations of the DM and the Dutch guilder had occurred before agricultural prices were set in a common unit of account.

which the franc, the mark, the lira, the Belgian franc and the florin are brought together."[15]

Ironically, it was France which first tested the ability of the European customs union to survive a parity realignment. On August 8, 1969, the French franc was devalued 12.5 percent. With agricultural prices in the common market unchanged in terms of the EUA, the devaluation would have implied a jump in agricultural prices on the French market. For reasons that are detailed in section 1.2.3.1, this was unacceptable to the French government. The solution was to insulate the French market through the introduction of a system of subsidies and export levies allowing cereal prices to remain unchanged in terms of French francs. Levies on French exports would prevent the rest of Europe from being flooded by French cereals that had become relatively cheaper; subsidies were designed to compensate foreign farmers for the lower price at which they could sell on the French market. Thus free trade, the cornerstone of the EEC, was temporarily suspended as a result of the realignment. The insulation of the French market caused great concern in the Community. According to *Le Monde* (August 13), the devaluation had "buried the common agricultural market."

The solution adopted for the French agricultural market facilitated the revaluation of the DM a few months later. This time, German farmers resisted the reduction in the DM price of their products implied by the revaluation. Once again, the solution was to keep domestic prices in Germany unchanged. To prevent the German market from being overloaded with imports from the rest of Europe, Germany was allowed to impose a tariff on agricultural imports and to grant farmers an export subsidy.

The rising concern that exchange rate fluctuations would jeopardize the working of the customs union and of the common agricultural policy was clearly stated in the 1969 Barre Report.[16] It was the first attempt to formulate a systematic and coherent approach to monetary unification in Europe: "The Commission estimates that a widening of the fluctuation margins for the exchange rates of member countries would pose important problems in the area of the common agricultural policy and in that of trade relations in the Community, and especially that it would compromise the further integration of markets."[17]

---

15 As quoted in Kitzinger (1973).
16 Raymond Barre was then one of the EEC Commissioners.
17 Commission Memorandum to the Council on the Coordination of Economic Policies

1.2.3   The Common Agricultural Market

The Treaty of Rome did not deal explicitly with the problem of Europe's agricultural markets: This was passed to a special conference meeting in Stresa (Italy) a year later. Two major policies emerged from the conference: the commitment to protect Europe's agricultural sector and the decision to create a unified market for agricultural products.[18]

European farmers were protected even before the creation of the EEC, as they are in many industrial countries. The two most widely used methods of protecting the agricultural sector are production subsidies and external tariffs. Production subsidies do not directly affect the level of consumption, but raise domestic production at the expense of imports. The transfer from taxpayers to farmers takes place at a deadweight loss equal to the cost of attracting new resources into the agricultural sector. This was the system used in the United Kingdom before it joined the EEC, under the name of "deficiency payments." The EEC opted instead for a variable-tariff system allowing food prices to be stabilized in the Community. The levy imposed on imports of agricultural products from the rest of the world is equal to the difference between the price fixed in the Community and the world price. In the absence of "lump-sum" transfers that would distribute income from consumers to farmers with no deadweight loss, a production subsidy is in principle superior to a levy: by not affecting consumption, it implies smaller welfare losses. Although this is an important argument against the variable levy, the comparison between the two

---

and Monetary Cooperation within the Community, *Bulletin of the European Communities*, Supplement, March 1968, p.5, our translation.

18 The rationale for Europe's agricultural policy is well documented by the following passage in the 1985 EEC report on the future of the Common Agricultural Policy (CAP): "The European Community is confronted with the question whether it wishes to maintain a substantial number of workers in agriculture. To that question there can only be a positive reply. The need to maintain the social tissue of the rural regions, to conserve the natural environment, and to safeguard the landscape created by two millenia of farming, are reasons which determine the choice of society in favour of a 'Green Europe,' which at the same time protects employment possibilities for those in agriculture and serves the long-term interest of all of Europe's citizens. An agriculture on the model of the United States, with vast spaces of land and few farmers, is neither possible nor desirable in European conditions, in which the basic concept remains the family farm." (Commission of the European Communities, *Perspectives for the Common Agricultural Policy*, July 1985.)

systems is less clear cut if it is costly to raise taxes to finance the subsidies; this introduces distortions elsewhere in the economy.[19]

What has attracted special criticism of the EEC is not so much the particular system chosen to protect farmers as the level at which prices have been fixed in the common internal market.[20] Since the late 1960s the EEC has moved from self-sufficiency to overproduction of most agricultural goods, and its major problem has become how to deal with excess supplies. Table 1.3 shows the degree of self-sufficiency, and the ratio of domestic prices in Europe to world prices, for a few products. Domestic prices are *intervention prices*, that is the price at which the Community guarantees to buy any excess supply, thus effectively putting a floor under the market price. The world price is the *entry price* net of tariff, which is used to determine the variable tariff rate to be applied on imports from the rest of the world. Entry prices are set slightly above intervention prices, so that market prices in Europe fluctuate inside a small band. The excess supply of food thus generated is removed from the market either through purchases by the Community, which then stores the products, or by granting farmers export subsidies equal to the tariff rate, called export restitutions.[21]

---

19 For a welfare comparison of the two systems see Josling (1971).

20 As described in a colorful comment in the *Financial Times* of November 24, 1987, "A camel is a horse designed by a committee. The CAP is EC's camel, though unlike the living variety it is not merely unattractive to look at but requires constant feeding as well."

21 Morris (1980) has computed the welfare cost of protecting farmers comparing the outcome of the CAP with the alternative of free trade in agricultural products. In 1978, for example, the transfer received by European farmers amounted to 1.4 percent of Europe's GDP—a very large number, given that, even including the transfer, agriculture accounts for less than 4 percent of total GDP. The cost of the transfer was 1.8 percent of GDP: 1.5 percent was paid directly by consumers through higher prices; an additional 0.3 percent was paid out of the EEC budget, and thus equally shared by all taxpayers, farmers included. The deadweight loss was estimated at 0.4 percent of Europe's GDP. As far as the EEC budget is concerned, the operation of the price-support mechanism (purchasing, storing and disposing of the stocks of excess production, and subsidising exports) absorbs most of its resources: In the 1985 it accounted for for 70 percent of the total budget. The cost of protection obviously depends on the value attached to the stocks cumulated by the EEC. There are two extreme views: One is that these stocks are temporary surpluses which can be disposed of at Community prices. The other— taken by Morris—is that these stocks have negative value: There is little prospect of ever selling them, and they involve a continuing and increasing storage bill.

Table 1.3
Prices and overproduction in the EEC

Commodity	Ratio of EEC intervention price to world market price[a]		Degree of self-sufficiency in the EEC	
	1976–80	1981–85	1976–80	1981–83
Milk[b]	4.76	n.a.	116	140
Butter	1.43	1.19	116	128
Wheat	1.07–1.40	.92–1.13	111	124
Beef	1.61	1.79	98	103
Sugar	2.04	1.66	119	141

a. The world market price is the EEC entry price net of tariff; where two figures appear, they correspond to the minimum and maximum price offered during the year. The degree of self-sufficiency is the percent ratio of domestic production to domestic consumption.
b. Powdered skim milk.
Sources: EC, *Yearbook of Agricultural Statistics*, various issues and *Annual Report on Agriculture–Agricultural Markets*, various issues. World prices are defined as follows. *Milk*: minimum offer price from third countries. *Wheat*: soft red winter II, import price c.i.f. in Rotterdam. *Beef*: import price c.i.f. in Rotterdam. *Sugar*: import price c.i.f. in London. *Butter*: import price c.i.f. in London of New Zealand butter.

The organization of the common market also has been criticized. However, the Community had to deal with a very special problem: the common agricultural market did not coincide with a common currency area. Food prices had to be set centrally in a unit of account, but in individual countries they had to be quoted in local currencies. It was easy to foresee that exchange rate realignments would mean trouble for the common market. In the next section we explain the effects of exchange rate realignments on the common market and on the EEC budget.

1.2.3.1 The Operation of Monetary Compensatory Amounts
In the common agricultural market, prices are set in a common unit of account, the ECU.[22] When prices are fixed in ECU, exchange rate realignments vis-à-vis the ECU are reflected instantaneously in the domestic-currency price of agricultural products. Input prices in the agricultural sector, however, do not react as fast. Nominal contracts, the cost of changing prices, and their interaction with pricing-to-market

---

22 The unit of account used in the common agricultural market was the EUA until 1978, and became the ECU at the start of the EMS.

introduce lags in the response of input prices to exchange rate changes. These differences in the response of input and output prices to a change in the exchange rate have always worried European governments. The common solution, illustrated by the devaluation of the French franc in 1969, has been the insulation of domestic agricultural markets from the effects of changes in nominal exchange rates. This solution was the opposite of instantaneous pass-through. After a realignment the *domestic*-currency price of agricultural products in the various countries is kept unchanged; the common ECU price is converted using the pre-realignment exchange rate instead of the new one. Because this system introduces a potential for arbitrage, it is supplemented by border levies and subsidies: the Monetary Compensatory Amounts (MCA). Countries whose currencies have depreciated relative to the ECU raise taxes on agricultural exports (negative MCA); revaluing countries instead pay farmers an export subsidy (positive MCA). Subsidies and tariffs are paid in and out of the EEC budget.[23] In order to understand how this mechanism works, it is instructive to go through a simple example.[24]

Suppose prices and exchange rates are normalized at 1, so that 1 ECU = 1 DM = 1 lira, and the intervention price for milk is 10 ECU per liter. A realignment occurs, implying a 10 percent appreciation of the Deutsche mark and a 10 percent depreciation of the lira, both relative to the ECU.[25] The intervention price for milk is unaffected by the realignment: Therefore, the price of milk after the realignment should fall to 9 marks in Germany and rise to 11 lire in Italy. However, domestic-currency prices are kept unchanged: After the realignment the price of milk in Germany stays at 10 DM, thus effectively rising from 10 to 11 ECUs; in Italy it stays at 10 lire, thus falling from 10 to 9 ECUs. The EEC eliminates the possibility of arbitrage profits by taxing milk exports from Italy and subsidizing milk exports from Germany. For each liter of milk that a German farmer exports to Italy, he receives 1 ECU (a positive MCA) from the EEC that compensates him for the lower price on the Italian market. Conversely, when an

---

23 MCAs also apply to non EMS-member countries, and to the UK; there are also special provisions for the lira, which fluctuates within a wider band. MCAs for Italy and the UK are variable over time and are recomputed weekly.
24 For a description of the working of MCA see Bundesbank (1984).
25 We thus assume, for simplicity, that the DM and the lira have equal weights in the ECU basket, which is not the case in reality.

Italian farmer ships milk to Germany he is taxed; the tax rate is also equal to 1 ECU (a negative MCA).

MCAs are important in realignment negotiations. The official communiqué that announces a realignment always contains an explicit reference to the problem of MCAs and, in particular, to how long countries should be allowed to keep MCAs on. Since the pass-through of exchange rate changes to agricultural prices is administered by the EEC, the timing of the pass-through is important to realignment negotiations. The communiqué usually sets a date before which an MCA should not be removed, nor agricultural prices adjusted. The minimum interval is usually one year. For example, the communiqués announcing the realignments of March 21, 1983 and April 6, 1986 both contain the following statement: "Notwithstanding other provisions, Member States participating in the exchange rate mechanism of the EMS for whom Monetary Compensatory Amounts are created or modified by these central rate adjustments, will not request changes in the Compensatory Amounts now introduced before the end of the current agricultural price fixing round, and the Commission will not make any proposal to that effect." Since five out of the eight big realignments have taken place in the spring or early summer, and prices in the common market are set annually in the spring, the MCAs introduced at the time of a realignment have remained in place for at least a year.

The elimination of positive and negative MCAs, and thus the pass-through of exchange rate changes to agricultural prices in the "strong-" and "weak-currency" countries, has not been symmetric. Table 1.4 shows the values of MCAs for four countries between 1974 and 1986. The values are always positive for the two countries whose currencies have constantly appreciated relative to the ECU, Germany and the Netherlands; they are negative for France and Italy because the lira and the French franc have constantly depreciated relative to the ECU.

The figure of 12 percent for Germany in 1974 indicates, for example, that agricultural prices in Germany were 12 percent higher than they would have been if the ECU price had been translated into DM at the current market exchange rate.[26] It is interesting to note that positive

---

26 The level of tariffs and subsidies in trade between any two European countries corresponds to the sum of the respective MCAs. Thus, for example, in 1974, a German farmer exporting butter to Italy received a subsidy equal to 28.3 percent of the price—the algebraic sum of Germany's positive MCA plus Italy's negative MCA; if the butter was shipped from the Italy to Germany, a corresponding tax was applied to the price received by the Italian exporter.

Table 1.4
Monetary compensatory amounts: percent divergence between market exchange rates and green rates—a positive MCA indicates that the green rate is undervalued

	Germany	Netherlands	France	Italy
1974/5	12.0	2.7	−13.3	−16.0
1975/6	10.0	2.0	0.0	0.0
1976/7	9.3	1.4	−14.9	−17.0
1977/8	9.3	1.4	−14.9	−17.0
1978/9	10.8	3.3	−10.6	−15.0
1979/80	9.8	1.9	−3.7	−4.0
1980/81	8.8	1.7	0.0	0.0
1981/2	3.2	0.0	0.0	−1.0
1982/3	8.4	5.4	−5.3	−1.4
1983/4	13.0	8.4	−9.5	−5.0
1984/5	7.9[a]	3.5[a]	−4.4	−1.8
	6.8[b]	2.6[b]		
1985/6	2.9[a]	2.9[a]	−1.0	0.0
	1.8[b]	1.8[b]		−7.3[c]

a. Dairy products.
b. All other products.
c. After the July realignment.
Source: EC, Directorate General for Agriculture, European Agricultural Guidance and Guarantee Fund, *Annual Report*, various issues.

MCA for Germany and the Netherlands never disappear.[27] In France and Italy, in contrast, negative MCA are periodically removed through price increases.

The asymmetric adjustment of MCAs is explained by the resistance of farmers in strong-currency countries to nominal price cuts. Downward price rigidity and the farmers' lobby make price cuts very difficult to implement. Negative MCAs, in contrast, are relatively easier to eliminate since they require price increases. As a result, market prices in Germany and the Netherlands are higher, on average, than in the rest of Europe.

For example, between 1979 and 1986 DM prices for dairy products were 10 percent higher on average than they would have been if the

---

27 There is only one occasion, 1981, when the subsidies to the Netherlands were set back to zero.

ECU had been translated into DM at the official exchange rate. Market prices in France and Italy were lower, but only by 5 percent because negative MCAs are eliminated faster. This asymmetry in the response of agricultural prices to nominal exchange rate changes has real effects on agricultural production in the EEC. It encourages production in strong-currency countries and discourages it in weak-currency countries. However, since the bias introduced is not symmetric in the two groups of countries, the system raises average intervention prices and thus encourages overproduction in Europe as a whole.

Milk and dairy products are one example of the bias introduced by the operation of MCAs. The cost of supporting these products accounts for one-third of the total cost of the CAP, and is the largest single item in the EEC budget: 20 percent of the total budget. Table 1.5 shows a breakdown by country of production of milk, and of the cost of supporting prices in this sector. Germany is both the largest producer and the largest recipient of EEC aid. The Netherlands produce as much milk as France, and receive the same share of total aid from the EEC. This is in sharp contrast to the relative size of the agricultural sector in the three countries. In 1984, for example, the value of total output in agriculture was almost twice as large in France as in Germany (40 billion ECUs compared with 28 billion), and almost four times as large in France as in the Netherlands.[28]

1.2.3.2 *Summary of the Effects of Exchange Rate Realignments on the Common Agricultural Market*

The European experience shows how difficult it is to run an international market in which prices are set in a common unit of account, when exchange rates fluctuate. This difficulty is an important motivation of Europeans' aversion to exchange rate fluctuations. To deal with exchange rate realignments the EEC had to set up a system of Monetary Compensatory Amounts that have three serious consequences:

1. MCAs shift production from the weak- to the strong-currency countries and thus have real effects on Europe's agricultural sector.

---

28 The system was reformed in 1984 (see Monetary Committee 1987). The main innovation was the introduction of rules for the automatic dismantling of MCA. It has been argued (see for example Boyd 1987) that the new system may make realignment negotiations more complicated, since German and Dutch farmers now form a strong lobby opposed to EMS realignments.

Table 1.5
Milk and dairy products: production and cost of price-support (1984–5)

	Germany	Netherlands	France
Output of storable milk[a] (share of total EC production)	30%	23%	24%
Cost of supporting the price of milk and dairy-products: purchases, storage, and export refunds (share of total EC costs)	30%	20%	20%

a. (Skimmed and whole powdered milk and condensed milk)
Sources: EEC, *Yearbook of Agricultural Statistics*; EEC, Directorate General for Agriculture, European Agricultural Guidance and Guarantee Fund, *Annual Report*, various issues.

Moreover, since the bias is not symmetric, MCAs encourage overproduction of food in Europe as a whole.

2. MCAs raise the cost of the EEC both by adding to the EEC budget directly and by encouraging overproduction of food.

3. MCAs effectively result in the suspension of free trade in agricultural products across Europe.

1.3 The Bretton Woods Experience and European Exchange Rate Initiatives in the 1970s

1.3.1 Europe under Bretton Woods

In the 1960s discussions of exchange rates in Europe were linked closely to the reform of the international monetary system. European institutions depended for their success on exchange rate stability. At the same time many participants in the Bretton Woods system perceived excessively rigid exchange rates as one of the reasons for its unsatisfactory performance: as we have seen, official proposals for wider exchange rate margins had circulated since 1964. In the debate over the reform of the Bretton Woods system two issues were of particular concern to Europeans: the "confidence problem" and the "redundancy problem," using Mundell's (1969a) terms. Although the two problems are closely related, we discuss them separately, because they were perceived somewhat differently by the two main actors in the EEC, France, and Germany.

1.3.1.1 International Reserve Assets and the Provision of International Liquidity

The confidence problem relates to the ability to exchange one reserve asset for another at a fixed price. It only occurs if there is more than one reserve asset, as in the second postwar period when central banks held reserves in dollars, sterling, and gold. Under Bretton Woods the world was dependent on U.S. deficits for the provision of international liquidity, but the liabilities of the U.S. central bank relative to its gold assets were increasing. Over time official holders of dollars began to fear that the Federal Reserve might not be able to keep the dollar price of gold unchanged. Thus a confidence problem was unavoidable in the Bretton Woods system: If U.S. deficits were eliminated, the world would be deprived of a major source of liquidity, with depressing effects on world trade and economic activity.[29] This dilemma was clearly anticipated by Triffin (1960), and can be traced back to Keynes' failure to win approval for his "bancor" plan at the Bretton Woods conference. Keynes' and Triffin's solution to the confidence problem was to "internationalize" foreign exchange reserves, assigning to the IMF and to a "world money" the task of meeting the liquidity requirements of the world economy.

In the 1960s the confidence problem was intensified by a sequence of U.S. balance of payments deficits that exceeded the world's need for additional reserves; it became a central issue in international monetary discussions.[30] The main discussants were France and the United States: Europeans rarely participated with a common position.[31] The French wanted to find a substitute for the dollar as an international reserve asset, and thus end the special privileges that the United States enjoyed as a reserve currency country. Initially, with Giscard d'Estaing as Finance Minister, the French favored the substitution of an international reserve asset for dollars. After 1966, when Debré took over Giscard's job, the French position hardened. France actively sought

---

29 A solution of course is that gold supplies, net of the stock of gold used to produce goods, increase just enough to meet the higher demand for reserves.

30 An early sign was the "gold crisis" of November 1960. The crisis led to the creation of a "gold pool," established by the United States and seven other countries for the purpose of stabilizing the free-market price of gold in London. The pool operated until March 15, 1968, when interventions were suspended and a two-tier market for gold was established.

31 On the international monetary discussions of the 1960s see Solomon (1977).

an increase in the dollar price of gold to ratify the loss in purchasing power of the dollar and to allow the transition toward a system solidly anchored to gold.[32] The Americans, who had originally tried to defend the status quo, eventually agreed with the proposal to create an international reserve asset, just as the French had turned against it.

The debate over how to solve the confidence problem provided an early argument in favor of monetary unification in Europe. Europeans, and the French in particular, resented the privileged position of the United States and the seigniorage accruing to them from the use of the dollar as an international reserve asset.[33] The argument that a monetary union in Europe would reduce seigniorage was made most forcefully by Giscard d'Estaing (1969):

Apart from the fact that the six Common Market countries may have their own reasons for achieving [a monetary union]—reasons which are linked to the good functioning of the Common Market itself—the present structure of world payments and reserves makes the absence of a single monetary instrument appear an anomaly. Such monetary union would limit the need for international liquidity. Some of the transactions now carried through international liquidities would then be carried through internal western European settlements. I am always impressed by the fact that when one speaks today about the problem of payments, or international monetary problems, Americans speak of the dollar, the British speak of the pound, and Europeans, all Europeans, speak of gold. The reason is not that we have gold mines; of all nations we have been said to have the fewest gold mines. Rather, it is because we desire to have an objective monetary representation of our own. Since we do not find it in either the dollar or the pound, we Europeans compensate by looking for it in gold. This is not a realistic view, however, because the reason for which Europeans are looking to gold is the same that could lead them to try to find a common monetary expression. It is desirable that the international community consider this union as an important means of improving the monetary system.

The agreement to create an international reserve asset that could be used along with gold and the dollar eventually came, but too late to avoid a crisis of confidence. In 1968 the countries belonging to

---

32 The French position on gold was influenced by the views of Rueff, who advocated a doubling of the price of gold. See Rueff (1967).
33 Sebastian (1985) provides an analysis of seigniorage and international monetary interactions.

the Group of Ten agreed to create a new facility based on Special Drawing Rights from the IMF, the purpose of which was "to meet the need, as and when it arises, for a supplement to existing reserve assets."[34] By that time, however, the convertibility of the dollar had been abandoned de facto.

1.3.1.2 The $N - 1$ Problem and the German Quest for Price Stability

In an N-country world, only $N-1$ countries need to peg their exchange rate: If they do, the balance of payments of the Nth country will automatically be in equilibrium. There is a "redundancy" problem: The world has one degree of freedom, in the sense that it has one more policy instrument than it has policy targets. The extra instrument can be assigned to fixing the world price level in terms of a preassigned bundle of goods, or to the price of gold if gold is at the center of the world monetary system. The redundancy problem is closely related to the confidence problem: If there are two reserve assets, dollars and gold, and the United States, the N-th country, freed from the balance of payments constraint, does not pledge to fix the price of gold, the confidence problem will arise. Mundell (1969b) describes the Bretton Woods system as one in which the United States, by fixing the price of gold, set the price level for the entire world: The other countries were left with the option of either pegging the dollar, in which case they lost all monetary autonomy or, if unwilling to accept the U.S. inflation rate, of realigning their exchange rate vis-à-vis the dollar.[35] Thus, to minimize exchange rate realignments, Europe and particularly Germany had to accept the inflation rate autonomously chosen by the United States.

From the first DM crisis of 1956–57,[36] German authorities constantly

---

34 I.M.F., *Annual Report*, 1968.

35 Hendrick Houthakker, who was member of the Council of Economic Advisers at the end of the 1960s, reports that at the time Europeans were ready to neutralize any change of the dollar price of gold, with changes of their currencies' price of gold of the same amount. "I asked him (the official in charge of international monetary affairs at the European Economic Commission) what Europe would do if the dollar were devalued under the rules of Bretton Woods. He stated flatly that all European currencies would be devalued by the same percentage on the same day." (Houthakker 1978, p. 54).

36 In 1955–56 Germany was running a current account surplus and inflation was accelerating: An attempt to slow down economic activity increasing interest rates added to the inflow of reserves through the capital account. The increase in interest rates was soon reversed, but in spite of all efforts to reduce the interest rate differential vis-à-vis foreign countries, and despite a ban on interest payments on deposits by nonresidents, speculative capital inflows accelerated in the anticipation of a DM revaluation. The

faced the choice between achieving their domestic inflation targets and losing monetary autonomy by remaining comitted to fixed exchange rates. Time and again the accumulation of reserves associated with a current account surplus would raise the German money stock: Attempts to sterilize the increase in reserves through a contraction of domestic credit would raise interest rates, thus accelerating the capital inflow and the accumulation of reserves. German authorities oscillated between the view that "the payments deficits of inflation-prone countries ought to be remedied mainly by their own efforts, and without prematurely easing the pressure on them by a DM revaluation," and the view that a revaluation was the only way out of the policy dilemma. The steps that eventually led to the DM revaluation of 1961 help us to understand the German problems during the Bretton Woods years.

In early 1960 the Bundesbank, worried by signs that the economy was moving beyond full employment, had tightened domestic credit: the discount rate was raised and banks' reserve requirements were increased. Capital started to flow in, and the introduction of a ban on the payment of interest to nonresidents again proved insufficient to stop it. Against the advice of the Bundesbank, the government decided not to revalue. The Bundesbank responded by abandoning its failed attempt to tighten monetary policy, admitting that it had "lost control over credit expansion." When the government objected to the turnaround in monetary policy because it endangered price stability, it was left with only one choice: Accept the revaluation. The decision to revalue was explained by Ludwig Erhard, the Economics Minister, on the following grounds: "From the start the federal government recognized the stability of money and prices as the overriding principle of its policy. If it wanted to fulfill this promise it could not hesitate to adopt a decisive measure of this kind."[37]

By the mid-1960s, the view that balance-of-payments disequilibria should be corrected by restrictive policies in the deficit countries was going out of fashion in Germany. In 1964 the German Council of Economic Experts called for a transition to flexible exchange rates:

crisis eventually ended with the devaluation of the French franc (August 2, 1957), and with the coordinated increase in British interest rates and a further reduction in German rates, in September.

37 For an account of the German policy dilemma in the 1960s, see Emminger (1977).

"the only one able to guarantee domestic price stability." The transition to fully flexible rates was seen as the only way to regain control of the domestic money stock. The following characterization of the necessary conditions for the functioning of a fixed exchange rate system illustrates the thinking that led to the end of the Bretton Woods system: "A system of fixed rates can only function so long as the key-currency country, by its domestic stability—that is monetary stability and economic stability in general—enables the other member countries to maintain fixed exchange rates without imposing undue strains on their own domestic stability."[38] The view that by the end of the 1960s the United States had stopped providing the public good of price stability, thus making membership in the Bretton Wood system unattractive, is also echoed by Harry Johnson: "So long as the United States maintained reasonable price stability, it suited the other major countries to live with the international financial dominance of the dollar, and to retain some autonomy of domestic policy on the basis of being able to change their national exchange rates against the dollar if necessary: once the United States became a potent source of world inflation, the question naturally arose of establishing a basis for common action to resist imported inflation."[39] Harry Johnson makes another important point: "The key question for the future is whether the prospect for continuing inflation in the United States is sufficiently strong and sufficiently distastful to European countries to make them willing to adopt a common currency in order to be able to counter American inflation by *harmonized* upward exchange rate flexibility." His argument in favor of monetary unification in Europe was dictated by the fear that an uncoordinated response to the dollar crisis would endanger the working of the EEC.

At the end of the Bretton Woods era the Germans shared the preoccupation expressed by Harry Johnson on the exchange rate question in Europe. On the one hand, a floating exchange rate vis-á-vis the dollar was seen as the condition for domestic price stability. On the other hand, German officials were worried about the disruptive effects on the customs union and on the common agricultural market of large fluctuations of intra-Community exchange rates.[40]

---

38 Emminger (1977).
39 H. Johnson (1973).
40 For an account of the German position see Kloten (1978).

1.3.2 European Exchange Rate Initiatives in the 1970s

With the exception of the DM revaluations in 1961 and 1969, and the French franc devaluation in 1969, intra-EEC exchange rates had been very stable throughout the first fifteen years of the Community. Exchange rate stability had been an important factor in the development of the customs union and of the common agricultural market. The temporary suspension of the common market—introduced to deal with the realignments of 1969—had signaled how difficult it was for the new institution to deal with nominal exchange rate fluctuations. On the eve of the collapse of Bretton Woods, monetary unification in Europe seemed within reach: The prospect of a European Monetary Union was officially discussed at the Hague Summit of EEC Heads of State in 1969, where an agreement was reached on the main principles, leaving to a special committee the task of deciding how to implement the transition.[41] As suggested by Harry Johnson, the acceleration of initiatives toward monetary unification in Europe in 1969–70 was probably motivated by the fear that the revaluation of European currencies vis-à-vis the dollar would be disorderly and would mark the end of the EEC. The active role played by Chancellor Brandt at the Hague Summit—he officially put forward the plan for monetary unification—probably also reflected the special interest of Germany in a *harmonized* European revaluation vis-à-vis the dollar.

The European response to the collapse of Bretton Woods was much less coordinated than had been suggested by the plan for monetary unification. In 1971, with the Smithsonian Agreements, fluctuation bands were widened to 4.5 percent; the new fluctuation bands implied an increase in the maximum excursion of bilateral exchange rates in the EEC from 3 to 9 percent, which was far too large for

---

41 At the Hague summit the six EEC countries agreed on the principle of monetary unification, but expressed divergent opinions on how to implement the transition. Two quite different views emerged. The French wanted the immediate abolition of fluctuation bands, and the transition to irrevocably fixed exchange rates; the Germans thought that precondition for a monetary union was the convergence of macroeconomic policies and performances, and the transfer of powers in the area of economic policy-making to the EEC Commission. The French thought that a clear committment to irrevocably fixed rates would be sufficient to force policy convergence; the Germans thought instead that irrevocably fixed rates were incompatible with decentralized policy-making, and put forth a programme of step-by-step transition toward supranational decision making first, and currency unification later.

the functioning of the common market. Europeans responded by setting up the so-called "snake-in-the-tunnel." The center of the tunnel
was represented by the parity of each currency vis-à-vis the dollar.
Around this axis, bilateral parities within Europe could fluctuate by
2.25 percent, thus reducing to one-half the excursion allowed by the
Smithsonian Agreements. The system lasted only one year, from April
1972 to March 1973: when European central banks stopped defending
the margins vis-à-vis the dollar, the snake left the tunnel and started
to float freely.

This "floating snake" lasted until 1979, but really never reached beyond the group of small countries surrounding Germany. Successive
attempts by France, Italy, and the United Kingdom to stay in the system always failed. The United Kingdom joined the system for less
than two months, from May to June 1972; Italy left in February 1973;
France left in January 1974, except for a brief interval between July
1975 and March 1976.[42] The DM was the only major currency in the
system, surrounded by three EEC "satellites"—the Benelux currencies
and the Danish kroner—and two non-EEC currencies, the Norwegian
and the Swedish kroner.

Thygesen (1979) suggests two reasons why the snake was unable to
keep the major currencies together: the asymmetry of the exchange
rate mechanism and the failure of exchange market intervention rules
to provide credibility to the fluctuation margins. The beginning of
the snake experiment had been accompanied by an important institutional change in Europe. European central banks had agreed to grant
each other unlimited financing for the purpose of intervention. The
new facility that was created, the Very Short Term Financing Facility, was administered by a new institution, the European Monetary
Cooperation Fund. The claims and liabilities among central banks re-
sulting from exchange market intervention were to be settled within
one month. This period, however, was too short to help member
countries get over a foreign exchange crisis. For example, the intervention mechanism proved unable to help Britain overcome the June
1972 crisis which forced it to drop out of the system.[43] The snake had
another drawback: it was based on a bilateral parity grid. Central
banks were required to intervene whenever they reached the bilateral

---

42 For a chronology of the snake see *European Economy*, no. 12, July 1982.
43 See Bank of England *Quarterly Bulletin*, September 1972.

Table 1.6
Germany: nominal and real effective exchange rates (indices: 1980 = 100)[a]

	World		Intra-EEC		
	Nominal	Real (WPI)	Nominal	Real (ULC)	(WPI)
1970	65.8	94.2	64.0	90.1	92.9
1978	95.4	104.0	95.3	98.8	104.2

a. ULC refers to competitiveness measured by relative unit labor costs; WPI refers to competitiveness measured by relative wholesale prices. The weighting scheme used to build the effective exchange rate accounts for competition in third markets.
Source: Banca d'Italia, *Servizio Studi*, own computations.

margin vis-à-vis another currency in the system. In practice this meant that whenever a weak currency hit the margin vis-à-vis the DM, its central bank was expected to intervene. The inability of the financing mechanism to provide sufficient credibility to the committment to defend the margin usually meant that the weak curency had to give up.

1.3.2.1 Concluding Remarks
Looking back at the European Exchange Rate experience in the 1970s, we are led to believe that the fear of a possible damage—to Germany's competitiveness—from an uncoordinated approach to the revaluation of European currencies vis-à-vis the dollar turned out to be well founded. The evolution of the nominal and real effective exchange rates of the DM between the end of Bretton Woods and the start of the EMS also confirmed the German worries of the early 1970s. Table 1.6 shows that the appreciation of the *nominal* effective exchange rate of the DM—both throughout the world and inside the EEC—was accompanied by a corresponding appreciation of the *real* effective exchange rate. This phenomenon is analyzed in greater detail in chapter 3.

The practice of accompanying intra-European exchange rate realignments with the introduction of MCA kept the common agricultural market alive, but the share of the total EEC budget absorbed by agriculture increased from 50 percent in 1965 to 80 percent in 1978.

2   What Is the EMS?

2.1 Introduction

The European Monetary System consists of an agreement among the central banks of the European Community to manage intra-Community exchange rates and to finance exchange market interventions.[1] Thus the exchange rate mechanism of the EMS is only one aspect of the system. Moreover, while only a subset of the EEC countries[2] participate in the exchange rate mechanism, all of them belong to the EMS. For example, the European Currency Unit (ECU), created with the EMS, is a monetary unit based on a basket of *all* EEC currencies (including sterling and the drachma which are not part of the EMS exchange rate mechanism).[3] Therefore the EMS is reminiscent of Bretton Woods, not only because the exchange rate regime incorporated in the two systems is similar—essentially both can be described as "adjustable pegs"—but also because both systems embody provisions and institutions for granting monetary support to member countries.

The Bretton Woods experience, and the proximate causes of its collapse, were vivid in the minds of European policymakers in the late 1970s when the EMS was being designed. Many of the central figures in the EMS negotiations—particularly French president Giscard d'Estaing and Otmar Emminger, president of the Bundesbank—had been an important part of the discussions over the reform of Bret-

---

1 For a description of the rules of the EMS see *European Economy* 12 (July 1982), EEC, Monetary Committee (1986), and Ungerer et al. (1983, 1986). For an "outsider's" view of the EMS, see Cohen (1981).

2 Germany, France, Italy, Belgium, Luxemburg, Denmark, the Netherlands, and Ireland.

3 As of September 1989, the currencies of the two new members of the EEC, Spain and Portugal, will also be included in the ECU basket, whether or not these two countries will decide to join the exchange rate mechanism of the EMS.

ton Woods that had taken place throughout the 1960s. Three weaknesses of the Bretton Woods system were in the minds of the EMS negotiators: (1) the asymmetric working of the system, which freed the United States from subjecting domestic monetary policies to the smooth functioning of the world monetary system, while shifting to other countries the burden of adjustment; (2) the difficulties of coping with a world of increasing capital mobility; and (3) the dramatization of parity realignments, which often motivated their postponement, leading to speculative attacks and to the buildup of large current account imbalances. Each of these weaknesses corresponded to the failure of one of the conditions required for the successful operation of an international monetary system based on a regime of fixed but adjustable parities.

To operate successfully, an adjustable peg needs three conditions (see Williamson 1977): (1) a set of rules governing monetary policy and exchange market interventions that determines whether the system works symmetrically or asymmetrically; (2) provisions for fending off speculative attacks and defending a parity grid; and (3) a set of rules for changing central parities. After an early period in which Bretton Woods worked as a "gold-exchange standard," where the United States pegged the dollar price of gold and the other countries simply pegged their currencies to the dollar, the Bretton Woods system had become a "dollar standard": that is, a system in which the United States would set monetary policy independently, without regard to the price of gold, and the other countries had the option of either passively pegging the exchange rate to the dollar or, if they were unwilling or unable to go along with U.S. monetary policy, of realigning their dollar parity. In this new situation the United States had no direct obligation toward the functioning of the system.

As we discussed in chapter 1, such an asymmetric situation could be attractive to the other members of the system only so long as the United States used its policy independence to provide a public good, price stability. As soon as the United States assigned monetary policy to domestic objectives and stopped providing a nominal anchor, the incentive for belonging to an asymmetric system vanished.

Capital flows were another constant source of concern in the Bretton Woods period. Originally the system had been designed for a world of low capital mobility. It had long been debated whether IMF financing could be used at all to meet the reserve needs associated with international capital flows. Article VI of the IMF Articles of Agreement stated that "a member country may not make use of the Fund's resources to meet a large or sustained outflow of capital, and the Fund may request a member to exercise controls to prevent such use of the resources of the Fund." Exchange controls were viewed as the proper instrument to use to stem speculative attacks. One explanation for this view is that IMF financing was ill-suited to meet a speculative attack. Even the "gold tranche,"[4] which was de facto a fraction of the country's reserves deposited at the IMF, was not readily available to respond to a capital outflow.[5] "Standby Arrangements" had originally been designed to provide a country with a ready-to-use line of credit. The arrangements were usually set up for drawings beyond the gold tranche, but there had been at least two occasions when a standby arrangement was set up for amounts within the gold tranche, simply to speed up the availability of funds. Standby's, however, were subject to conditionality, and were only considered after a review by the IMF of the country's policies and prospects "in relation to the objectives and purposes of the Fund," and accorded "in consideration of the policies and intentions" set forth in a letter by the authorities of the drawing

---

4 Each member country of the Bretton Woods system had to deposit with the IMF a "quota," proportional to its economic size. The quota had to be paid 25 percent in gold, and the remaining 75 percent in the country's own currency. Through this deposit, and in the spirit of convertibility, the country made its own currency available to the other members of the fund to finance their balance of payments needs. The quota was also used to determine the amount and terms of financing that each country could obtain from the Fund. All IMF financing facilities are "swap" facilities: A country in need of foreign exchange purchases the specified amounts of the currencies it needs from the IMF using domestic currency, thereby increasing the IMF holdings of its own currency, over and above the 75 percent of the original quota and decreasing the fund's holdings of the currencies being purchased. At the end of the financing period, the country "repurchases" its own currency, using the same quantities of foreign exchange that it obtained in the first place, thus reestablishing both its own original position vis-à-vis the fund, and the fund's holdings of the other currencies.

5 In the early years of the IMF, drawings from the gold tranche required the preparation by the staff of the Fund of a recommendation to the board; only after this recommendation had been considered at a board meeting, could the required currencies be drawn. The whole process took about a week. Drawings from the gold tranche were speeded up in 1964, when approval no longer required an official meeting of the Board; the actual availability of funds, however, still required approximately three days. (See Horsefield and Lovasy 1969). Drawings from the gold tranche became legally immune from challenge only after the 1969 changes in the IMF Articles of Agreement.

country. The Bretton Woods system was very far from the automatic provision of financing necessary to fend off a speculative attack.[6]

In the Bretton Woods system, parity changes were essentially unilateral actions. While in principle the position of gold as a numeraire allowed any country, including the United States, to devalue relative to the others, the United States was de facto prevented from changing the price of dollars relative to any other currency in the system, while the other countries could unilaterally decide on a parity change. The Articles of Agreement permitted parity changes only to correct a "fundamental disequilibrium," but the Fund's role was often limited to rubber-stamp parity realignments. At the time of the 1949 devaluation of sterling, for example, "the Managing Director of the Fund was informed by the Chancellor of the Exchequer on September 15 that the U.K. government intended to devalue sterling by approximately 30 percent. Formal notification of the proposal to establish a new par value was submitted to the Fund on September 17, and on the afternoon of that day the Executive Board concurred in the proposal." (de Vries 1969). Parity realignments of less than 5 percent did not even require a decision by the Fund, provided that the country taking action had never previously changed its parity. This was the case of the DM revaluation of 1961, for example, which was unilaterally decided by the German government without consulting the Fund.

The experience of the Bretton Woods system thus presented the EMS negotiators with three problems: the design of intervention rules, and thence the choice over the degree of symmetry of the system; the creation of mechanisms and institutions for financing exchange market intervention; and a code of conduct for the realignment of central parities. In the next three sections we discuss how these problems were dealt with in the EMS.

2.2 Intervention Rules

The first step taken by the European Council of Ministers in designing the EMS was the creation of a new monetary unit, the ECU. The ECU is a composite unit of account, made up of a basket of specified amounts of each Community currency, as shown in table 2.1. Since the number of units of each currency in the ECU is fixed, the weights of the various currencies change over time, as intra-European exchange

---

6 For an illustration of the procedures involved in granting a standby arrangement see Gold (1970).

rates fluctuate.[7] This is particularly true of the weights of currencies like the pound, which belong to the ECU but not to the exchange rate mechanism of the EMS. Exchange rate fluctuations thus could move the composition of the ECU far away from the initial set of weights which were based on the economic size of the various countries. To correct this, the units of each currency that make up one ECU are reviewed every five years, or on request, whenever the weight of any currency has changed by more than 25 percent. As table 2.1 shows, an exchange rate devaluation relative to the ECU decreases a currency's weight: The weight of the French franc, for example, was about 20 percent at the start of the system and had reached 16.7 percent before the ECU update in 1984, but returned to 19 percent in 1986.[8] The ECU serves four functions in the EMS. It is a reserve asset and a settlement instrument for transactions among the Community's central banks. This "official" function is similar to that of the SDR in the Bretton Woods system; we discuss it in section 2.3. In addition, the ECU provides a numeraire for the exchange rate mechanism, the basis of the "indicator of divergence" and the unit of account for the intervention operations in the EMS.

EMS intervention rules work as follows: Each Community currency has an *ECU central rate*, expressed as the price of one ECU in terms of that currency. ECU central rates are fixed and are revised only when there is a realignment. The ratio of any two ECU central rates is the *bilateral central rate* of any pair of currencies which together form the *parity grid* of the system. By joining the exchange rate mechanism of the EMS a central bank agrees to keep its market exchange rate vis-à-vis any other currency participating in the mechanism within preassigned margins from the *bilateral central parity*. The parity grid thus is the core of the exchange rate mechanism of the EMS; in this mechanism the ECU is no more than a numeraire. The bilateral margins are set at 2.25 percent on each side of the central parity, so that the width of the fluctuation band for any bilateral rate is 4.5 percent. The lira is allowed to fluctuate in a larger band, 12 percent wide; the

---

7 ECU weights are computed in the following way: let z_i be the *units* of currency i in one ECU. The weight of currency i in the ECU basket is given by $w_i = z_i S_i$, where S_i stands for the price of one ECU in terms of currency i.

8 The ECU was created as part of the EMS agreements on December 5, 1978, by superseding the European Unit of Account. The first revision of weights occured in 1984 when the drachma was introduced into the basket as a result of Greece's accession to the EEC. The next revision is scheduled for 1989; at that time the escudo and the peseta will also be added to the basket.

Table 2.1
Composition of the European currency unit[a]

	National currency units		Weights (percent)			
	(1979)	(1984)	(1979)	(1984)		(1986)
Belgian franc	3.66	3.71	9.3	8.1	8.2	8.4
Danish krone	0.217	0.219	3.1	2.7	2.7	2.8
French franc	1.15	1.31	19.8	16.7	19.0	19.1
Deutsche mark	0.828	0.719	33.0	36.9	32.0	33.3
Irish pound	0.00759	0.00871	1.1	1.0	1.2	1.2
Italian lira	109.0	140.0	9.5	7.9	10.2	9.5
Luxembourg franc	0.14	0.14	0.4	0.3	0.3	0.3
Netherlands guilder	0.286	0.256	10.5	11.3	10.1	10.6
Pound sterling	0.0885	0.0878	13.3	15.1	15.0	13.7
Greek drachma	—	—	—	—	1.3	0.9

a. The table shows the compostion of the ECU-basket in 1979, and the revision that took place in 1984. It also shows the weights of each currency in 1979, in 1984—before and after the revision of the composition of the basket—and in 1986.
Source: Ungerer (1986).

pound and the drachma belong to the ECU basket, and thus have an ECU central rate but do not observe the exchange rate margins.

While a parity grid is in force, each central bank fullfills its obligation not to go beyond the margins by intervening in the foreign exchange market. Intervention is compulsory only when two currencies reach their bilateral margin, that is when the bilateral exchange rate diverges by 2.25 percent from the central parity. This is called *marginal intervention*. Marginal intervention must be carried out by both central banks involved, in the currency at the opposite bilateral limit. Financing for marginal intervention is unbounded: while there are obviously no limits to the purchase of the weaker currency by the central bank that issues the stronger currency, there are also no limits to the sales of the strong currency by the "relatively weaker" central bank. As we illustrate in section 2.3, that is because, for the purpose of marginal intervention, the strong central bank undertakes to grant its weaker partner an unlimited credit line.

The EMS agreements also allow central banks to intervene in buying and selling each other's currencies *intra-marginally*, that is before the outer limits of the bilateral band have been reached. In this case, however, intervention is subject to the approval of the central bank whose currency is being sold or bought. There are no provisions for the automatic financing of intra-marginal intervention. Intervention in non-Community currencies—usually in dollars—is always permitted, and not subject to mutual authorization. The data we report in chapter 4 show that marginal intervention accounts for only a fraction of total intervention. Another significant fraction is represented by intra-marginal intervention and is carried out by the central banks that issue the relatively weaker currencies.

2.2.1 The Divergence Indicator

In addition to the rules for marginal intervention, there is within the EMS (EC Monetary Committee 1986, p. 48, article 3) an indicator which signals the divergence of each currency from its ECU-central rate. When this divergence indicator crosses a threshold, a country is expected to act through "diversified intervention, measures of domestic monetary policy, changes in central parities, or other measures of economic policy." None of these actions is compulsory, however, in contrast to the obligation to intervene arising when a currency reaches a *bilateral* margin.

The indicator was designed to single out the currency diverging from the mean, and to impose upon it the burden of adjustment. In reality, it has played almost no role in the system: As we mentioned earlier, the indicator bears no obligations; moreover, it is ill-designed to single out divergencies from the mean.[9] The value of the indicator of divergence for a currency i at each point in time is

$$a_t^i = \sum_j w_t^j d_t^{j,i} \tag{2.1}$$

where w_t^j is the weight of currency j in the ECU basket, defined in footnote 7, $d_t^{j,i}$ is the deviation of currency j from its central parity vis-à-vis currency i, the sum is over all currencies in the basket, and,

9 For an analysis of the properties of this indicator, see Rey (1982), Salop (1981), Spaventa (1982), and Masera (1987).

by definition, $d^{i,i} = 0$.[10] The threshold of the indicator is set at

$$a_i^* = 0.75(2.25(1 - w_i)) \tag{2.2}$$

that is, 75 percent of the divergence that would be observed if currency i had deviated by the full 2.25 percent margin from *all* other currencies in the system. Therefore, in a situation where the bilateral exchange rates of all other $N-1$ currencies were at the respective central parities, the indicator of divergence would call for action when the ith currency has used only a fraction (75 percent) of its bilateral bands vis-à-vis all other currencies. The indicator thus would seem more restrictive than the obligation to intervene when a currency reaches the bilateral bands. However, since ECU-weights differ across currencies and vary over time, the indicator does not function in the same way for all currencies. Consider the following example, adapted from Salop (1981). Currency A and currency B have reached their bilateral 2.25 percent margin, while their divergence from all other currencies is less than 2.25 percent. From equation (2.1), the value of the divergence indicator for currency A is

$$a_A = 2.25w_B + x_A(1 - w_A - w_B) \tag{2.3}$$

where x is the weighted average of the divergence of currency A from the central parity vis-à-vis third currencies, whose weight in the ECU basket is $(1 - w_A - w_B)$. Using equation (2.1) we can ask for what value of x does currency A reaches its threshold. Let x_A^* indicate the value of x for which $a_A = a_A^*$. From equations (2.1)–(2.3) we know

$$x_A^* = 2.25(0.75 - \frac{0.25w_B}{1 - w_A - w_B}) \tag{2.4}$$

for every value of w_a, x_A^* is a decreasing function of w_B. By symmetry we can compute the required average divergence of currency B from the other currencies of the system that makes that currency's divergence indicator reach its threshold. Using this expression and equation (2.4), we can compute the ratio of the average deviations of these two currencies with respect to the rest of the system that makes

---

10 Adjustments are made for the lira—whose band is wider—and for the currencies that belong to the ECU but are not part of the exchange rate mechanism of the EMS.

the two divergence indicators reach their thresholds

$$\frac{x_A^*}{x_B^*} = \frac{1 - w_B/\alpha}{1 - w_A/\alpha} \tag{2.5}$$

Where $\alpha = 3(1 - w_A - w_B)$. The larger the relative size of country A, the larger the lefthand side of equation (2.5); that is, the larger is the allowed deviation of currency A relative to the other currencies in the system before the two divergence indicators cross their thresholds.

Because currencies' ECU-weights are not equal, the divergence indicator of a currency with a small weight in the ECU can reach the threshold under conditions in which the indicator for a currency with a large weight would not. At the beginning of the EMS the combined weight of the DM and the guilder—two currencies that tend to move very closely together—was 43 percent; this almost ensured that the indicator would never single out Germany and the Netherlands as the divergent countries. The phenomenon is aggravated by the increase over time of the weights of strong currencies, as shown in table 2.1.[11] While applauded by some as an important innovation[12] the indicator of divergence has played no role in the EMS. This has been the result not only of the unattractive features of the indicator, but also of the absence of any real obligation associated with having reached the threshold.

2.3 The Very Short Term Financing Facility

There are three financing facilities in the EMS: the Very Short Term Financing Facility (VSTF); the Short Term Monetary Support (STMS), and the Medium Term Financial Assistance (MTFA). The first two are administered by central banks; the third is administered by the EEC Council of Ministers. The STMS is designed to provide short term

---

11 As Spaventa (1982) shows, two currencies can also reach their bilateral margin before either of the two has reached its threshold of divergence. In the limiting case, a currency with a weight of 50 percent would pull along the whole basket, and could never be pushed to its ECU-margin. Moreover, while two currencies sit at their bilateral margin—without either having reached the threshold—a third currency, though keeping within the bilateral margins vis-à-vis the first two, may reach its threshold. These undesirable features are of course aggravated by the presence in the ECU of currencies that do not belong to the exchange rate mechanism.

12 See, for example, van Ypersele [1985].

Table 2.2
The working of the Very Short Term Financing Facility[a]

Central Bank of Denmark		European Monetary Cooperation Fund		Bundesbank	
Assets	Liabilities	Assets	Liabilities	Assets	Liabilities
−1 (liability with the EMCF) +1 (check Bundesbank)		+1 Denmark	+1 Bundesbank	+1 (deposit with the EMCF)	+1 (check to Central Bank of Denmark)
−1 (foreign exch. mkt. sale of DM)	−1 counterpart of foreign exchange mark. intervention				

a. Transactions above the dotted line correspond to the opening of the credit line by the Bundesbank. Transactions below the line take place when the Danish central bank intervenes in the foreign exchange market.

financing for balance of payments needs due to transitory difficulties; the MTFA is designed to provide longer term financing.

The VSTF is meant to provide credibility to bilateral EMS parities by securing unlimited financing for marginal intervention. It consists of mutual credit lines among the central banks of the system. Since marginal intervention is compulsory, and must be carried out for unlimited amounts by the two central banks whose currencies have reached the bilateral margin, these credit lines are automatic and unlimited.

We describe how the VSTF works, and how marginal intervention affects the money supplies in the two countries whose currencies have reached the bilateral margin, by means of an example illustrated in table 2.2. Consider the case where the DM and the Danish krone have reached their bilateral limit, with the krone in a relatively weaker position. For the purpose of marginal intervention the Danish central bank draws on its credit line with the Bundesbank, typically by writing a check on the Bundesbank. The use of the credit line results in an increase in the liabilities of the Bundesbank and in the assets of the Danish central bank. The transaction is recorded in the accounts of the European Monetary Cooperation Fund (EMCF), which show a liability vis-à-vis the Bundesbank and an asset vis-à-vis the Danish central bank. Thus the transactions produce a monetary expansion in Germany and a monetary contraction in Denmark.[13] The credit lines mature 45 days after the end of the month in which the intervention has taken place, and can be renewed for a further period of three months at the request of the debtor central bank. While the initial credit line is unlimited, renewal is not: it cannot exceed a ceiling equal to the country's quota in the Short Term Monetary Support facility.[14] Beyond the first deadline, financing of marginal intervention thus is no longer unlimited. When the credit falls due, the Danish central bank must repay the Fund in DM at least up to 50 percent of its debt; the rest can be paid back in ECUs.[15] Central banks can also use the credit lines of the VSTF for intramarginal intervention, but in this case access to the VSTF is not automatic: It is subject to the authorization of the central bank whose currency is being drawn.[16] In September 1987, with the Nyborg agreement, the use of the Very Short Term Financing Facility has been extended. Credit lines for marginal intervention have been extended by one month—they now mature 75 days after the end of the month following the one in which the intervention has taken place—and the amount that can be renewed has been increased to twice the country's quota in the STMS.

---

13 There are also a number of minor complications, arising from the fact that the accounts of the fund are kept in ECUs. The interest credited to the two ECU accounts in the fund is computed as the weighted average of domestic money-market rates across Europe, using ECU weights.

14 These quotas are remarkably smaller than the resources European countries can draw on from the IMF—limited to an yearly maximum of 90 percent of each country's quota (except in "special circumstances"). The ratios of the IMF quotas to the quotas in the STMS—computed for 1987, applying an ECU-SDR exchange rate of 1.1196—are: Benelux, 4.431; Denmark, 3.29; France, 3.08; Germany, 3.71; Ireland, 4.10; Italy, 2.998; Netherlands, 4.669, U.K., 4.256.

15 EEC central banks have ECU deposits with the European Monetary Cooperation Fund (created with a deposit by each central bank) of 20 percent of their gold reserves plus 20 percent of their dollar reserves. These ECUs are used primarily as a means of settling debts arising from intervention.

16 Between March 1979 and September 1987, the VSTF had been used to finance intramarginal intervention only in four occasions. See Masera (1987).

2.4 Provisions for Changing Central Parities

One of the weaknesses of the Bretton Woods system had been the
lack of a set of rules for changing central parities: Parity realignments
were dramatized and often delayed, leading to the buildup of large
imbalances. In the end, the decision to change the parity was essentially unilateral; thus there was no check on a country's incentive to
use a parity realignment to gain an advantage at the expense of its
partners. In the snake, parity realignments were essentially unilateral
decisions by Germany and had often resulted in the abandonment
of the system by one or more of its members.[17] EMS realignments
only gradually became collective decisions. The first realignment in
September 1979 largely repeated the snake pattern: One country, Germany, took the initiative of calling a meeting at which it presented a
complete set of new parities. It was then realized that this method
could not work a second time, as the number of parties around the
table and their relative importance were very different from those of
the snake. The following two realignments were essentially unilateral (Denmark, November 1979; Italy, March 1981); no meeting was
called, only one currency was involved; and no policy measures were
discussed. The Community procedures were limited to giving a sort
of "multilateral approval" to the decision taken by one member. After these three realignments, however, the procedure became one of
collective decision, making it much closer to those of other Community areas, such as trade and agriculture.[18] The general perception of
realignment meetings, whose organizational aspects are unfortunately
not public knowledge, is that the actual outcome rarely meets the request of member countries in full. The representatives of countries
seeking changes in the parities of their own currencies often emerge
from the negotiations with a somewhat different grid of parities from
the one they were seeking at the start. There are three noteworthy
aspects of these meetings. First, as we discussed in chapter 1, there
is the impact of the realignment on the common agricultural market;
the provisions for eliminating the monetary compensatory amounts
introduced at the time of a realignment are important issues in the

17 For example, the realignment of August 1977 resulted in a 5 percent devaluation of
the Danish and Norwegian kroner, while Sweden decided not to go along and abandoned the system.
18 For this "insider's" account of EMS realignments, see Padoa Schioppa (1985).

negotiations. Second, weak-currency countries always seem to ask larger devaluations than Germany is prepared to accept.[19] Third, the setting of monetary targets surprisingly is not an integral part of the negotiations, while exchange rate rules and monetary rules in principle should be set jointly.

2.5 Are EMS Exchange Rate Rules Really Important?

The choice between the two systems—bilateral parity grid, or ECU-parities only—was the main issue in the negotiations over the design of the EMS. When it first launched the EMS, the EEC Council of Ministers stated that "the ECU will be at the center of the system" (EC Monetary Committee 1986, p. 47, paragraph 1). Some participants in the negotiations, the French in particular, took this statement at face value, that is as indicating that the obligation to intervene should arise only with respect to a divergence from the central ECU rate. They wanted no bilateral obligations. However, this view was defeated and eventually abandoned by the French themselves.[20] As we have already noted the ECU is currently devoid of any meaningful role in the exchange rate mechanism. The EMS ended up functioning exclusively around the parities' grid mainly because one of the major partners in the negotiations, the Bundesbank, resisted joining a system characterized by intervention rules that would be able to single out *the* divergent currency—as opposed to a pair of divergent currencies—in the fear that its domestic monetary policies would be made vulnerable by such rules.[21] An additional reason for the abandonment of an ECU-based system is that central parities and target zones defined around a basket of currencies are too cumbersome to work with, as the simple algebraic examples in section 2.2.1 should have suggested.

While solutions existed for the more technical drawbacks of an ECU-based system,[22] "it was hardly the technical issues that decided the choice of the bilateral parity grid." What eventually decided the issue

---

19 An exception is the January 1987 realignment, when apparently Denmark and Belgium initially opposed the devaluation of their currencies.

20 For a reconstruction of this debate see *European Economy*, 12 (July 1982) and Ludlow (1982).

21 See, for example, Rieke (1979).

22 For example, the problem of different weights can be solved by applying to the high-weight currencies ECU margins that are narrower than those applied to the low-weight currencies.

was "the firm resistance of the Bundesbank officials, supported by the Dutch and the Danes, to any triggering of mandatory interventions by movements in a currency's ECU rate. It was clear that the DM was prone to diverge upwards and that an ECU-based system would push Germany more often to the front line of intervention with unfortunate consequences for monetary stability." (Thygesen 1979)

Finally, one frequently held view in the debates on the EMS which we find most misleading is that the establishment of the ECU as the centerpiece of the EMS exchange rate mechanism could per se eliminate the type of asymmetries that plagued the Bretton Woods system. That view relies on the belief that pegging exchange rates to a weighted average of the currencies in the system can provide the nominal anchor, or the standard. That view is incorrect because, for the equilibrium of the system to be well defined, all *but one* member should peg their exchange rates to the common weighted average. The point can be illustrated with reference to a system limited to two currencies—say, the French franc and the DM. Let α and $(1 - \alpha)$ be the weights of the franc and the DM in the ECU basket. The price of one ECU in terms of francs and marks respectively is

$$FF/ECU = [1 + (1 - \alpha)/\alpha DM/FF]/\alpha$$
$$DM/ECU = [1 + \alpha/(1 - \alpha)FF/DM]/(1 - \alpha)$$

where DM/FF is the price of francs in terms of DM—and FF/DM is its reciprocal. It is apparent that pegging the franc-ECU rate is equivalent to pegging the DM/FF rate. Thus one country is free to determine monetary policy independently Hence an ECU-based EMS can reproduce exactly the asymmetries of the dollar standard. These asymmetries could be eliminated in two ways. One is the establishment of exogenously fixed and commonly negotiated targets for the ECU, or for any member currency that the "free" central bank should follow. The other is the adoption of a commodity standard; that is a commodity, or a basket of commodities, whose nominal price all central banks are required to peg.

3

The Macroeconomic Impact of the EMS: Exchange Rates

3.1 The Issues

The main features of the exchange rate mechanism of the EMS are the bilateral fluctuation bands and the possibility of realignments. Indeed, from March 1979 to December 1987 there were 10 realignments of bilateral central rates; only in 1980 and 1984 did bilateral central rates remain unaffected. Since bilateral fluctuation bands of 4.5 percent (12 percent for Italy) are relatively wide, this experience raises the question of whether the exchange rate mechanisms put in place by the EMS affect nominal exchange rate fluctuations at all, or whether they are simply a "veil" over a system of de facto floating exchange rates. Are the EMS realignments simply accomodating the unstoppable market forces, without even delaying inevitable exchange rate changes caused by divergent monetary policies?

Krugman (1988a, 1988b) provides the framework for discussing the effects of bilateral fluctuation bands, or nominal "target zones." Suppose that the bands were fully credible, that is the probability of realignments is zero. Then when nominal exchange rates reach bilateral fluctuation limits, asset market equilibrium requires the distortion of the relation between the nominal exchange rate and "fundamentals" like monetary and fiscal policies. The expectation that monetary policy will be endogenously changed to validate the existing regime once the limits of the fluctuation bands are reached strengthens the exchange rate in the proximity of the devaluation limit and weakens it in the proximity of the revaluation limit, independently of what happens to "fundamentals." In this sense the fluctuation bands induce a distortion in the relation between exchange rates and fundamentals. As Krugman shows, these mechanisms ensure that the mere presence of

fluctuation bands significantly affects the expected time to reach fluctuation limits: In this sense exchange rates are "stabilized" by credible
bands. As the probability of realignments when exchange rates reach
the fluctuations limits exceeds zero, the stabilizing effect of the bands
decreases to the point where exchange rates within the bands behave
as in a pure floating regime. Thus the exchange rate system in the
EMS, if at all credible to the public, should have stabilized bilateral
nominal exchange rates. In section 3.2 we survey the evidence on the
changes in the stochastic behavior of bilateral nominal exchange rates
after March 1979.

What effect does the EMS have on real variables? As we noted in
chapter 1, one of the apparent motives behind the political support for
the EMS was the belief that stabilizing nominal exchange rates could
achieve a stabilization of relative prices within Europe. This implies
a belief that a change in the *nominal* exchange rate regime can have
important *real* effects, such as stabilizing the relative prices of goods
produced in different countries.

There is substantial professional interest in the real effects of alternative nominal exchange rate regimes.[1] The evidence from the comparison of the Bretton Woods era with the flexible exchange rate years
suggests that nominal exchange rate regimes might be associated with
significant real effects: Mussa (1986) studies the behavior of different
price indices in different time periods and different countries, and
finds that relative prices appear to be more stable during periods of
stable nominal exchange rates with remarkable regularity. Stockman
(1983) performs statistical tests on a large sample of countries, during
fixed and flexible exchange rates, and finds that, after controlling for
country-specific real shocks and for the higher volatility of worldwide
shocks in the 1970s, the return to flexible exchange rates still explains
40 percent of the increased volatility of real exchange rates. Dornbusch
and Giovannini (1988) argue that the different behavior of exchange
rates after the collapse of the Bretton Woods period supports the view
that goods prices adjust more slowly than asset prices.

Did the EMS achieve a stabilization of relative price levels of member countries? Under one interpretation of the evidence on the behavior of real exchange rates before and after 1973, the advent of floating
rates was just an endogenous response to large exogenous real shocks:
The monetary discipline imposed by fixed exchange rates simply was

---

1 See Baxter and Stockman (1987) for comprehensive empirical studies on the behavior
of real macroeconomic variables across alternative nominal exchange rate regimes.

not sustainable after 1973. The EMS experience challenges this interpretation. The EMS—a partial return to fixed exchange rates—was created at the time of the second oil shock and lasted throughout the unprecented U.S. fiscal expansion and the ensuing fluctuations of the real dollar exchange rate. Thus the presence of macroeconomic instability in the world economy since 1979 appears to invalidate the argument that the EMS is an endogenous response of monetary institutions to the world environment. For this reason evidence from the EMS is particularly relevant to the general question of the real effects of nominal exchange rate regimes. In section 3.3 we survey the evidence on the behavior of aggregate relative prices.

In the last section of this chapter we turn to the behavior of effective real rates. Two interesting issues concerning effective rates arise. First, as Canzoneri (1982) showed, an exchange rate union which seeks to stabilize bilateral rates within itself can destabilize the multilateral rates of its members by destabilizing the exchange rate vis-à-vis the rest of the world. Second, can the EMS be interpreted as a device for stabilizing the DM effective exchange rate? During the collapse of the Bretton Woods system, the DM was a pole of attraction of international capital flows, and appreciated *both* vis-à-vis the dollar and vis-à-vis the other European currencies. From Germany's perspective, the establishment of the EMS could represent a way to achieve more substantial exchange rate stability through a sort of "European Alliance" for limiting the damaging effects of extreme dollar-DM fluctuations.

3.2 The Stochastic Properties of Bilateral Nominal Rates

In this section we offer evidence on the changes in the stochastic behavior of bilateral nominal rates in Europe after March 1979. This evidence can be used to determine whether the exchange rate mechanisms put in place by the EMS affected central banks' policies at all, and if those mechanisms were deemed credible by the public. The alternative hypothesis is that, after joining the EMS, central banks did not change policies appreciably and exchange rate realignments simply accomodated the trend divergences of different countries' monetary policies.

Several authors have offered empirical evidence closely related to ours. Rogoff (1985a) studies the variance of the forward rate prediction error for France and Italy vis-à-vis Germany and compares it with the variance of the forward rate prediction error for the dollar/DM, pound/DM and yen/DM exchange rates.[2] He shows that changes in both the franc and the lira exchange rates relative to the Deutsche mark are significantly more predictable after the beginning of the EMS than during the period from February 1974 to February 1979. Artis and Taylor (1988) show that changes in nominal bilateral exchange rates of European currencies vis-à-vis the DM display a smaller variance after March 1979.

Since we are concerned about the variance of exchange rates around their conditional expectations rather than around the unconditional mean, we need an exchange rate forecasting model. We estimate the following prediction equation:

$$1n(S_{t+1}/S_t) = \alpha + \beta 1n(F_t/S_t) + \varepsilon_{t+1} \tag{3.1}$$

where S is the price of a DM in terms of each of the currencies in our data set, and F is the 1-month forward exchange rate. The choice of the DM as the numeraire currency is justified by our general hypothesis—supported in a number of chapters in this book—that the EMS is effectively centered around the DM. The empirical evidence of section 3.4, however, provides additional information about the other European cross rates by reporting the changes in behavior of effective rates.

Numerous empirical studies[3] have rejected the hypothesis that the forward rate is an unbiased predictor of the future spot exchange rate. Thus we do not restrict (α, β) to equal $(0,1)$ as Rogoff (1985a) did. However, many authors have shown that the forward premium contains relevant information for forecasting changes in the spot exchange rate.[4] Equation (3.1) is thus still an acceptable forcasting equation, even though the unbiasedess hypothesis is rejected.

We estimate equation (3.1) using monthly data over the EMS period (March 1979 to September 1987) and over the period preceding the EMS (from June 1973—the start of the period of generalized floating—to February 1979). The currencies included in our sample are the Belgian Franc, the Dutch guilder, the French franc, the Italian lira, and the pound sterling. The data sources are specified in the Appendix.[5] From each subsample we obtain the estimated residuals, which we plot in

---

2 He also computes the root mean square error of forecasts obtained from an unrestricted vector autoregression, over a one-month horizon and a 12-month horizon.

3 See, for example, Hansen and Hodrick (1980) and Cumby and Obstfeld (1981).

4 See Hodrick and Srivastava (1984) and Cumby and Obstfeld (1984).

5 Data for the Danish krone is not available for most of the first subsample.

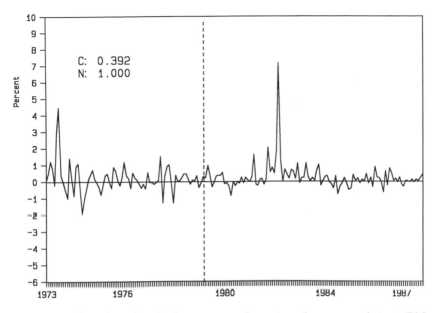

Figure 3.1 Belgian franc (nominal): percentage change in exchange rate relative to DM.

figures 3.1 to 3.5. These series have, by construction, a mean of zero. The null hypothesis is that the variance of exchange rate surprises has not changed in the more recent period. This hypothesis is tested with a standard F-test (see Hogg and Craig 1970, chapter 10) and with a nonparametric rank test proposed by Hajek and Sidak (1967) and applied by Artis and Taylor (1988) to EMS exchange rates. Unlike the F-test, the rank test is based on the assumption that exchange rate forecast errors are unconditionally Cauchy distributed. This assumption is suggested by an extremely high coefficient of kurtosis of the distribution of exchange rate forecast errors. In each figure we report the marginal significant level for the null hypothesis that the variance of exchange rate surprises has not changed in the two periods, versus the alternative that the variance during the EMS is lower. The letter N stands for the F-test (based on normality), while the letter C stands for the rank test (based on a Cauchy distribution).[6]

Figure 3.1 reports unanticipated changes in the Belgian franc/DM rate. The null hypothesis, that the variance of unanticipated changes

---

6 Bollerslev (1987) performs tests of convergence of bilateral exchange rates in Europe where the conditional expectation of exchange rate changes is zero (a random walk model) but conditional variances change over time.

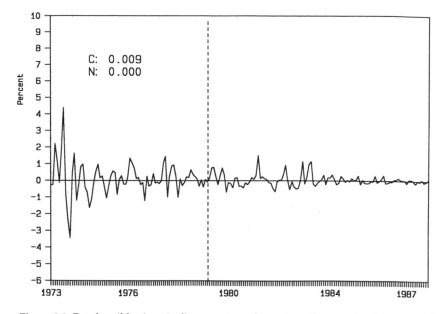

Figure 3.2 Dutch guilder (nominal): percentage change in exchange rate relative to DM.

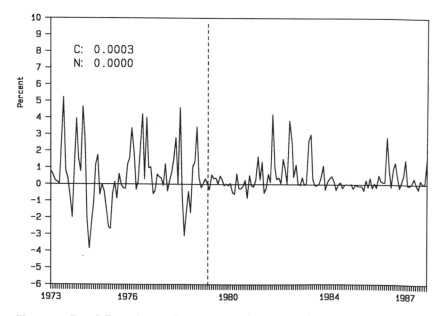

Figure 3.3 French Franc (nominal): percentage change in exchange rate relative to DM.

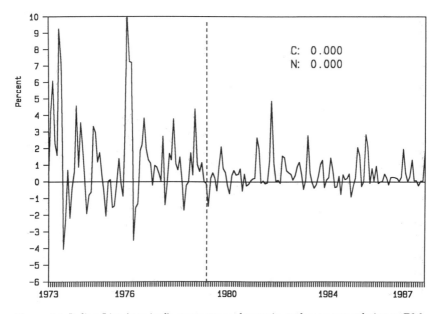

Figure 3.4 Italian Lira (nominal): percentage change in exchange rate relative to DM.

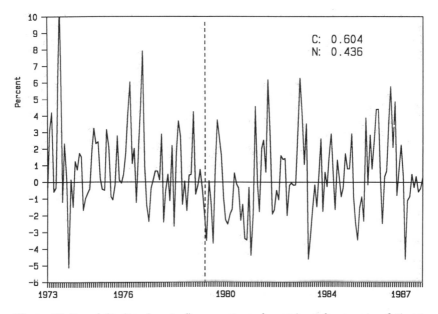

Figure 3.5 Pound Sterling (nominal): percentage change in exchange rate relative to DM.

in the Belgian franc/DM rate has not changed during the EMS, clearly is not rejected by the data. The lack of rejection is accounted for by two facts: First, the Belgian franc did not fluctuate against the DM during the whole period preceding the setup of the EMS, being one of the currencies that belonged to the snake agreement. Second, the devaluation of 6.5 percent of February 22, 1982 was not reflected in the forward rate prevailing at the end of January 1982, and thus it contributes disproportionately to the variance during the EMS.

Figure 3.2 reports the same calculation for the Dutch guilder, which also belonged to the snake from April 1972 to February 1979. Contrary to the case of the Belgian franc, the variance of the Dutch guilder/DM forecast errors does appear to decrease during the EMS years: The null hypothesis is strongly rejected. The same result is evident in the case of the French franc and the Italian lira, reported in figures 3.3 and 3.4, respectively. In figure 3.5 we perform the same test on a European currency that did not belong to the exchange rate arrangement: the British pound. The figure and the tests indicate no appreciable change in volatility in recent years. These findings are similar to those of Rogoff (1985a) and Artis and Taylor (1988), who used different data sets and different samples.

In summary, the evidence on bilateral nominal exchange rates suggests that the EMS has decreased the volatility of bilateral DM rates significantly, at least in the case of the Guilder, the French franc, and the lira. This would happen if (sterilized or nonsterilized) intervention by these four countries actively sought the stability of bilateral rates, and if the EMS fluctuation bands were, at least to some extent, deemed credible by the public.

3.3   Has the EMS Affected Real Exchange Rates?

Have the nominal exchange rate rules of the EMS affected real variables, such as relative prices or output in different countries? This is an important question. Whether relative prices are affected by nominal exchange rate regimes is the first issue to be settled when analyzing alternative exchange rate regimes. Yet so far there have been very few systematic attempts at determining the real effects of exchange regimes.[7] In this section we provide additional evidence on

---

7 The only systematic work we are aware of is the paper by Baxter and Stockman (1987). Stockman (1987c) studies—among other things—the evidence on the effects of

the question; we concentrate on the changing behavior of bilateral real exchange rates after the start of the EMS.

First we obtain plots of changes in real exchange rates from 1960 to the present. This long interval allows us to compare the behavior of real rates over different regimes, including the Bretton Woods period and the snake. The real exchange rates are the log of relative wholesale prices (see the Data Appendix for the sources) and are computed using monthly data. Complete series were available for Belgium, France, Italy, the Netherlands, Britain, and the United States; we plot them in figures 3.6 to 3.11. As in section 3.2, real exchange rates are computed relative to the DM, and are first-differenced. In each figure we highlight the period during which each currency was part of the European snake and of the EMS.

For all currencies changes in real bilateral rates during the Bretton Woods years are noticeably smaller than in the subsequent period, except for the clearly identifiable instances when the DM was revalued (March 1961, October 1969, May 1971) or when other currencies were devalued (sterling: November 1967; French franc: August 1969). Two facts emerge from these figures. First, the behavior of real exchange rates is almost identical to the behavior of nominal rates; we interpret this phenomenon as a strong indication of the presence of price stickiness.[8] Second, the volatility of the (real) Belgian franc and Dutch guilder relative to the DM do not appear to differ noticeably in the snake and in the EMS period. Similarly, the pound sterling rate and the dollar rate do not display any significant change in volatility after 1979. The dramatic increase in the volatility of the dollar/DM rate after the collapse of the Bretton Woods system is especially noteworthy.

In table 3.1 we report the results of tests that the variance of unanticipated changes in the bilateral rates of the DM has not decreased after 1979, relative to the 1973–1978 period. The tests are constructed analogously to those in the previous section. We estimate forecasting equations separately from 1973:6 to 1979:2 and from 1979:3 to 1987:9. The variables that we use for the forecasts are lagged realizations of real exchange rate changes (from 1 to 12 lags) and the forward premium defined in equation (3.1). From the estimates of the parameters of the forecasting equations we obtain estimates of real exchange rate

---

monetary policies on real activity.

8 See Flood (1981), Dornbusch and Giovannini (1988), and Giovannini (1987, 1988a) for a discussion of the empirical evidence on prices and exchange rates and price stickiness.

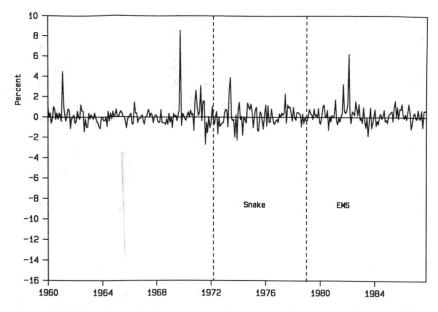

Figure 3.6 Belgian Franc (real): percentage change in exchange rate relative to DM.

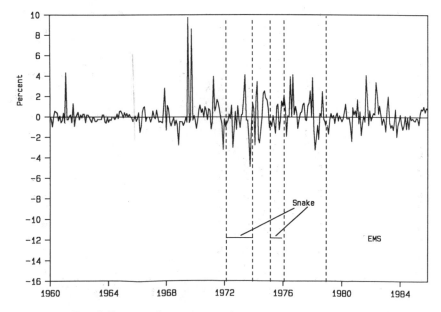

Figure 3.7 French Franc (real): percentage change in exchange rate relative to DM.

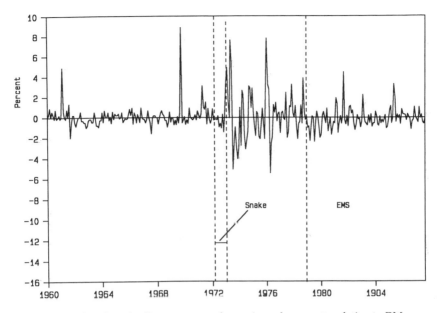

Figure 3.8 Italian Lira (real): percentage change in exchange rate relative to DM.

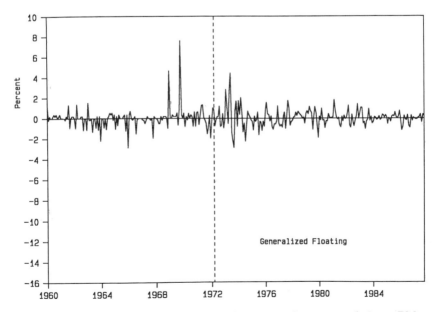

Figure 3.9 Dutch guilder (real): percentage change in exchange rate relative to DM.

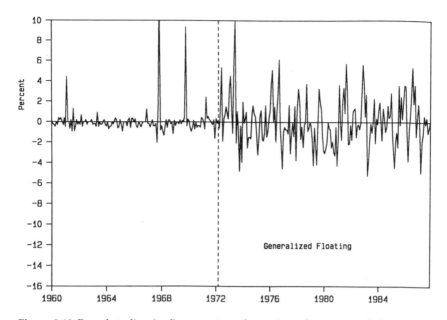

Figure 3.10 Pound sterling (real): percentage change in exchange rate relative to DM.

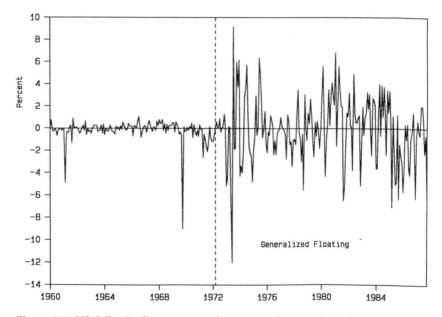

Figure 3.11 US dollar (real): percentage change in exchange rate relative to DM.

Table 3.1
Tests of no change in the variance of unanticipated changes of real DM
rates during the EMS[a]

Currency	F test	Rank test
Belgian franc	0.998	0.600
Dutch guilder	0.245	0.279
French franc	0.000	0.0003
Italian lira	0.000	0.003
Pound sterling	0.897	0.714

a. Marginal significance levels for the null hypothesis of no change in variance, vs. alternative of higher variance during EMS period.

surprises. The results by and large confirm our observations about figures 3.6–3.11: Because of the high volatility of *unanticipated* changes which characterizes exchange rates, the actual exchange rate changes very much resemble the unanticipated exchange rate changes used for the tests. We find that only in France and Italy is the volatility of unanticipated real exchange rate changes significantly lower after 1979 than during the previous six years. This result may support the hypothesis that the EMS has contributed to a decrease in volatility of relative prices of German, Italian, and French goods.

Consistent with Rogoff (1985a) and Artis and Taylor (1988), our findings show that a nominal exchange rate regime like the EMS is associated with significant real effects, namely a decrease in the variance of unanticipated relative price changes.[9]

3.4   Effective Exchange Rates

This section documents the changes in the stochastic properties of effective real exchange rates of EMS countries. Effective rates are geometric averages of bilateral real rates, computed using the weights reported in table 3.2. These weights are obtained from the IMF Multilateral Exchange Rate Model (MERM) and take into account the global

---

9 Stockman (1987a,b) has suggested that relative prices could be less volatile in a fixed exchange rate regime because of the presence of (actual and expected) controls in international payments. In Italy capital controls have been loosened since the start of the EMS. Yet the volatility of the real lira/DM rate has decreased. See chapter 7 for a description of capital controls in Europe. See also Eichengreen (1988) for similar results concerning the behavior of real exchange rates during the interwar years.

Table 3.2
Weights for multilateral exchange rates (base year: 1977)[a]

	Bel	Fra	Ger	Ita	Jap	NL	Swe	UK	US
Belgium	–	0.212	0.262	0.105	0.082	0.105	0.028	0.024	0.183
Denmark	0.022	0.101	0.136	0.127	0.106	0.042	0.090	0.086	0.290
France	0.058	–	0.236	0.185	0.128	0.049	0.027	0.049	0.267
Germany	0.058	0.201	–	0.150	0.151	0.073	0.048	0.057	0.261
Italy	0.035	0.207	0.263	–	0.131	0.042	0.024	0.058	0.239
Netherlands	0.076	0.165	0.240	0.143	0.081	–	0.026	0.038	0.230
United Kingdom	0.049	0.126	0.171	0.087	0.166	0.058	0.045	–	0.298

a. The weights in each country's index are read from the rows of the table.

effects of changes in the relative price of output in any two countries. Thus they are designed to measure a country's competitiveness relative to its trade partners. The partner countries we include for each currency cover about 80 percent of the original MERM weights.

As we pointed out in section 3.1, stabilizing certain bilateral exchange rates does not necessarily imply stability of the overall competitive position of a country. This is because—as Canzoneri (1982) pointed out—foreign exchange intervention by the countries that belong to the exchange rate union affects the supply of their assets relative to the rest of the world, and might destabilize their exchange rate with respect to the countries outside the union.

We look first at the evidence on unanticipated changes in real effective exchange rates. We compute them as the residuals in forecasting regressions which include lagged changes in real exchange rates (from one to twelve lags) and the differential between the country's one-month Euro interest rate and the Eurodollar interest rate, equal to the forward exchange premium. As before, we estimate the forecasting equations over two samples: 1973:6 to 1979:2 and 1979:3 to 1987:6. The results are reported in table 3.3. The table shows that for all countries except Italy there is no significant decrease in the volatility of unanticipated changes in real effective exchange rate. In the case of Italy the F-test suggests a fall in volatility; the rank test does not detect any difference across the two subsamples.

The measures of volatility we have analyzed come from data that has been made stationary by first-differencing. First-differencing the real exchange rate eliminates most of the low-frequency components

Table 3.3
Tests of no change in the variance of unanticipated changes of effective real rates during the EMS[a]

Currency	F test	Rank test
Deutsche mark	0.637	0.701
Belgian franc	0.874	0.275
Dutch guilder	0.818	0.747
French franc	0.786	0.681
Italian lira	0.002	0.385
Pound sterling	0.994	0.926

a. Marginal significance levels for the null hypothesis of no change in variance, vs. alternative of higher variance during EMS period.

of the series. Indeed, it could be argued that those low-frequency components are worthy of special attention.[10] Williamson (1985) suggests that while exchange rate *volatility* (measured by the standard deviation of unanticipated exchange rate changes) might have a negative impact on trade and welfare, exchange rate *misalignment* (that is prolonged deviations of the exchange rate from some fundamental level) are likely to bring about the largest costs. Recent research by Krugman and Baldwin (1987), Baldwin (1986), Dixit (1987), and especially Krugman (1988b) provides the first attempt at formalizing the linkage between the uncertainty and slow mean-reversion in exchange rate movements and the speed of adjustment of intersectoral factor movements and investment.

Although the concept of exchange rate misalignment is clearly not well defined,[11] the evidence on long-run movements of effective real exchange rates is interesting. Here we use the simplest possible measure of long-run fluctuations: the standard deviation of the *level* of the real exchange rate.[12] Table 3.4 reports standard errors of effective

---

10 Huizinga (1987) reports evidence suggesting that the levels of real exchange rates might be stationary, although the rate at which they revert to mean is very slow.

11 It is unclear, for example, whether or not the term misalignment implies some concept of temporary market disequilibrium.

12 Williamson (1985) offers a survey of alternative measures of exchange rate misalignment. For empirical work on exchange rate misalignment, see Bean (1987), De Grauwe (1986), De Grauwe and Bellefroid (1986), and De Grauwe and Verfaille (1987). Edison and Fisher (1988) apply explicit models of long-run fluctuations of exchange rates to test for EMS convergence.

Table 3.4
Standard errors of real effective exchange rates (in percent per month)

Currency	60:1–71:8	60:1–79:2	79:3–85:12
Deutsche mark	3.5	12.3	10.9
Belgian franc	1.8	3.4	14.1
Dutch guilder	4.6	8.1	9.2
French franc	2.9	5.2	11.1
Italian lira	2.7	3.8	6.1

Source: IMF, IFS. Real exchange rates are constructed using WPIs, with weights from table 3.2.

exchange rates from 1960 to 1985. Standard errors are calculated for the EMS years and the years preceding them, including the Bretton Woods years, from January 1960 to August 1971. (The numbers in the table are standard errors of the log of the real exchange rates.) A remarkable fact emerges: For all countries except Germany, there has been an increase in the volatility of real effective exchange rates in the recent years.[13] In the case of the DM, the volatility of the effective rate decreases by about 11 percent when we compare the EMS period with the 20 years preceding it. Thus the table indicates that in Germany, unlike in the other EMS countries, fluctuations of the real exchange rate are lower in the period after 1979 than in the previous twenty years.

Table 3.5 helps to interpret the results from the previous table. We compute the correlation between the effective rates used in table 3.4 and effective rates that include only EMS partner countries, also obtained from the original weights of table 3.2. Table 3.5 shows that in the 1960s and 1970s the correlation between the EMS index and the global index is highest for Germany and the Netherlands. The high correlation for Germany indicates that the other EMS currencies with the exception of the Dutch guilder did not follow the large appreciation of the DM vis-à-vis the dollar during the collapse of the Bretton Woods system. This phenomenon is clearly attenuated in the recent years. The correlation between the EMS and the global index for Germany turns negative, indicating that the EMS might have limited the effects of the fluctuations of the dollar/DM rate on Germany's competitiveness.

---

13 Since we know very little about the small-sample properties of these statistics, we do not attempt to provide formal tests of significance of these changes in variances.

Table 3.5
Correlations between "Global" and EMS real effective rates

Currency	1960:1–1979:2	1979:3–1987:9
Deutsche mark	0.910	−0.051
Belgian franc	0.295	0.958
Dutch guilder	0.922	−0.160
French franc	0.848	0.423
Italian lira	0.795	−0.657

Source: As in table 3.4. The "EMS" real effective rates are computed including only Belguim, France, Germany, Italy, and the Netherlands.

The German experience contrasts sharply with that of Belgium. In Belgium the standard error of the log of the real exchange rate has increased by a factor of four since the beginning of the EMS. Part of this increase in volatility certainly can be attributed to the increase in the correlation between the global and the EEC real exchange rate indices for Belgium.   Given that Belgium is one of Germany's major trading partners (accounting for 12 percent of Germany's intra-European trade), this has been an important factor in stabilizing Germany's real exchange rate.

The French and Italian experience falls somewhere in the middle. The fall in the correlation between the global and the EEC indices—even becoming negative in the case of Italy—is consistent with the observation that during the EMS these countries found their currencies placed between the dollar and the DM.[14] But apparently it has not been enough to stabilize these countries' overall competitiveness.

3.5   Summary of the Evidence

A number of important facts emerge from the data. First, the stochastic behavior of nominal bilateral rates of European currencies relative to the DM has changed since 1979, except in the case of the Belgian franc. (Belgium was a member of the snake since April 1972.) Second, the reduced volatility of nominal exchange rate innovations is associated with the reduced volatility of real exchange rate innovations. This is consistent with evidence reported by Stockman (1983), Mussa (1986),

---

14 In chapter 6, we further explore the asymmetric behavior of European exchange rates relative to the dollar and discuss possible explanations for it.

Baxter and Stockman (1987), and Dornbusch and Giovannini (1988). Although our empirical analysis, like most of the others just cited, does not yield formal tests of the hypothesis that nominal exchange rate regimes have real effects, we believe that it constitutes the necessary departure point for deeper empirical analyses of the real effects of alternative exchange rate regimes.

Finally, we find that while the innovations of first-differences in real effective rates do not significantly change after the start of the EMS, the volatility of the levels of real effective rates increases for all countries except Germany. In the case of Germany, the lower volatility of the level of the real exchange rate may be explained by the change in correlation between the global competitiveness index and the index of competitiveness vis-à-vis EMS partners: 0.91 during the 1960s and 1970s, and −0.51 in recent years. The change in the correlation between the two indices suggests that since the beginning of the EMS, European currencies *on average* have stayed closer to the DM, thus contributing to the stabilization of Germany's global competitiveness. This is just the opposite of the early 1970s when the fall of Bretton Woods was acompanied by an appreciation of the DM *both* in Europe and vis-à-vis the United States. This provides some support for the "European Alliance" view of the EMS: the interest that Germany had in the creation of the system was "to limit the detrimental effects of dollar disturbances." (Thiel 1987, p. 17).

A comparison between the two episodes of dollar depreciation in the late '60s and after 1985 shows the extent to which the EMS has stabilized Germany's overall competitiveness. From November 1969 to March 1973 the DM appreciated by 25 percent vis-à-vis the dollar: this was accompanied by an 18.6 percent worsening of Germany's overall competitiveness. From January 1985 to December 1987 the DM appreciation was similar—27 percent—but this time it was accompanied by a loss of competitiveness only half as large, 9 percent.

Appendix: The Data

Nominal exchange rates	(spot and forward)	Data Resources Inc.: FACS Databank.
Real exchange rates	(nominal exch. rates)	IMF, *IFS* line rf.
	(wholesale prices)	IMF, *IFS* line 63.

Nominal exchange rates are monthly observations of spot and forward rates recorded at 11:30 EST. The nominal exchange rates used to compute real exchange rates are monthly averages. Effective real exchange rates are computed using the weights from the IMF Multilateral Exchange Rate Model (MERM), as specified in the text.

4   Is Europe a Greater Deutsche-Mark Area?

4.1   Introduction

Regimes of fixed exchange rates, like the Bretton Woods System, or of limited exchange rate flexibility, like the EMS, raise the question of symmetry. Who runs monetary policy and who sets exchange rate parities? If exchange rates are determined exogenously by a mechanical rule, is monetary policy run by one country or by all members of the system? In chapter 2, we found that the "symmetry" of the exchange rate rules was very much at the center of EMS negotiations. However, in the current system there is no provision for enforcing symmetric foreign exchange market intervention. We concluded that in a symmetric ECU-based system, there are $N-1$ bilateral exchange rates to be pegged by N member countries. In this chapter, we discuss evidence that bears directly on the question of whether the EMS is characterized by a "center country"—Germany—which manages its own supply of money and assumes that, given the DM bilateral rates, other countries will accommodate its monetary policy. We begin by looking at how exchange rate intervention in the EMS has actually worked. Next we ask what the observable implications of symmetric and asymmetric exchange rate regimes are. In the next two sections, we evaluate these implications empirically.

Our interpretation is that the EMS reproduces the historical experiences of fixed exchange rate regimes. Germany is the center country; it runs monetary policy for the whole system, similarly to the United States during the early Bretton Woods years. When the other countries are unable or unwilling to go along with Germany's monetary targets, they let their exchange rates depreciate relative to the DM.[1]

---

1 This intepretation is at odds with a commonly held view that the EMS could be

4.2   Evidence from Foreign Exchange Market Intervention Data

This section discusses the evidence from foreign exchange market intervention data. Our original dataset were daily intervention volumes reported by the central banks of the countries members of the EMS and broken down by "type" of intervention.[2]

Table 4.1 reports cumulative intervention figures as percentages of total intervention by all countries in each subperiod.[3] In the period from January 1983 to March 1985 there was a general appreciation of the dollar on an effective basis.[4] In the second period, from April 1985 to April 1986, there was a downward trend of the dollar effective exchange rate index.[5] The three panels of the table contain data on intervention at the margin of bilateral fluctuation bands (which is carried out in EMS currencies), on intramarginal intervention in EMS currencies, and on dollar intervention, respectively.

The rules of the EMS, described in chapter 2, were designed with the explicit purpose of "sharing the burden of adjustment." Intervention at the margin—when two currencies reach the limit of the bilateral fluctuation band—is compulsory. It has to be carried out by both central banks involved, using each other's currency. Furthermore, it is supported by the Very Short Term Financing Facility described in chapter 2.

Table 4.1 shows that the two countries most involved in intervention at the margin were Belgium and France. The negative signs in Table 4.1 indicate a *sale* of foreign exchange by the central bank: For example, the first figure for Belgium ((−)0.554) indicates that the Belgian central bank undertook 55.4 percent of all marginal interventions carried out between January 1983 and March 1985. The sign is negative, indicating that during this period the Belgian franc frequently hit

---

interpreted as a sort of "cooperative" regime. Melitz (1985), for instance, claims that the EMS is an "exchange rate union" and that a sharp distinction should be made between an exchange rate union and a Bretton Woods type of arrangement, "where one country—namely, the one that is supposed to issue the reserve currency—stands in an asymmetric relation vis-à-vis all of the rest." (p. 486).

2 These data are also used by Scholl (1981), Micossi (1985), and Caesar (1986).

3 See notes to the table.

4 During that interval there was one EMS realignment which took place in March 1983 and involved a revaluation of the DM vis-à-vis all EMS partners.

5 In that period there were two realignments: July 1985 (lira devalued) and April 1986 (general DM revaluation).

Table 4.1
Central Bank intervention in the EMS

	Jan. '83–Mar. '85	Apr. '85–Apr. '86
Marginal intervention (in EMS currencies)		
Germany	(−) 0.093	(−) 0.031
Netherlands	(−) 0.039	(−) 0.108
France	0.313	0.861
Italy	0.000	0.000
Belgium	(−) 0.554	0.000
Intra-marginal intervention (in EMS currencies)		
Germany	0.000	0.000
Netherlands	0.006	0.051
France	0.637	(−) 0.647
Italy	0.073	(−) 0.079
Belgium	0.283	(−) 0.224
Intervention in U.S. dollars		
Germany	(−) 0.645	(−) 0.076
Netherlands	(−) 0.009	0.092
France	(−) 0.303	0.142
Italy	0.012	(−) 0.592
Belgium	(−) 0.030	(−) 0.097
Summary		
Intervention at margin	0.196	0.429
Intra-margin intervention	0.196	0.250
Dollar intervention	0.608	0.321

Source: See Scholl (1981), Micossi (1985), and Caesar (1986). The data used to construct this table are cumulative intervention figures expressed in U.S. dollars. Negative signs indicate foreign exchange sales by the central bank of the corresponding country. Each entry represents the share of intervention of that country in the total volume of intervention during the given interval, that is in the sum of the absolute values of the entries of that column.

the bottom of the band relative to another currency in the system. This currency was often the French franc: Over the same period the Banque de France was responsible for sizeable interventions (31.3 percent of the total) in the opposite direction. Notice that the Bank of Italy, which enjoys a wider fluctuation band, never intervened at the margin.

The second panel reports data on intra marginal intervention. It shows that Germany—at least during the years reported in our table— has on average kept no positions in other EMS currencies for the pur- pose of intervention. This strongly suggests that Germany might not intervene in the EMS when the DM is within the bilateral fluctuation bands of its partner currencies.

The other important piece of evidence on intramarginal intervention comes from the bottom panel of the table: Intramarginal intervention is as significant in volume as are intervention at the margin and inter- vention vis-à-vis the dollar.[6] In the second panel we can see that the direction of intramarginal intervention changed between the first and the second period. As we document in chapter 6, the strength of the dollar between 1983 and 1985 was associated with a weak DM within the EMS: the table shows that all the other central banks in the sys- tem were purchasing DMs. After April 1985, when the dollar started falling, the signs in the table change: A weak dollar was associated with a strong DM inside the EMS; all other central banks (with the exception of the Netherlands) intervened, selling DMs.

The third panel of the table reports dollar intervention. The large dollar sales by the Bundesbank, especially during the period of dollar appreciation, might have been motivated by the objective of avoiding the strains within the EMS associated with fluctuations of the dol- lar exchange rate.[7] With the data in table 4.1, however, we cannot determine whether dollar intervention by the Bundesbankbank was motivated by the desire to avoid exchange rate strains in the EMS or

---

6 For another discussion of the growing importance of intramarginal intervention, see Ungerer *et al.* (1986).

7 Notice that the dollar interventions by the other central banks are generally consistent with their intramarginal interventions. When the dollar starts falling, for example, France sells DMs and buys dollars: the DM sale supports the franc inside the EMS, and the dollar purchase is an attempt at slowing down the fall in the dollar, which is ultimately responsible for the weakness of the French franc relative to the DM. Italy is an exception: When the dollar starts falling, the Bank of Italy intervenes, selling *both* dollars and EMS currencies (presumably DMs and Dutch guilders).

by the desire to avoid big fluctuations in relative prices with a large trading partner—the United States—along with the assumption that other European authorities would accomodate. The important lesson from Table 4.1 apparently is that the burden of EMS-related intervention was shared very unevenly among EMS countries: Most of the intramarginal intervention was carried out by countries other than Germany, while Germany intervened only when bilateral fluctuation margins were reached.

4.3   Intervention and Sterilization

In the presence of domestic sterilization, intervention rules are useless in determining whether an exchange rate union is symmetric or not. We show this by means of a minimal "accounting" model of international money market equilibrium with two countries.[8] We use the term "accounting" since all the stress of the model is on the accounting relationships between foreign exchange reserves, domestic credit, foreign exchange intervention, and sterilization. Money demand and portfolio disturbances are given exogenously, and the only "behavioral" relation we posit is an interest-elastic money demand equation.

Money demand equations in the home and foreign country (whose variables are starred) depend on an exogenous velocity shock, v, and nominal interest rates

$$M = -v - ai \qquad M^* = -v^* - ai^* \tag{4.1}$$

The central bank's balance sheet implies

$$M = D + R \qquad M^* = D^* + R^* \tag{4.2}$$

where D and D^* are home and foreign domestic credit, and R and R^* are foreign exchange reserves. We assume that D and D^* are the sum of an exogenous component and a component that is proportional to

---

8 Central banks' interaction in a two-country world is studied in Girton and Henderon (1976). Their model allows for imperfect asset substitutability and for the presence of an outside reserve asset. Marston (1980) analyzes how sterilization policies affect the impact of various disturbances on balance-of-payments flows. De Grauwe (1975a, 1975b) and Aoki (1977) explore the effects of sterilization on the stability of reserve flows.

foreign exchange reserves

$$D = \overline{D} - bR \qquad D^* = \overline{D}^* - b^*R^* \qquad 0 \leq b, b^* \leq 1 \tag{4.3}$$

where b and b^* are the sterilization coefficients. International portfolio equilibrium is specified as follows

$$i = i^* + x \tag{4.4}$$

where x is an exogenous disturbance representing shifts in investors' preferences for domestic and foreign assets. Equation (4.4) reveals the two main simplifications in this model. First, in order to highlight as clearly as possible the interactions of foreign exchange intervention and sterilization, x is given exogenously, although in principle it should be determined by expectations of exchange rate changes or risk premia. These variables are normally linked to monetary changes. This implies that in our model x can only represent a portfolio shift associated with exogenous taste shocks which are orthogonal to monetary fundamentals, or that expectations of exchange rate changes are not linked to fundamentals.[9] The growing consensus among empirical researchers is that monetary authorities have been unsuccessful at controlling risk premia by means of sterilized foreign exchange market intervention; see for example Obstfeld (1982, 1983). Our assumption that x is exogenous matches these findings.

Second, there is no explicit treatment of capital controls. As we argue in chapter 7, the effect of capital controls on interest rates can best be studied using an explicitly intertemporal general-equilibrium model. The partial equilibrium model in this chapter, while a useful benchmark for analyzing the interaction of intervention and sterilization on balance-of-payments flows and money supplies, cannot simply be extended to incorporate capital controls. By contrast, the effects of capital controls are very visible, at least in a subset of the data we analyze in this chapter, and will have to be taken into account in the empirical analysis.

As in all fixed exchange rate models, the $N-1$ problem is also present: there are eight endogenous variables but only seven equations. We need an equation specifying a foreign exchange market intervention rule. Here we are not concerned with how these rules are

---

9 A similar argument, of course, applies to the velocity shocks.

created, but only how these rules interact with sterilization coefficients in the final equilibrium. We assume

$$R = g(R - R^*) \qquad 0 \le g \le 1 \tag{4.5}$$

When $g = 0$, all the adjustment is borne by the foreign country. When $g = 1$, only the domestic country adjusts.

The solution of the model yields

$$M = (1 - \Phi)\overline{D} + \Phi\overline{D}^* - \Phi\left[(v - v^*) + ax\right] \tag{4.6a}$$

$$M^* = (1 - \Phi)\overline{D} + \Phi\overline{D}^* + (1 - \Phi)\left[(v - v^*) + ax\right] \tag{4.6b}$$

$$i = -a^{-1}\left[(1 - \Phi)(\overline{D} + v) + \Phi(\overline{D}^* + v'')\right] + \Phi x \tag{4.6c}$$

$$i^* = -a^{-1}\left[(1 - \Phi)(\overline{D} + v) + \Phi(\overline{D}^* + v^*)\right] - (1 - \Phi)x \tag{4.6d}$$

where

$$\Phi = \frac{g(1 - b)}{g(1 - b) + (1 - g)(1 - b^*)} \tag{4.7}$$

Equations (4.6) and (4.7) show that the effects of foreign exchange market intervention rules on the countries' money supplies can be eliminated completely by sterilization policies. The correlation between domestic credit and the domestic money stock is a function of both countries' sterilization parameters, together with the parameter of the intervention rule. For any given intervention rule—that is for any value of g—if the foreign country sterilizes all reserve flows, $b^* = 1$ and $\Phi = 1$. In this case, the foreign money stock is perfectly correlated with $\overline{D}^*$. The home money stock, however, is also only affected by $\overline{D}^*$, but not by $\overline{D}$. When the home country sterilizes all reserve flows, the foreign country has to accomodate home monetary policy entirely and has no control over its money stock. With complete foreign-country sterilization, the home-country offset coefficient is equal to 1.[10]

So far the two countries are perfectly symmetric: Either one can be placed at the center of the system by an appropriate choice of intervention and/or sterilization rules. However, the distribution of the shock x may be the source of asymmetries whenever central banks are con-

---

10 This happens only if $b < 1$. In the case where both b and b^* equal 1, there is no solution to the system.

cerned about fluctuations in their foreign exchange reserves, or when they face constraints in the amount of international borrowing they can undertake to finance balance-of-payments deficits. Suppose that the distribution of x is not symmetric around zero; that is investors' preferences are biased towards the foreign country, for example. Consider the effects on foreign exchange reserves of a positive realization of x, which is equivalent to a shift away from home-country bonds

$$\frac{dR}{dx} = -\frac{g}{g(1-b) + (1-g)(1-b^*)} < 0 \tag{4.8a}$$

$$\frac{dR^*}{dx} = \frac{1-g}{g(1-b) + (1-g)(1-b^*)} > 0 \tag{4.8b}$$

a positive realization of x reduces reserves at home, and raises them by the same amount abroad. Equation (4.8a) also shows that for any given value of b^* and g—provided $g > 0$—the loss of reserves by the domestic central bank is larger the higher b is (i.e., the more the domestic central bank attempts to sterilize) and is minimized by setting $b = 0$. In general, for a given probability distribution of x, the variance of reserve flows is larger as the sterilization coefficients get higher. If the distribution of shocks is asymmetric, and if central banks do not have access to unlimited credit lines, then a country more likely to face adverse international portfolio shifts will not follow a policy of sterilization, since that policy would increase the probability of large reserve losses. Therefore asymmetric portfolio shocks, coupled with constraints on the size of reserves shortfalls, are likely to give rise to asymmetric monetary systems, where the strong currency central bank affects the system's supply of money more than any other central bank.[11] By contrast, weak-currency countries that are prevented from

---

11 The observation that reserve constraints can generate asymmetries, and in particular a global deflationary bias, has a long tradition in international economics. See, for example, Triffin (1960), Katz (1972), Yaeger (1976, pp. 403–405), and Argy (1981). A recent restatement of that problem is in Wyplosz (1988). This point is reinforced if the level of reserves affects x. Collins (1986) estimates the determinants of the forward premium in the run-up to an EMS realignment, and shows that the most important variables in determining the evolution of the premium are the level and the rate of depletion of central bank reserves in the country whose currency is expected to devalue. It is easy to show that, if x is a function of an exogenous component and R (x should be a decreasing function of R), then the size of the response of R to a change in x is always larger than the expressions on the right-hand side of equations (4.8a) and (4.8b).

unlimited borrowing will choose not to sterilize, leaving to strong-currency countries that do not have to face binding borrowing constraints the option of controlling domestic interest rates.

This section delivers a number of strong empirical implications that could be exploited to determine whether the EMS can be considered a greater DM area. Equations (4.6c) and (4.6d) suggest that, in an asymmetric system, interest rates respond asymmetrically to international portfolio shocks. Equations (4.6a), (4.6b), (4.8a), and (4.8b) imply that the center country, by sterilizing foreign disturbances, attempts to control its own money supply while the "satellite" countries, by avoiding the sterilization of international reserve flows, attempt to control their foreign exchange reserves. In other words, the values 0 and 1 of the sterilization coefficient imply two different objectives for monetary authorities: control of foreign exchange reserves when $b = 0$ and control of the money stock when $b = 1$.

4.4 Interest Rates

Equations (4.6c) and (4.6d) reveal that home and foreign interest rates are the sum of two components: a common component reflecting money demand and supply disturbances and an asymmetric component reflecting international portfolio disturbances. Suppose that, either by foreign exchange market intervention rule or by sterilization practice, the foreign country is the center of the system: that is $\Phi = 1$. In this case, the common component reflects only money demand and supply disturbances in the foreign country; the international portfolio component is reflected only in the home interest rate, but does not affect the foreign rate. Thus the center country's interest rates are only affected by money market conditions in that country, and all international portfolio shocks, originating either from expected exchange rate changes or from movements in risk premia, are reflected entirely in the other country's interest rates.[12]

The asymmetric behavior of interest rates in response to interna-

---

12 As equations (4.6c) and (4.6d) clearly show, there might be cases where covariations between money-demand shocks and international portfolio disturbances do not produce the perfectly asymmetric interest rate pattern discussed above. Consider for example a portfolio shock that is perfectly correlated with the disturbance in the domestic money market, that is $x = a^{-1}v$. In this case foreign interest rates are unaffected by the disturbance *independently* of sterilization and intervention practices, even if these implied perfect symmetry, that is $\Phi = 1/2$.

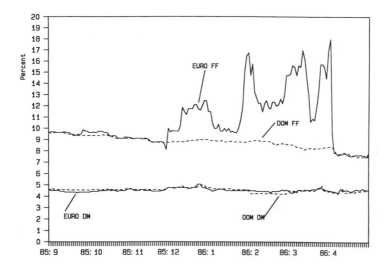

Figure 4.1 French and German offshore and domestic interest rates: 1-month deposits.

tional portfolio shocks seems to us the most robust and most easily verifiable implication of our analysis in the previous section: In an asymmetric system, interest rates in the center country should be relatively unaffected by international portfolio disturbances.

An analysis of interest rate movements in the periods preceding EMS realignments should help us to determine whether Germany is the center country. These periods are typically characterized by interest rate movements that are attributed to expectations of EMS realignments.[13] As we show in chapter 6, the exact timing of EMS realignments is often determined by a crisis in the dollar exchange rate: It is a common empirical observation that these crises raise the demand for DMs relative to other European currencies, and can therefore approximate the portfolio shocks of the model. Figure 4.1 shows the one-month Euro-franc and Euro-DM interest rates, with their domestic equivalents, for the period preceding the April 1986 realignment. Euro interest rates strikingly confirm the asymmetries predicted by the model, in the case where Germany is the center country. In the five months before April 1986, the Euro-franc rate increases dramatically, by up to 8 percent per annum, but the DM rate falls by less than 50 basis points. However, the domestic rate in France is almost

---

13 See, for example, Collins (1984).

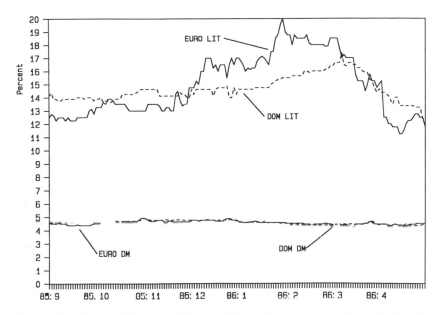

Figure 4.2 Italian and German offshore and domestic interest rates: 3-month deposits.

unaffected, evidence of the power of capital controls.

Figure 4.2 shows domestic and Euro rates on 3-month deposits for the DM and the lira. Here again the DM rates are unaffected by the expectation of the EMS realignment. On the other hand in Italy, where capital controls had been relaxed in October 1985,[14] the expectation of a realignment moves both domestic and offshore rates. Indeed after October 1985 the domestic rate exceeds the offshore rate. Similar patterns can be observed around all other EMS realignment dates, or other periods of turbulence in the foreign exchange markets.

Table 4.2 offers additional evidence on the difference in interest rate volatility across Germany, France, and Italy. The table reports the standard errors of residuals from forecasting equations of 1-month interest rates, domestic and offshore.[15] The residuals from forecasting

---

14 The compulsory financing of export credits in foreign currency had been lifted; see table 7.1b.

15 Using monthly data, we project (the log of 1 plus) interest rates on a constant, a time trend, seasonal dummies, and four months' lags of: the dependent variable; (the log of 1 plus) the U.S. Treasury bill rate; the log of the effective exchange rate; the log of industrial production; the change in base money; and the change in foreign exchange reserves at the central bank.

Table 4.2
Volatility of interest-rate innovations[a]

	Domestic rate	Offshore rate
GERMANY		
Sample	79:3–86:8	79:3–86:8
$\bar{R}^2$	0.989	0.987
D.W.	2.090	2.113
Std. (residual)	0.003	0.003
FRANCE		
Sample	79:3–86:6	79:3–86:6
$\bar{R}^2$	0.966	0.720
D.W.	2.051	2.084
Std. (residual)	0.006	0.030
ITALY		
Sample	79:3–86:1	79:3–86:1
$\bar{R}^2$	0.986	0.845
D.W.	1.991	1.989
Std. (residual)	0.003	0.021

a. Summary statistics for the forecasting equations of 1-month money market and European interest rates. See footnote 15 for the list of right hand side variables.

equations are estimates of unanticipated movements in interest rate. The table shows that our estimates of the volatility of unanticipated interest rate movements in Germany differ dramatically from those in France and Italy. While the standard errors of onshore and offshore DM rates are both equal to 0.3 percent per annum, the standard error of the French domestic rate is twice as much, while the standard error of the French offshore rate is ten times larger! In the case of Italy, while the domestic interest rate displays the same volatility as the German interest rate, the offshore rate is seven times more volatile. Thus table 4.2 broadly confirms the evidence from the specific events in the foreign exchange markets reported in figures 4.1 and 4.2. The volatility of German interest rates is dramatically smaller than that of French and Italian offshore rates. Domestic rates in France and Italy are much less volatile than their offshore counterparts, although the French domestic rates are still twice as volatile as the German domestic rates.[16]

Overall, the data on interest rates suggest that only Germany sets monetary policy independently. Italy and France can either acco- modate German monetary policies perfectly or decouple domestic and foreign interest rates, at least temporarily, by resorting to capi- tal controls.

4.5   What Can We Learn from Estimates of Reaction Functions?

In our accounting model, the crucial determinants of the working of the exchange rate union are the parameters b and b^*, measuring the extent to which reserve inflows and outflows are sterilized by the two central banks. Hence the most straightforward empirical test of the "Greater DM Area" hypothesis appears to be the estimation of sterilization coefficients for the various central banks. A comparison of the magnitude of these coefficients would indicate the extent to which each country controls its own domestic money base.

The estimation of behavioral equations of central banks has a promi- nent place in empirical research in international economics. Work on the classical gold standard (Dutton 1984, Pippenger 198, and Good- hart 1972) has employed estimates of behavioral equations to deter- mine whether the Bank of England abided by various definitions of the "rules of the game." (This question is very similar to the issues we are exploring in this chapter.) Equations specifying decision rules for the supply of domestic credit in relation to changes in foreign reserves have been used in various contexts. Herring and Marston (1977) and Obstfeld (1980, 1983), among others, estimate reaction functions jointly with capital flows equations to determine the degree to which domes- tic credit expansions in Germany are offset by international capital flows. More recently Mastropasqua, Micossi, and Rinaldi (1988) and Roubini (1988) have estimated sterilization equations for a number of European countries, with the apparent objective of determining whether the Bundesbank—perhaps unlike its partner central banks— has maintained control over its own supply of money.

The common specification of these reaction functions assumes that the rate of growth of domestic credit is set by the central bank as a

---

16 We have also found that the volatility of interest rates in Germany during the EMS period has decreased dramatically relative to the preceding ten years; conversely, the volatility of French rates has increased, while that of Italian rates has decreased.

function of the rate of growth of international reserves, (various definitions of) the GNP gap, inflation, seasonal dummy variables, and
time trends. It appears, however, that once foreign exchange reserves
are correctly defined, the estimate of the coefficient of the balance of
payments in these equations is always insignificantly different from
−1 for all countries. This result was obtained by Obstfeld (1983)
for Germany, using Bundesbank data,[17] and by Herring and Marston
(1977), Neumann (1984), and Roubini (1988) for a number of European
countries, using IMF data. The results of Micossi, Mastropasqua, and
Rinaldi (1988), who also use IMF data, show that estimates are very
sensitive to the way in which one accounts for the changes in the
domestic-currency value of foreign exchange reserves that arise from
exchange rate fluctuations rather than from foreign exchange market intervention.[18]

When the estimate of the coefficient on the change of foreign reserves is insignificantly different from −1, these authors conclude that
central banks fully sterilize reserve flows. Since a coefficient insignificantly different from −1 is typically found for all European countries,
the conclusion would be that all countries fully sterilize reserve flows.
However, the model in section 4.2 suggests that full sterilization of
reserve flows is not an equilibrium, since every international portfolio
shock would have an infinite impact on intra-European reserve flows,
as equations (4.8a) and (4.8b) indicate. While capital controls might
decrease these impact coefficients somewhat, full sterilization by all
EMS members is clearly not a sustainable equilibrium. This raises
questions about the reliability of estimates of central bank behavioral
equations, and of using them to determine whether or not the EMS is
an asymmetric exchange rate union.

We immediately question the plausibility of the specification of the
reaction function described above when we move away from the sim-
plified illustrative model of section 4.2.[19] In a more general and much

17 Obstfeld computed a corrected measure of domestic credit growth to account for
changes in reserve requirements at commercial banks.
18 The point, suggested by Roubini (1988), is that valuation effects should be netted
out since they do not lead to changes in the monetary base. If, however, one uses IMF
data—as these authors do—there is no clean way to do it because there are no data that
allow valuation effects to be separated from other items in the balance sheet. Some of
our estimates also indicated that the results vary widely with the choice of instruments,
and of right-hand-side variables.
19 This section, and the following one, draw heavily from Giovannini (1986), who

more realistic environment, with a number of exogenous shocks and a rich dynamic structure, central banks that set domestic-credit growth mechanically—by responding only to the current realization of the output gap, reserves, and the inflation rate—would surely not behave optimally. They would miss out on opportunities to affect their targets by exploiting correlations among other variables in the economy, their targets (either the domestic money stock or foreign exchange reserves), and the instrument at their disposal, domestic credit. Thus, if central banks are assumed to behave rationally, the simple reaction functions studied in the empirical literature are likely to be misspecified. They exclude all variables correlated with the monetary authorities' targets, to which the central bank should respond in order to improve control of its target variables. This observation was made by Sims (1980), who suggested that these behavioral equations in a sense are "necessarily" misspecified, because they need "incredible" exclusion restrictions to achieve identification.

The difficulties in specifying and estimating structural reaction functions, together with the problems in interpreting the estimates of correctly specified equations, lead us to study the reduced-form properties of the data. Our objective is to pinpoint the implications for reduced-form of two alternative assumptions about the behavior of central banks: either (1) central banks target a domestic variable, like the money supply,[20] or domestic interest rates; or (2) they target foreign exchange reserves.[21]

Suppose the task of monetary authorities is to minimize the expected square deviations of two target variables, a domestic target (like money or interest rates) and a foreign target (like reserves), from a given level. We formally state the problem as follows

$$\text{MIN}_{t-1} E \left[(\varepsilon/2)(Y_{1t} - \overline{Y}_1)^2 + ((1 - \varepsilon)/2)(Y_{2t} - \overline{Y}_2)^2 \right] \qquad (4.9)$$

subject to

$$Y_{it} = A_i(L)Y_{1t-1} + B_i(L)Y_{2t-1} + C_i(L)X_t + D_i(L)Z_t + u_{it} \qquad (4.10)$$

---

applied linear-quadratic control theory to determine whether England and Germany followed the "rules of the game" during the International Gold Standard. His findings, that Germany did follow these rules but that England did not, are suggestive of the fact that the gold standard might also have worked asymmetrically.

20 $b = 1$ in the model of section 4.3.

21 Equivalent, in our model, to $b = 0$.

Where Y_1 and Y_2 are the two target variables, and $\overline{Y}_1$ and $\overline{Y}_2$ their desired values. X is the instrument, domestic credit, Z is a vector of exogenous variables seasonals and lagged endogenous variables, determined jointly with the targets and instruments which also help to predict the target variables; and u are unobservable disturbances. The authorities are assumed to solve equations (4.9) and (4.10) by choosing a feedback rule

$$X_t = \Theta + \Gamma_1(L)Y_{1t-1} + \Gamma_2(L)Y_{2t-1} + \Omega(L)Z_t \tag{4.11}$$

Taking the first-order conditions from equations (4.9) and (4.10), substituting for X from equation (4.11), and expressing all variables as deviations from the respective means, the following reduced-form equations are derived

$$Y_{1t} - Y_{2t} = \psi_1(L)Y_{1t-1} + \psi_2(L)Y_{2t-1} + \psi_3(L)Z_t + u_{1t} - u_{2t} \tag{4.12}$$

$$Y_{1t} = (1 - \varepsilon)\left[\psi_1(L)Y_{1t-1} + \psi_2(L)Y_{2t-1} + \psi_3(L)Z_t\right] + u_{1t} \tag{4.13}$$

where

$$\psi_1(L) = \frac{A_1(L)C_2(L) - A_2(L)C_1(L)}{\varepsilon C_1(L) + (1 - \varepsilon)C_2(L)}$$

$$\psi_2(L) = \frac{B_1(L)C_2(L) - B_2(L)C_1(L)}{\varepsilon C_1(L) + (1 - \varepsilon)C_2(L)}$$

$$\psi_3(L) = \frac{D_1(L)C_2(L) - D_2(L)C_1(L)}{\varepsilon C_1(L) + (1 - \varepsilon)C_2(L)}$$

Equations (4.12) and (4.13) state that, under the assumptions of the model, the two target variables move proportionally, with a coefficient of proportionality equal to their relative importance in the central banker's objective function. In the extreme case where one target variable—say Y_1—carries all the weight in the objective function, that target becomes uncorrelated with any variable in the information set. This is the well known result from optimal control theory, pointed out by Sargent and Wallace (1976) and Sargent (1976), and by Cooley and Leroy (1985).

The reduced form in equations (4.12) and (4.13) suggests a test of the model. According to it, the disturbances of the two equations are orthogonal to the variables on the right hand side. Thus the model imposes $2 \times K$ orthogonality conditions on the data, where K is the number of variables on the right hand side of the two equations. On the other hand, there are only $K + 1$ parameters to estimate. Hence the remaining $K - 1$ orthogonality conditions can be tested. Instead of implementing this test directly, we simplify the estimation further; we are not interested in the values of the ψ, so we substitute equation (4.12) into (4.13)

$$Y_{1t} = (1 - \varepsilon)(Y_{1t} - Y_{2t}) + \eta_t \tag{4.14}$$

where η is a composite disturbance term. We estimate equation (4.14) using a subset of the right-hand side variables in equations (4.12) and (4.13).[22] In this equation, the model is tested by projecting the estimates of η onto the remaining instruments. If these projections differ significantly from zero, the model is rejected.

Finally, before testing the model we need to address the choice of data. First we must identify an appropriate domestic target: We use both the stock of high-powered money and the domestic money market rate, since the operating procedures of central banks in these countries often involve explicit targeting of domestic interest rates. Second, we must measure valuation effects on foreign exchange reserves appropriately. These must be netted out of the changes in foreign exchange reserves expressed in domestic-currency terms. We use two different methods: First we subtract changes in the "other items" line of central banks' balance sheets in *International Financial Statistics* from changes in foreign exchange reserves. The other items line contains both valuation effects on foreign exchange reserves and additional items unrelated to foreign exchange gains. Then we subtract monthly estimates of foreign exchange gains or losses from changes in foreign exchange reserves, obtained by interpolating an unpublished quarterly series of valuation adjustments of foreign exchange reserves, for all three countries.[23]

In the data, the variable Y_1 is the monthly rate of change of the domestic money stock, or the domestic money market rate. The vari-

---

22 We should stress that equation (4.14) is not a structural or behavioral equation, but simply an implication of the reduced form of the model.

23 This series was kindly made available to us by the staff of the research department at the Bank of Italy.

Table 4.3a
Estimates and tests of the linear-quadratic control model: Germany[a]

	Reserves less other items		Reserves less valuation effects	
	Money target	Int. rate target	Money target	Int. rate target
$1-\varepsilon$	.738	.312	.892	.663
(std. err.)	(.195)	(.047)	(.054)	(.058)
$\bar{R}^2$	.130	.207	.800	.502
Q	.000	.021	.220	.017
F	.000	.000	.065	.009
χ^2	.000	.000	.098	.030

a. Sample: 1979:12 to 1987:12. The line denoted by Q, F, and χ^2 report the marginal significance levels of the corresponding test statistics. The Q statistic tests for zero autocorrelation of η at lags.

able Y_2 is the change in foreign exchange reserves relative to the stock of high-powered money. Z contains a trend, seasonal dummies, and lagged values of: the domestic money market rate (in the case where Y_1 is high powered money); or the stock of high powered money (in the case where Y_1 is the domestic money market rate); the rate of growth of industrial production; and the rate of change of the exchange rate (relative to the DM for France and Italy, and relative to both the franc and the lira for Germany).

We first estimate $(1-\varepsilon)$ and the residuals η using as instruments the seasonal dummies and the other variables in Z, lagged from seven to twelve months. Then we project our estimates of η onto the variables in Z, which were not used as instruments in the previous step, lagged from one to six months. The test of the model (the null hypothesis) is that the coefficients of these instruments are all jointly zero. This hypothesis is tested using an F-test and an asymptotic chi-square test.

The results are reported in the three panels of table 4.3. The model is rejected at the 5 percent marginal significance level in all but two cases: the third column of panels (a), Germany, and (b), France. The estimates of the relative weight of the external target $(1-\varepsilon)$ is, surprisingly and in contrast to the results surveyed above, generally higher in Germany than in France or Italy. These estimates do vary substantially, depending on the definition of the target variables and the type of data used for foreign exchange reserves. The lack of uniform and positive results might be caused by a number of specification

Table 4.3b
Estimates and tests of the linear-quadratic control model: France[a]

	Reserves less other items		Reserves less valuation effects	
	Money target	Int. rate target	Money target	Int. rate target
1–ε	.376	.146	.520	.284
(std. err.)	(.059)	(.041)	(.073)	(.049)
$\bar{R}^2$	.407	.139	.483	.226
Q	.033	.000	.398	.000
F	.003	.000	.080	.000
χ^2	.015	.000	.114	.000

a. Sample: 1979:12 to 1987:10. See note to table 4.3a.

Table 4.3c
Estimates and tests of the linear-quadratic control model: Italy[a]

	Reserves less other items		Reserves less valuation effects	
	Money target	Int. rate target	Money target	Int. rate target
1–ε	.607	.594	.540	.570
(std. err.)	(.092)	(.063)	(.080)	(.079)
$\bar{R}^2$	.314	.444	.256	.239
Q	.000	.000	.000	.000
F	.008	.000	.002	.000
χ^2	.029	.000	.014	.001

a. Sample: 1979:12 to 1987:7. See note to table 4.3a.

problems, in addition to the data problems mentioned above. The desired values for the target variables may not be constant: this would likely happen when the stock of high powered money or the domestic interest rate are intermediate targets. The constancy of the desired values for the target variables is the restriction that yields the proportional movement of Y_1 and Y_2. Also the objective functions might be misspecified.[24]

Therefore, we conclude that there is still no reliable evidence that

---

24 An interesting alternative to the present setting would be to assume that central banks minimize the probability that foreign exchange reserves fall below a certain value, together with the square deviations of the domestic target from its desired value.

allows us to identify differences in monetary-policy rules in France, Germany, and Italy.

4.6   Concluding Remarks

This chapter uses analysis and empirical evidence to complement the information on the institutional features of the EMS that we offer in chapter 2. The combined results from these two chapters are as follows:

• The institutional features designed to achieve symmetry in the EMS are not working appropriately. The divergence indicator is unbalanced, contains currencies outside the EMS, and does not bind member central banks to any action. The provision for marginal intervention, although symmetric, is rarely resorted to effectively, since the largest fraction of EMS intervention apparently is intramarginal.

• Foreign exchange market intervention rules can be made completely ineffective by domestic monetary policies. Thus achieving symmetry in the exchange rate mechanism does not imply, per se, that the $N-1$ problem is solved symmetrically. Indeed, symmetric foreign exchange market intervention rules do not solve the $N-1$ problem at all. Therefore the most important area for future institutional improvements of the EMS is likely to be the setting of monetary rules.

• In Europe, de facto, the $N-1$ problem is solved asymmetrically: Germany is the center country, and countries such as Italy and France peg their currencies to the mark. The strongest evidence in support of this proposition comes from the behavior of interest rates in the weeks preceding EMS realignments. While in a symmetric regime the German rates would decrease as much as the French or Italian rates would increase, in reality the German rates are hardly affected by expectations of changes in the DM price of the lira or the French franc.

• Models of the behavior of central banks do not provide any reliable empirical results yet. While ad hoc reaction functions, in addition to being most likely misspecified, tend to yield unrealistically high estimates of sterilization coefficients, the model which we believe to effectively improve upon many of the limitations of behavioral equations is rejected by the data.

Appendix: The Data

Interest rate forecasting equations

Domestic interest rates (including U.S. T-bill rate)	IFS line 60c.
Effective exchange rates	IFS line amx.
Industrial production	IFS line 66.
Monetary base	IFS line 14.
Reserves	IFS line 11.
Offshore interest rates	DRI FACS Data Bank.
Daily interest rates	DRI FACS Data Bank.

Sources are common for all countries. Monthly Italian offshore rates are computed using forward exchange rates and interest rate parity.

Linear-quadratic control model

Foreign assets	IFS line 11–16c-17r
High-powered money	IFS line 14.
Money market rate	IFS line 60b.
Industrial production	IFS line 66c.
Exchange rate	IFS line rb.

5

The Bundesbank's Reputation and the European Disinflation: Theory and Empirical Evidence

5.1 Introduction

Since the beginning of the 1980s, the countries belonging to the European Monetary System have experienced a large fall in inflation. This chapter evaluates the role of the exchange rate regime in their disinflation experience.

Professional views of the role of the exchange rate regime in a disinflation, and the actual experiences, differ widely. On the one hand, experiences such as the Southern-Cone "new style" IMF plans, where the exchange rate was used to stop very high inflation rates, were viewed as negative. They are criticized by Dornbusch (1982) among others. Critics point to the disruptive effects of the large appreciation in the real exchange rate, which was eventually unsustainable, and to the lack of credibility of the exchange rate targets. On the other hand, Bruno (1986) suggests that exchange rate policy might have had an important role in the successful Israeli stabilization.[1] The positive role of exchange rate policy in the Bolivian stabilization is also stressed by Sachs (1986).

In the case of the EMS experience, most observers tend to conclude that the exchange rate regime helped the high-inflation countries. Fischer (1987) describes the EMS as "an arrangement for France and Italy to purchase a commitment to low inflation by accepting German monetary policy." Even in countries considering EMS membership, the main advantages of membership are associated with Germany's reputation. *The Economist* (September 21, 1985) writes, "If sterling does join, the biggest change will be the transfer of responsibility for

---

[1] For an analysis of the role of the exchange rate regime in the Israeli disinflation, see Cukierman (1987).

Britain's monetary policy from the Bank of England to the Bundes-bank which, as the central bank keenest on sound money, sets the pace for other to follow. This would be a blessing: Tory governments may like appointing City gents as governors of the Bank, but Mr. Karl Otto Poehl would do a better job." *The Financial Times* (September 28, 1987) writes: "In place of money supply targetry, long since discredited, we would have that unflinching guardian of monetary rectitude, the Bun-desbank, standing as guarantor against Britain's endemic propensity to genererate double-figure rates of inflation."

This chapter starts by illustrating theoretical arguments in favor of pegging the exchange rate to bring down inflation. We model the inflation process as being determined crucially by price setters' ex-pectations. Authorities willing to bring the inflation rate down face the problem of affecting the public's expectations. The arguments in favor of exchange rate pegging rely on the credibility of the central bank's commitment to the exchange rate target. As we will show, there is still no compelling proof that exchange rate targets are more credible than monetary targets, although the perceived "costs" of re-alignments and the much greater publicity of exchange rate targets relative to monetary targets might explain this puzzle.

We will provide empirical evidence to highlight the shifts in infla-tionary expectations after the start of the European Monetary System. Sometime after the start of the EMS, there seems to be weak evidence of a fall in inflationary expectations. However, this shift in expecta-tions could have been caused by dramatic and endogenous shifts in domestic policies that may have been induced by the EMS.

5.2   The Disinflation of the 1980s

At the time when the EMS was set up, the big difference in macro-economic performance across Europe was in the rates of inflation. In 1979–80, CPI inflation was 5 percent in Germany and 15 percent on average in the rest of Europe, with peaks of 20 percent in Italy and the United Kingdom. Figures 5.1 through 5.4 show the behavior of CPI inflation in four European countries, and compare it with the inflation rate in Germany. In the 1980s European inflation rates converged fast. By 1986 the inflation differential with Germany was down to 3 per-cent for most countries. Even in Italy, the traditionally high-inflation member of the group, the inflation differential with Germany does not

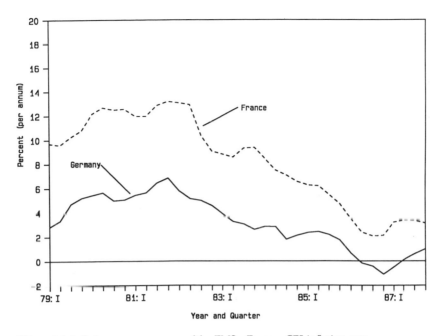

Figure 5.1 Inflation convergence and the EMS—France: CPI inflation rate.

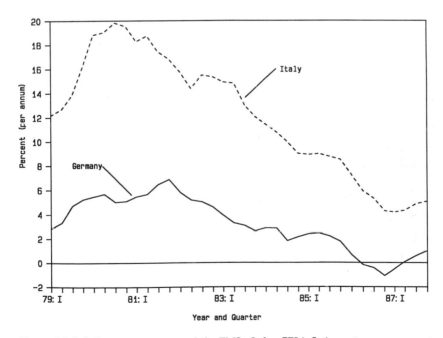

Figure 5.2 Inflation convergence and the EMS—Italy: CPI inflation rate.

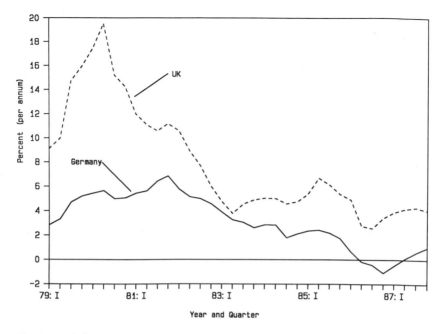

Figure 5.3 Inflation convergence and the EMS—UK: CPI inflation rate.

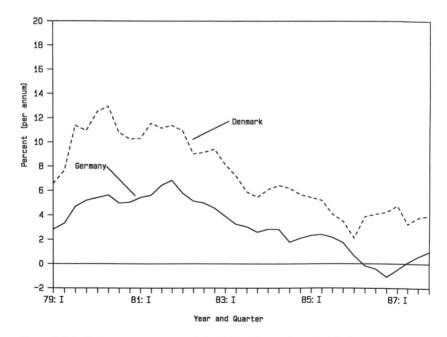

Figure 5.4 Inflation convergence and the EMS—Denmark: CPI inflation rate.

exceed 5 percent. Given that Germany has achieved zero growth of consumer prices, that result is quite remarkable.

The disinflation of the 1980s has been accompanied by large swings in competitiveness across Europe. In fact it has been argued that real exchange rate appreciation has been a crucial factor in the disinflation. In figures 5.5 through 5.8 we show the behavior of two real exchange rate indices relative to Germany: In each case, both for the value-added deflator and for unit labor costs, the index is the ratio of the real effective exchange rate of each country (as reported in the I.M.F. *International Financial Statistics*) to the real effective exchange rate of Germany. The index measures competitiveness relative to Germany, accounting for competition in world markets (an increase in the index indicates a real appreciation relative to Germany). The most interesting comparison is the one between Italy and the United Kingdom. The real appreciation of sterling was important in the Thatcher disinflation: The swing between 1979 and 1980 is about 80 percent, according to both measures. By 1987, however, U.K. competitivenesss relative to Germany had returned to 1979 levels. The U.K. experience contrasts sharply with the Italian one. Throughout the 1980s Italy experienced a slow, continuing real appreciation relative to Germany. The cumulative loss of competitiveness is about 10 percent if computed using unit labor cost and slightly higher if GDP deflators are used instead.

Developments in other countries are less clearcut. In France, competitiveness relative to Germany fell in the first three years of the EMS. There was a sharp recovery around the March 1983 realignment and a further fall in the more recent years. The competitiveness of Denmark relative to Germany closely follows its different exchange rate policies. The depreciations of the early years of EMS membership produced large gains in competitiveness relative to Germany. Following the change in government of November 1982, when a fixed parity vis-à-vis the DM became the goal of Danish monetary policy, competitiveness began to fall sharply.

5.3   Arguments in Favor of Exchange Rate Pegging

Consider a country suffering from high inflation and wishing to reduce it. If the money supply is used as the nominal anchor, then the exchange rate is endogenous; if the exchange rate is the anchor, the money supply is endogenous. The choice of a nominal anchor makes

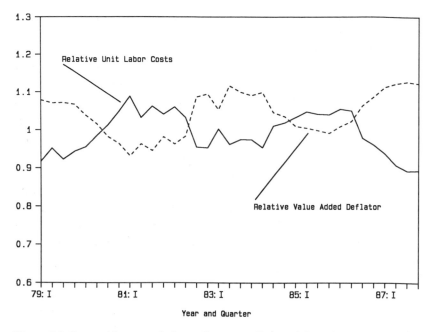

Figure 5.5 Competitiveness relative to Germany—France: bilateral real exchange rates from IMF effective indices.

little difference in the steady state, but has important consequences during the transition, since the output cost of disinflating—the "sacrifice ratio"—is different in a money supply strategy relative to an exchange rate strategy.[2] There are two reasons why the output cost may be lower in the exchange rate strategy.

The first was pointed out by Fischer (1988a). If goods prices are sticky, a reduction in the rate of money growth raises real interest rates, thus inducing a recession.[3] Were it possible to accompany the reduction in the rate of money growth with a once-and-for-all increase in the stock of money to accomodate the increase in money demand, the recession could be avoided. The likely outcome, however, is the

---

2 Dornbusch (1986a) discusses the linkages between exchange rate policies and inflation. See also the models by Gylfason and Lindbeck (1986, 1987), and Howitt (1987).

3 A reduction in the rate of money growth decreases inflationary expectations and increases money demand. Given the real stock of money and sticky prices, nominal interest rates need to increase to equilibrate the money market. Since inflationary expectations are down, the increase in nominal rates is reflected in an increase in real interest rates.

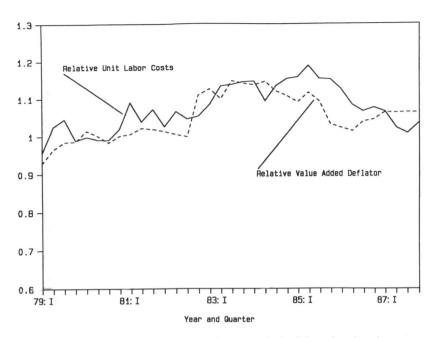

Figure 5.6 Competitiveness relative to Germany—Italy: bilateral real exchange rates from IMF effective indices.

undermining of the credibility of the whole program by the once-and-for-all increase in the money stock. As Fischer shows, a disinflation strategy that fixes the nominal exchange rate could be more attractive than one that fixes the rate of money growth, since in the former case the required fall in the stock of money is smaller. With wage stickiness as the major cause of the recession, a smaller fall in the money supply tends to make the sacrifice ratio smaller.[4]

Monetary targeting and exchange rate pegging might also have different effects in a disinflation because of the credibility of monetary versus exchange rate targets. This is the focus of the current chapter. Before illustrating the effects of alternative exchange rate regimes on expectations, we discuss how price setters' expectations are formed,

---

4 A formal welfare analysis of the effects of exchange rate pegging is carried out by Helpman and Razin (1987), who apply a model where individuals have finite expected horizons, but where nominal prices are perfectly flexible, and therefore the type of inertia associated with price expectations we concentrate on in this chapter is absent. Their model highlights the issue of sustainability of the stabilization policy and the time patterns of fiscal and monetary policies that can validate the exchange rate freeze.

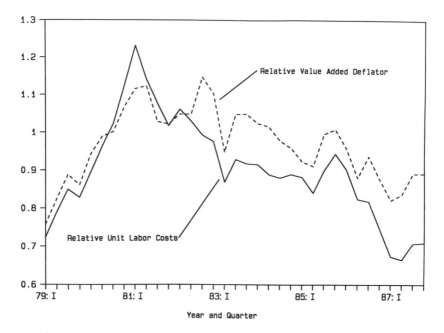

Figure 5.7 Competitiveness relative to Germany—UK: bilateral real exchange rates from IMF effective indices.

and the credibility problem of central banks.

Suppose the central bank announces its money growth target before wage contracts are signed. Once the contracts are signed, if the central bank reneges on the preannounced target, real wages fall and output rises. If the central bank has an incentive to raise output, it will indeed renege on its announcement. Aware of this incentive, unions will set wages at the level where the central bank's utility from one more unit of output exactly matches its marginal disutility of more inflation. In the ensuing equilibrium the union has been effective at eliminating the chance of being caught by surprise inflation, the central bank is frustrated in its attempt to raise output, and the inflation rate is "too high."[5]

If the interaction between the public and the central bank is like a

---

5 Notice that while it is optimal to promise zero money growth ex ante, it is not optimal to fullfill the promise: This is an example of the dynamic inconsistency of optimal plans, first pointed out by Kydland and Prescott (1977), Calvo (1978), and Fischer (1980). The papers by Barro and Gordon (1983a, 1983b) apply that idea to the macro models studied in this chapter.

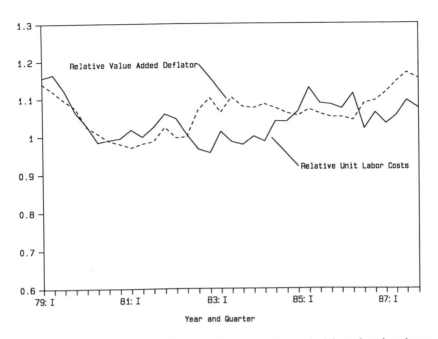

Figure 5.8 Competitiveness relative to Germany—Denmark: bilateral real exchange rates from IMF effective indices.

series of one-shot games with no memory, there is no way out of the deadlock. But if the interaction is repeated over time and the public keeps track of the central bank's record, the outcome of the one-shot game can be improved upon. Reputation is the mechanism through which better outcomes can be sustained.[6]

An interesting situation—and one that is directly relevant to our discussion—is the case of a new incoming government that wants to bring inflation down. When the new administration takes office, the public is uncertain about its true preferences; that is, whether this is really a "tough" government or just another "wet" government pretending to be tough. A wet government might also have an incentive to act tough for some time to try to fool the public, postponing the day when it creates a big inflation. The only thing the tough government can do is to reduce the growth rate of money and stick to it, waiting for the public to convince itself that it is really tough. The cost of acquiring such reputation is a recession, which occurs because money is

---

6 See Backus and Driffil (1985) for an analysis of reputational equilibria. Melitz (1988) applies the concept of reputational equilibrium to the EMS.

tight, but expectations have not adjusted fully. The slower the public in revising its expectations, the longer the recession. The latter can be shortened by making it deeper. If the tough government at the beginning of its term acts even tougher than it would under normal conditions, then it will take less time for the public to be convinced that it is indeed faced with a tough government. A wet government might have an incentive to act tough for some time, but it is unlikely to be ready to accept a very deep recession just to fool the public.[7]

The difficulties in breaking the expectations' inertia described here arise in a regime where the monetary authority targets the rate of money growth. Would targeting the exchange rate instead improve the chances of successfully fighting inflation?[8] To answer this question, we need to consider alternative exchange rate arrangements. In particular, we need to take into account the interactions between the public and the monetary authority in each country, and among monetary authorities in different countries. We simplify the analysis by ruling out the reputation-building effects described earlier, and discuss a two-country monetary system in a static setup.[9] In the next section we show that an extension of the model to the multi-period case can account for some of the empirical regularities we noted above.

The models we analyze rely on two crucial assumptions. First, expectations affect price dynamics because wages cannot fully and instantaneously react to current information.[10] Second, price setters have

---

7 Barro (1986) shows the need to create a recession to establish a reputation. The tradeoff between the length and the size of the recession is discussed in Vickers (1987).
8 In this chapter, and particularly in our empirical analysis, we concentrate on the strategic interactions between governments and price setters—where the success of a disinflation hinges on the government's ability to affect expectations—and on the advantages from pegging the exchange rate that are associated with the endogenous adjustment in expectations. As we shall see below, alternative exchange rate regimes can also affect the convergence of inflation rates among member countries through channels that are independent of the public's expectations, by imposing different constraints on monetary authorities and affecting their incentives to inflate. Collins (1988) concentrates on these effects in her discussion of the European disinflation. Her conclusion is that they do not provide a strong enough argument to explain the convergence of inflation rates in the 1980s. Our empirical analysis, designed to identify the endogenous shifts in expectations, will control explicitly for the effects studied by Collins.
9 These two countries could be affected equally by rest-of-the-world shocks, and constitute a separate region.
10 The implicit assumptions of all models in this section is that the first-best equilibrium, full wage and price flexibility, cannot be attained for exogenous technological constraints, and that (at least some) goods markets are not competitive. For a survey

Table 5.1
The Canzoneri-Henderson 2-country model

$y = -(w - p)(1 - \alpha)/\alpha - x$	(5.1)
$y^* = -(w^* - p^*)(1 - \alpha)/\alpha - x$	(5.1')
$y - y^* = \delta(e + p^* - p)$	(5.2)
$m - p = y$	(5.3)
$m^* - p^* = y^*$	(5.3')
$\Omega = -\sigma(n - k)^2 - (q)^2$	(5.4)
$\Omega^* = -\sigma(n^* - k^*)^2 - (q^*)^2$	(5.4')
$q = p + \beta(e + p^* - p)$	(5.5)
$q^* = p^* + \beta(p - e - p^*)$	(5.5')

rational expectations. The first assumption gives monetary authorities the power and the incentive to affect real variables, like employment and international competitiveness. The second assumption gives rise to strategic interactions between the public and the monetary authorities; the public, by trying to guess the authority's reactions, can jeopardize—or speed up—the efforts of the monetary authority. In the presence of nominal stickiness (wages are predetermined), equilibria are affected crucially by the type of exchange rate regime postulated, that is by the "rules of the game" between monetary authorities. With symmetric flexible exchange rates, gains and losses are shared equally among the various countries. Gains and losses, however, are not shared equally if the exchange rate regime is asymmetric. To illustrate these points, we adopt the two-country model laid out in table 5.1, studied extensively by Canzoneri and Henderson (1988a, 1988b). The two countries are symmetric. All variables are in logs and expressed as deviations from their means. The supply functions (equations (5.1) and (5.1')) relate output to real product wages, and include a disturbance, x, that allows us to study the strategic interaction between the two countries in response to common real shocks, such as a worldwide supply shock. The level of the real exchange rate determines how demand gets allocated between the outputs of the countries (equation (5.2)). Domestic and foreign money are the only

---

on the empirical evidence on sticky prices, see Blanchard (1988) and Dornbusch and Giovannini (1988).

assets, and they are not traded. If we allowed additional assets in the model, it would become necessary to assume capital controls. Later on we discuss the issue of international capital mobility in this context. Money demand (equations (5.3) and (5.3$'$) is an increasing function of the level of income. The central banks' objectives are described by equations (5.4) and (5.4$'$): they are quadratic in the deviations of employment from a target and in the level of the consumer price index, defined in equations (5.5) and (5.5$'$). The target employment levels, k and k^* exceed the natural rate, which in this model equals 0. k and k^* represent the central banks' attitudes toward expansionary policies.[11] The exchange rate enters the authorities' objective function because a real appreciation lowers the domestic CPI.

The model is closed with equations specifying how wages are set. We assume that unions set them before the realizations of exogenous shocks, trying to minimize the fluctuations of employment around equilibrium. Under perfect foresight, this implies $n = n^* = 0$.[12] Employment is determined by the demand for labor implicit in equations (5.1) and (5.1$'$). However, the optimal level of wages is not independent of the exchange rate regime. To identify the possible advantages of exchange rate pegging, we compare the benchmark flexible exchange rate regime with two asymmetric regimes, managed and fixed exchange rates. In studying each regime, we only look at time-consistent Nash equilibria. We assume that each central bank sets monetary policy, taking as given (1) price expectations in the domestic labor market, thus giving rise to a time-consistent equilibrium; and (2) the partner country's money supply, thus giving rise to a Nash equilibrium in the international interaction.

5.3.1 Flexible Exchange Rates

In the flexible exchange rate regime, each central bank sets its own money supply taking the partner's as given. The exchange rate is endogenous. It is straightforward to show that minimization of the unions' loss function implies the following wage-setting rule:

---

11 These attitudes might be motivated by the presence of distortions in the economy, which move equilibrium output inside the production possibility frontier.
12 Prices, on the other hand, are perfectly flexible in this model.

$$w = (m)^e \tag{5.6}$$
$$w^* = (m^*)^e \tag{5.6'}$$

Substituting these expressions in equations (5.1) and (5.1'), and assuming perfect foresight, one obtains the Nash equilibrium

$$n = n^* = -\Phi x \tag{5.7}$$
$$q = m = \frac{\sigma}{\varepsilon + \alpha} k - \Phi x \tag{5.8}$$
$$q^* = m^* = \frac{\sigma}{\varepsilon + \alpha} k^* - \Phi x \tag{5.8'}$$

where

$$\Phi = \left[1 - \frac{\varepsilon(\varepsilon + \alpha)}{\sigma + (\varepsilon + \alpha)^2} \right]^{-1} \frac{(\varepsilon + \alpha)}{\sigma + (\varepsilon + \alpha)^2} \quad \text{and} \quad \varepsilon = \frac{(1 - \alpha)\beta}{\delta}$$

In the absence of a common supply shock (when $x = 0$), employment in both countries equals the natural rate but inflation is positive. When $x = 0$, equilibrium inflation is a function of central banks' incentives to "fool" the public with surprise monetary expansions, and of the incentives to export inflation to the rest of the world via a real exchange rate appreciation. The first effect can be isolated by setting $\beta = 0$, so that $\varepsilon = 0$. When $\varepsilon = 0$, countries have no incentive to export inflation to the rest of the world, since—as shown in equations (5.5) and (5.5')—a real exchange rate appreciation does not affect the domestic CPI. The larger the relative weight of the employment target in central bankers' objectives (σ), and, of course, the larger the desired employment level in the two countries (k and k^*), the larger the inflation bias. With $\varepsilon = 0$, inflation just equals what Barro and Gordon obtain in their closed-economy model.

International interactions affect equilibrium inflation to the extent that changes in the real exchange rate affect consumer prices in the two countries. The presence of international interactions actually *lowers* inflation in a Nash equilibrium: This effect is represented by the ε term in the coefficients of k and k^* in (5.8) and (5.8').

A further illustration of the contractionary bias associated with international interactions under flexible exchange rates is provided by the analysis of the effects of the negative worldwide supply shock x. Notice that x, on impact, lowers output and increases prices in both countries. In equilibrium, however, the contractionary effect on output and employment is preserved, while prices actually fall in both countries. Once again, this results from the contractionary bias of flexible exchange rates. In the response to the negative supply shock, each central bank tries to contract money more than the other, to engineer a real exchange rate appreciation, and to dump on the partner part of the cost of the disinflation. Since the two countries are identical, however, the equilibrium turns out to be just a worldwide deflation.

5.3.2   Managed Exchange Rates

In a flexible exchange rate regime, each central bank takes the other partner's money supply as given; therefore, it believes that a change in its own money stock can affect the exchange rate. Because the exchange rate feeds back into domestic prices, the central bank believes that monetary policy can improve the output-price level tradeoff. In contrast, in a regime of managed exchange rate the two countries perceive different tradeoffs.[13] One country (the Nth country) sets its own money stock, assuming the partner country will accomodate perfectly (given the exchange rate). Therefore it attempts to maximize its objective function subject to the world economy's tradeoff between output and the price level. The other country, on the contrary, believes—as in the case of flexible rates—that it can affect the price level with a smaller output loss by changing the exchange rate.

A model where one country gives up control of the exchange rate and controls its money supply, whereas the other $N - 1$ countries control the price of their currencies in terms of the Nth currency, appears to be useful in explaining the Bretton Woods system. Although the numeraire of the Bretton Woods system was gold, and thus there was a theoretical possibility of affecting all countries' exchange rates independently by changing their gold price, the dollar price of gold was regarded very much as the cornerstone of the whole system. A change in the dollar/gold parity was considered a de facto abandonment of the regime.[14] The role of the dollar must be contrasted with the ability that countries other than the United States had to affect their exchange

---

13 This model is motivated and analyzed by Giavazzi and Giovannini (1989). See also Kenen (1987) for interesting discussions of the relevance of asymmetric models of international monetary systems.
14 See Solomon (1977), for example.

rates.[15] Harry Johnson's (1972) description of the nature of the Bretton Woods system, which he refers to as the reserve currency system, confirms this view.[16]

As we discuss at length in chapters 3 and 4, asymmetry is also the central feature of the European Monetary System. However it remains to be seen whether the managed exchange rate regime discussed here is the appropriate model of the EMS. It is not clear, for example, how much independence countries other than Germany have in changing their currency parities vis-à-vis the DM. As we shall see, this question crucially affects the benefits in terms of "imported reputation" that countries can obtain by pegging their exchange rates.

Under managed exchange rates, optimal wage setting implies

$$w = (m^{*e} + e^e) \tag{5.9}$$

$$w^* = (m^*)^e \tag{5.9'}$$

where a $*$ now denotes the country that controls the money supply. Proceding as in the case of flexible rates, the Nash equilibrium in the managed exchange rate regime is

$$n^* = -\alpha \Gamma \Delta^{-1} \left[\varepsilon(\alpha + \varepsilon) + (\alpha + \varepsilon)^2 + \sigma \right] x \tag{5.10}$$

$$n = -\alpha \Gamma \Delta^{-1} \left[\varepsilon(\alpha + \varepsilon) + (\alpha + \varepsilon)^2 + \sigma(1 - \varepsilon/\alpha) \right] x \tag{5.10'}$$

$$q^* = \frac{\sigma}{\alpha} k^* - Ax \tag{5.11}$$

$$q^* = \frac{\sigma}{\varepsilon + \alpha} k^* - Ax + \Gamma \Delta^{-1} \varepsilon \sigma (\alpha + 2\varepsilon) x \tag{5.11'}$$

$$(e + p^* - p) = -\Gamma (\beta \Delta)^{-1} \varepsilon \sigma (\alpha + 2\varepsilon) x \tag{5.12}$$

---

15 The IMF Annual Reports of 1964 and 1965 admitted the use of exchange realignments for adjusting external imbalances and, indeed, countries other than the United States changed their gold parity (that is their dollar exchange rate) on several occasions between 1949 and 1969: 1949, realignment of several European currencies; 1957, devaluation of the French franc; 1958, devaluation of the French franc; 1961, revaluation of the DM and the Dutch guilder; 1967, devaluation of the pound; 1969, revaluation of the DM.

16 "In a reserve currency system, the adjustment problem operates asymmetrically: the non-reserve currency countries can adjust against the rest of the world by changing their par values in terms of gold, but the reserve currency country cannot do this unilaterally, for a variety of reasons."

where

$$\Delta = \Gamma\alpha\varepsilon\left[\sigma + \alpha(\alpha + \varepsilon)\right] + \left(\sigma + \alpha^2\right)\Gamma\left[\sigma + (\alpha + \varepsilon)^2\right]$$
$$\Gamma = \left[\delta\beta\left(1 - \alpha\right) + \alpha\right]$$
$$A = 1 + \alpha^2\Gamma\Delta^{-1}\left[\varepsilon\left(\alpha + \varepsilon\right) + (\alpha + \varepsilon) + \sigma\right] - \Gamma\varepsilon\sigma\left(\alpha + \varepsilon\right)$$

The Nash interaction under managed exchange rates gives rise to two interesting properties. The first is pointed out by Canzoneri and Henderson (1988b). Consider the first term on the right hand side of equations (5.11) and (5.11'). In the Nth country the inflationary bias associated with the central bank's incentive to raise output is larger than in the flexible rates regime and is the same as if the country were a closed economy. The asymmetric position of the Nth country prevents it from attempting to affect the real exchange rate in order to improve its tradeoff between output and prices. As we have seen above, the public's recognition of such an incentive is precisely what keeps price expectations lower under flexible exchange rates, relative to the closed-economy case. On the other hand, the incentive to affect the exchange rate is still present in the country that controls the exchange rate, and this helps to keep price expectations down. This country is indifferent between flexible and managed rates. As Canzoneri and Henderson point out, the result suggests that managed exchange rates are an inferior regime if the problem is correction of the "domestic" inflationary bias. A country that joins a stable monetary area but maintains the ability to affect the exchange rate does not improve upon the flexible rates outcome. In the Nth country, on the contrary, price expectations are higher than under flexible rates because the public recognizes that the central bank has lost the ability—and thus the incentive—to affect the real exchange rate.

The other property of a regime of managed exchange rates, pointed out by Giavazzi and Giovannini (1989), is associated with the effects of real shocks. As shown by equation (5.12), in response to a worldwide supply shock that hits identical countries, the real exchange rate always moves. A negative supply shock brings about a real appreciation for the country that controls the exchange rate. The opposite happens after a positive supply shock.[17] Furthermore, as a result of

---

17 In this model, the real exchange rate moves as long as $\varepsilon > 0$, that is as long as a real appreciaton affects prices. The same results would obtain if imported materials were used in the production of domestic output.

supply shocks, the country controlling the exchange rate is always better off relative to the country controlling the money supply. In a managed exchange rate system, the country controlling the exchange rate is successful in its attempt to run a "beggar-thy-neighbor" policy. By controlling the exchange rate, this country is able to affect prices at a comparatively lower cost in terms of output, because part of the output cost of stabilizing prices is shifted abroad.

5.3.3   Fixed Exchange Rates

The lesson from the analysis of flexible and managed rates is that the strategic interaction among countries gives rise to a contractionary bias; this partly offsets the domestic inflationary bias associated with the central banks' incentive to affect real wages when nominal wages are preset. As Rogoff (1985b) has pointed out, this is an example of a second-best situation where adding one inefficiency improves welfare. Controlling the exchange rate instead of the money supply, as in the managed exchange rate regime described above, does not help to bring down expectations. Private agents know that the central bank is not constrained in any way and can change the nominal exchange rate to affect output and inflation, just as under flexible exchange rates it can change the nominal money supply. From the viewpoint of a central bank in search of an exchange rate regime that would stabilize expectations, and thus help it to disinflate, there is no difference between flexible rates and a managed rates regime in which it retains the ability to affect the exchange rate.

We might now ask how a regime where countries have no ability to independently affect the exchange rate would work. In this section we turn to the analysis of a regime of *fixed* exchange rates. While this is an extreme case, it helps us to highlight the payoffs from giving up monetary independence.

What is the outcome of fixed rates in the two-country model shown here? Assume that the "*" country sets monetary policy, and the partner country accommodates any change in m^* by changing m accordingly. Ignoring real shocks, the equilibrium is:

$$n = n^* = 0 \tag{5.13}$$

$$q = q^* = \frac{\sigma}{\alpha}k^* \tag{5.14}$$

Comparison of equations (5.8$'$) and (5.14) clearly points to the conditions for fixed exchange rates to be an attractive option for a central bank facing a credibility problem. Under flexible rates, the equilibrium price level in the domestic country is $[\sigma/(\varepsilon + \alpha)]\,k$. Under fixed exchange rates, the domestic central bank loses all power to affect the domestic price level, and this is simply equal to the price level prevailing in the foreign country. If the foreign central bank does not suffer from a credibility problem (so that $k^* = 0$), fixed rates remove the domestic inefficiency. The domestic central bank acquires the reputation of the foreign central bank and price expectations are automatically stabilized. The closer the foreign to the domestic country, the less attractive a system of fixed exchange rates. Pegging to a country whose central bank faces a credibility problem similar to the one faced at home clearly does not help. For pegging to be an attractive option, the "credibility gap" must be sufficiently large. Fixed exchange rates remove all strategic interactions and, as we have seen, strategic interactions dampen the domestic inflationary bias. The condition for fixed rates to be superior to flexible rates is

$$\frac{k - k^*}{k^*} > \frac{\varepsilon}{\alpha} \qquad\qquad\qquad (5.15)$$

Fixed exchange rates are superior to flexible rates if the credibility gap is large relative to the incentive to affect the exchange rate under flexible rates.

This result leaves two open questions. First, what incentives does the center country have to form such an arrangement? Equation (5.14) indicates that the value of the loss function in the center country is higher under fixed exchange rates than under flexible rates. The model we use here cannot justify the participation of the center country in such an arrangement, because the countries are perfectly symmetric. Two types of asymmetries can justify the participation of the center country. The first is economic size: if the center country is much larger than the partner(s), it is nearly indifferent among alternative exchange rate arrangements. This explains why, for example, the United States has no objections to Bolivia pegging its currency to the dollar.[18]

The second argument, more suited to the EMS experience, has to

18 This is Mundell's (1968) "optimal division of the burden of adjustment."

do with asymmetric effects of common exogenous shocks. For example, if a common external shock tends to change the exchange rate between the two countries, the center country might find it desirable to participate in an arrangement for limiting exchange rate flexibility (the evidence on real exchange rates in chapter 3 could provide some support for this view).

The second question left open is the extent to which the exchange rate peg is perceived as binding by the monetary authorities and the public. Why should exchange rate targets be more credible than money supply targets? Pegging the exchange rate can only enhance the credibility of the central bank under two conditions: (1) exchange rate changes are in some sense "costly" to the central bank; (2) it is easy for the public to monitor the central bank's motivations to change the exchange rate.

Let us start from point (2). The ability to monitor the central bank's motivations to change the exchange rate depend on the information available to the central bank and to the public, and on the central bank's use of its private information. Canzoneri (1985) discusses the role of private information when a central bank has a money supply target.[19] He assumes that the central bank can, and is expected to, play a socially desirable stabilization role. He argues that modern democracies most likely have found ways to avoid time inconsistent behavior by central bankers. "Surprise" monetary expansions, if properly identified, can be minimized; however, cheating is harder to monitor. The central bank could make good use of its private information. Canzoneri studies the most relevant case: velocity shocks. Whenever the public cannot verify the central bank's private forecasts of velocity shocks, the central bank can rationalize ex post a larger than expected monetary expansion as justified by the need to accommodate the forecast of an unusually large and negative velocity shock. Therefore, if forecasts of velocity shocks are private information, there is no way to limit the central bank's incentive to overexpand.

What happens in a regime of pegged exchange rates? Given the exchange rate target, the central bank's only task is to accommodate all fluctuations in money demand freely. Velocity shocks are accommodated automatically under pegged exchange rates. Therefore, under pegged exchange rates the central bank cannot justify unanticipated

---

19 He analyzes a closed-economy model; however, his arguments can be transposed immediately to the open economy.

exchange rate depreciations as being motivated by the need to acco-modate forecasts of larger-than-usual contractions in velocity. This is one argument that makes an exchange rate target more credible than a money-supply target.[20]

In addition, if the central bank faces costs of changing the exchange rate, the credibility of an exchange rate target is enhanced. This is point (1). There are likely to be two types of costs: the costs of the "routine" (convincing the partners that an adjustment is needed, and negotiating the appropriate size of parity realignments) and the costs in terms of disruption of the system (too frequent adjustments of ex-change rates imply de facto abandoning the system). In Europe, the costs of abandoning the EMS are perceived to be very high. The French experience in the mid 1980s, to be described in section 5.5, vividly illustrates the public perceptions of these costs.

Thus the argument that exchange rate pegging is a superior strategy for fighting inflation is rather weak, because it relies on the assumption that exchange rate targets are more "visible" or credible than mone-tary, or interest rate, targets, and cannot explain the motivations of the center country to participate in such an arrangement. However, these theoretical drawbacks notwithstanding, the EMS might still have played a role in the disinflation of countries other than Germany. The absence of a strong theoretical argument makes the empirical analysis even more important. Before turning to the data, we will describe next a dynamic extension of the pegged exchange rate regime we have just studied. This extension allows for periodic exchange rate adjustments, and divergences between domestic and foreign inflation rates.

5.4 The Effects of Periodic Parity Realignments

The static models discussed in section 5.3 are useful in highlighting the basic effects of international monetary policy interactions on in-

---

20 With sticky prices, there might be disturbances requiring changes in the country's real exchange rate, brought about by changes in the nominal rate. Theoretically, this opens up the possibility that the central bank might be trying to fool the public when it announces that the exchange rate realignment is just the optimal response to a real shock. We believe that, while such theoretical possibilities could be constructed, the central bank would find it much harder to be believed if it claimed that its own fore-casts of these real shocks differed significantly from the public's. Furthermore, the least controversial stabilization role of the central bank is associated with the smooth functioning of the money markets. We discuss real shocks further below.

dividual countries' inflation. Some of their predictions, however, are at odds with the simple empirical facts we described in section 5.2. In particular, in a regime of fixed exchange rates, countries' inflation rates converge completely and the real exchange rate is unaffected; in section 5.2 we pointed out that convergence of inflation rates between Germany and the other countries is far from complete, and that bilateral real exchange rates have fluctuated considerably.

Here we extend the fixed exchange rate model of the previous section to account for periodic exchange rate realignments.[21] This is clearly desirable, since periodic realignments do characterize the EMS experience. We take the foreign country as given, set its inflation rate at zero, and ask whether a country caught in a "high-inflation deadlock" can gain from pegging its exchange rate to the low-inflation foreign country and realigning the exchange rate every T periods. Then we ask whether such a regime produces fluctuations of the real exchange rates and inflation rates similar to those discussed in section 5.2.

We assume a log-linear relationship between output supply, inflation, and the terms of trade described by an expectational Phillips curve. The reduced-form relation between output and inflation is equivalent to that implied by the one-shot model used above. With pre-set nominal wages, an increase in the price level lowers product wages and raises output. A real appreciation reduces the relative price of imported inputs and also raises output.[22] The supply equation is

$$y_t^s = \left(\pi_t - \pi_t^e \right) / \alpha - \gamma z_t \tag{5.16}$$

with $\alpha, \gamma > 0$; y is output, π is the inflation rate—the rate of increase of the output deflator—π^e the private sector's expectation of π, conditional on information available, and z is the level of the real exchange rate, measured as the relative price of foreign output in terms of domestic output. All variables are expressed as deviations from their

---

21 The exchange rate can be changed every T periods.

22 This supply function can be derived by considering the problem of competitive firms with a decreasing returns-to-scale technology, using domestic labor and foreign output as factors of production and facing a given world price of imported intermediate goods. Firms contract on nominal wages with workers before prices are set. This supply function is the only one consistent with the central banker's objective function specified below. If the supply equation were due to informational problems, as in Lucas (1973), the optimal policy would be that of eliminating randomness in monetary policy.

steady-state values.

Money demand is simply a function of the level of income

$$y_t^d = m_t - p_t \tag{5.17}$$

Under rational expectations the two conditions that have to hold for equilibrium are

$$\left(\pi_t - \pi_t^e\right)/\alpha - \gamma z_t = m_t - p_t \qquad \pi = \pi_t^e \tag{5.18}$$

The first describes equilibrium in the goods market; the second derives from the assumption of rational expectations which, in the absence of stochastic shocks, is equivalent to perfect foresight.

The central banker's instantaneous loss function is quadratic in the inflation rate and in the deviation of output from a target level

$$L_t = (1/2) \left[\pi_t^2 + \sigma \left(y_t - k_t\right)^2\right] \tag{5.19}$$

with $\sigma; k > 0$. The target level of output k is positive and exceeds the natural rate $(y = 0)$.

The central bank minimizes the present value of the sum of future losses

$$\underset{\{\pi_t\}}{\text{MIN}} \int_o^\infty L_t e^{-\rho t} dt \tag{5.19'}$$

Where ρ is the instantaneous utility discount rate. The loss function is minimized by choosing a path for π_t subject to a different set of constraints, depending on the international monetary regime. In studying each regime we concentrate only on the discretionary equilibrium, where the central bank chooses π taking π^e as given.

We discuss the monetary authority's choice between two regimes: flexible exchange rates and a regime where the exchange rate is pegged to a foreign currency, and periodically realigned. In the flexible rates regime with perfect foresight, the real exchange rate is constant and equal to 0. With z_t constant, there are no state variables in L_t. Minimization of (5.19') is therefore identical to minimization of equation (5.19).

Minimizing equation (5.19) subject to equations (5.16), (5.17), and (5.18), and to $z_t = 0$, yields the following optimal inflation rate

$$\hat{\pi}_t = \sigma k/\alpha \qquad\qquad\qquad (5.20)$$

Since in equilibrium $\hat{\pi}, \pi^e, z = 0$, and therefore $y = 0$, the central banker fails to move output away from the natural rate, but his incentive to do so results in a positive equilibrium level of inflation.[23]

The value of the instantaneous loss function in equilibrium is

$$\hat{L}_t = \left(1 + \sigma/\alpha^2\right) k^2/2 \qquad\qquad\qquad (5.21)$$

The higher the incentive to raise output via inflation surprises (that is the lower α), the larger the central bank's loss. In this Cournot-Nash equilibrium, where the central bank takes the public's expectation of inflation as given, the perception by the central bank of an output-inflation tradeoff different from the equilibrium one constitutes the source of inefficiency. With $\alpha = 0$ the value of the loss function remains positive, since monopolistic price setting is always present.

The inefficiency arising from the incentive to inflate would be removed if the central bank could be forced to choose $\pi = 0$. In the absence of reputational effects, however, such precommitment would not be credible. As equation (5.21) shows, the inefficiency of the Nash equilibrium would also be reduced if the weight of inflation in the central bank's loss function, $1/\sigma$, relative to the incentive of creating inflation, $1/\alpha$, could be increased somehow. This idea lies behind the suggestion to appoint a "conservative" central banker, or to introduce a nominal target in the central bank's objective function.[24]

A natural candidate for a nominal target is the exchange rate. If the central bank pegged the domestic currency to that of a foreign country where monetary policy integrity was known not to be dented by foreign influences, then it might be able to reduce the inefficiency loss. This might work because the choice of pegging the exchange rate could raise the cost of inflation: With a fixed nominal exchange rate, any inflation differential vis-à-vis the foreign country translates into changes in the real exchange rate and therefore into fluctuations in the level of output.

In the pegged exchange rate regime, we assume that the nominal

---

23 This is the result first obtained by Barro and Gordon (1983b), and is consistent with the analysis of section 5.3 above. See in particular equation (5.8) describing equilibrium inflation under flexible exchange rates, and the discussion that follows.
24 This observation is due to Rogoff (1985c).

exchange rate between the two countries is fixed for intervals of length T.[25] The T-intervals are exogenously given and are justified by fixed costs of publicly announcing a new peg. There are two important aspects to this definition of the pegged exchange rate regime. First, the central bank does not attempt to manipulate the exchange in order to achieve a better output-inflation tradeoff: That is, it does not attempt to run a "beggar-thy-neighbor" policy. This contrasts with the strategic interaction between the central bank and the private sector. Second, there is no international trade in assets, since there are no assets except money, and moneys are not tradeable internationally. In the presence of other assets capital controls would be needed since, as Obstfeld (1988) showed, with perfect capital mobility pegged exchange rate rules may produce multiple equilibria. We do not address these issues here: We ask instead whether pegged exchange rates are preferable in a situation where the central bank retains some degree of monetary autonomy through the operation of capital controls.

At the beginning of every interval of length T, a nominal exchange rate realignment sets the real exchange rate back to a preassigned level z_0. What is z_0 determined by? For the regime of pegged exchange rates to be sustainable, the central bank should not accumulate or decumulate foreign exchange reserves forever. Since the change in reserves is assumed to depend on the level of the real exchange rate, z_0 has to be such that the net accumulation of foreign exchange reserves within each interval is zero.

Within each interval, the change in the real exchange rate is

$$\dot{z}_t = -\pi_t \tag{5.22}$$

Given that in every T-interval the central bank faces the same problem, we restrict the horizon of the objective function to be T, without any loss of generality. To further simplify matters, we take the utility discount rate to be equal to zero. Therefore the central bank's problem becomes

$$\underset{\{\pi_t\}}{\text{MIN}} \int_0^T L_t dt \tag{5.23}$$

---

25 T cannot be zero, since this would be identical to a flexible exchange rate regime; we assume T to be less than infinity to allow the domestic inflation rate to differ from the inflation rate abroad.

subject to equations (5.5), (5.17), and (5.22). The solution is carried out in Appendix A and yields the following optimal path for inflation:[26]

$$\dot{\pi}_t = (z_0 + k/\gamma) \left[c_1 \mu_1 exp\, (\mu_1 t) + c_2 \mu_2\, (\mu_2 t) \right] \quad 0 \le t \le T \tag{5.24}$$

Notice that the optimal inflation path depends on the real exchange rate chosen at every realignment date. As mentioned before, z_0 is determined by the sustainability condition, *given* the optimal inflation path. This prevents the central banker from choosing z_0 directly as a control variable in his minimization problem.[27] The sustainability condition can be written as

$$\int_0^T \dot{R}_t dt = \int_0^T \delta z_t dt = 0 \tag{5.25}$$

where R is the stock of foreign exchange reserves.[28] Equations (5.25), (5.24), and (5.22), are solved for z_0, whose expression we report in Appendix A.

The choice between flexible and pegged exchange rates is determined by the difference between the value of the loss function in the two regimes. In the case of flexible rates, the value of the loss function is computed by substituting equation (5.20) into the objective function in equation (5.23), given the equilibrium condition $z_t = 0$. In the case of pegged exchange rates, we compute the path of the real exchange rate associated with the optimal inflation path in equation (5.24); both are then substituted into the objective function in equation (5.23), using equation (5.5) and the equilibrium conditions equation (5.18). The final result is

$$\int_0^T \hat{L}_{peg}(t)dt - \int_0^T \hat{L}_{flex}(t)dt = k^2 F(T) \tag{5.26}$$

where $F(0) = 0$, and the expression for F is reported in Appendix A. For $T = 0$, pegged exchange rates coincide trivially with flexible rates.

---

26 The values of the parameters in equation (5.24) also appear in Appendix A.

27 If the central bank chose both z_0 and π, any level of inflation would be sustainable, given the appropriate choice of z_0. All the discipline arising from the pegged exchange rate regime would vanish.

28 The accumulation equation implicit in equation (5.25) assumes that foreign exchange reserves do not yield interest.

With T positive, the pegged exchange rate regime achieves a smaller loss than flexible rates.

The intuition for this result is the following: When the nominal exchange rate is fixed, even for short periods of time, the weight of inflation in the loss function increases relative to the flexible exchange rate regime; non-zero rates of inflation bring about changes in the real exchange rate and further deviations of output from the target level. As in Rogoff's conservative central banker, increasing the weight of inflation in the authorities' loss function reduces the equilibrium loss.[29]

This model has two empirical implications for the effects of a transition to a regime of pegged exchange rates. The first implication concerns the impact on expectations. On average, expected and actual inflation between realignments is lower than under flexible rates. Under flexible exchange rates the equilibrium inflation rate (equation (5.20)) is constant; when the exchange rate is pegged, the equilibrium inflation rate, given by equation (5.24), is no longer constant.[30] But the *average* inflation rate between realignments is lower under pegged than under flexible rates: since output fluctuates under pegged exchange rates but is flat under flexible rates, and since the equilibrium loss is smaller in the pegged rate regime (as we have shown), the average inflation rate must be lower under pegged exchange rates. However, inflation at home remains higher than in the rest of the world. Therefore, when periodic realignments are allowed for, inflation rates do not need to converge internationally.

The second empirical implication regards the real exchange rate. Between realignments, the real exchange rate appreciates, since the domestic country has a higher inflation rate than the rest of the world and the nominal exchange rate is fixed.

Both empirical implications of the periodic realignments model largely agree with the regularities we described at the beginning of this chapter. In the next section we perform some formal empirical analysis to assess whether the reputational effects of alternative exchange rate regimes can actually be observed in the data.

---

29 See Giavazzi and Pagano (1988b) for a similar result.

30 The intuition runs as follows: With a fixed nominal exchange rate all differences between inflation at home and abroad translate into movements of the real exchange rate, and thus into fluctuations of output. A constant inflation differential would give rise to cumulative real appreciation, and thus to a trend deviation of output from equilibrium. Because the loss function assigns symmetric weights to positive and negative deviations of output from equilibrium, a constant (non-zero) inflation rate cannot be optimal.

5.5   Empirical Evidence

In sections 5.3 and 5.4 we showed that pegging the exchange rate to a low-inflation country can help to break the inertia associated with inflation expectations *if* the central bank gives up the right to change the exchange rate at will. Under these conditions, price-setters' expectations adjust endogenously, and the equilibrium rate of inflation for the country pegging the exchange rate is lower than in a regime of flexible rates. On the other hand, the center country faces a higher inflation rate than in the flexible rates regime.

Whether or not the exchange rate targets of the EMS are perceived by member central banks and by the public to be binding remains largely an empirical question. In particular, the model we used is silent on the question of credibility of the exchange rate targets. In this section we measure the shifts in expectations associated with the institution of the EMS and their impact on inflation rates.

We concentrate on the joint dynamics of wages, prices, and output, and identify the role of the EMS in the European disinflation by exploiting the empirical implications of the Lucas "critique." In his celebrated Carnegie-Rochester paper,[31] Lucas pointed out that statistical relationships between macroeconomic time series are affected by policy regimes, and therefore cannot be used to predict the effects of changes in policy. This proposition implies that, if we can clearly identify changes in policy regimes, we can use empirical shifts of the statistical relations among economic time series to provide evidence on the effects of the new regimes.

How can the Lucas critique help in assessing the effects of the EMS in the European disinflation?[32] We specify a reduced-form system of equations for the dynamics of prices, wages, and output. This reduced form is consistent with general models of wage and price setting characterized by short-run nominal rigidities and forward-looking behavior, as are the models we used in sections 5.3 and 5.4. In these reduced forms, we control for shifts in price and wage inflation caused by monetary policy and by changes in aggregate demand and costs originating from fluctuations of foreign final goods' prices and imported commodities' prices. The parameters of the reduced forms, as

---

31 Lucas (1976).

32 Blanchard (1984) studies shifts in the Phillips curve and the term structure equation in the United States during the new monetary policy "regime" after 1979.

well as their lag structure, depend on stochastic properties of exogenous variables and on the policy regime of the economy, both of which
affect expectations and the behavior of price setters. If we can control
for all variables that influence the joint dynamics of prices and wages,
a change in the policy regime will generate an adjustment in expectations; a change in the behavior of price setters; and, as a consequence,
a shift in the parameters of the reduced-form equations. Therefore,
any systematic failure of our statistical model—estimated over the period preceding the EMS—to predict price and wage inflation during
the EMS is an estimate of the quantitative role of the exchange rate
regime in the disinflation. If our reduced-form equations overpredict
inflation in the EMS period, we will tend to conclude that the EMS
has had a positive effect on the disinflation by shifting inflation expectations downward and therefore decreasing the output cost of the
inflation reduction.

Our statistical model of wage-price dynamics is specified as follows:[33]

$$Y_t = A(L)Y_{t-1} + B(L)Z_{t-1} + u_t \tag{5.27}$$

where $A(L)$ and $B(L)$ are polynomials in the lag operator, $Y_t = [p_t, w_t, y_t]'$
is the vector of the endogenous variables: price inflation, wage inflation, and output growth.[34] The vector Z_t contains a constant, a linear
time trend, seasonal dummies and other dummies (specified below),
money growth, the relative price of imported raw materials, and the
relative price of imported finished goods (in rates of change). These
two last variables capture demand and supply effects in the international transmission of price disturbances.[35]

The most important feature of equation (5.27) is that the variables
in Z, other than the trend and the dummies, are assumed to be determined outside of the system.[36] This limits the number of parameters
to be estimated, and as a result contains the sampling error in the dynamic simulations we perform below. The assumption that the vari-

---

33 See also Branson (1984) for an analysis of vector-autoregressive models of the open
economy. Branson's focus, unlike ours, is the structural interpretation of the estimated
coefficients, and covariance matrix of residuals.

34 The variables are (quarterly) changes in the logs of prices, wages, and real GDP.

35 See appendix B for a description of the data we use.

36 Here we follow Blanchard (1986), who uses similar models to study wage and price
inflation in the United States.

ables in Z can be left out of the vector-autoregression is warranted if the variables in Z_t correlated with u_t affect Y only with a lag. Plausibly, money growth and the relative price of imported intermediate and final goods (which are affected by movements in the nominal exchange rate) are correlated with innovations in output growth and wage and price inflation. On the other hand, the assumption that the Z variables affect Y with at least a one-quarter lag is consistent with the view that prices and wages are predetermined with respect to money growth and relative prices of imported intermediate and final goods, and that output responds slowly to changes in those variables.

Here we do not make any attempt to provide "structural" interpretations of the system of equations (5.27). In particular, we do not use our reduced-form equations to address the questions raised, for example, by Blanchard and Summers (1986) and Bean, Layard, and Nickell (1986) about the peculiar behavior of the European Phillips curves. According to Blanchard and Summers, the nature of wage bargaining in Europe produces hysteresis in employment. In their view European countries have faced high and persistent unemployment in the 1980s because of negative aggregate demand shocks (accommodation to the monetary contraction in the United States and domestic fiscal conservatism) coupled with increases in real wages, that have validated the increase in unemployment. The statistical model of wage-price inflation and output growth we use appears ill suited to capturing the effects discussed by Blanchard and Summers. The model instead is designed to capture the formation of expectations in wage and price setting.

Our basic strategy is to estimate equation (5.27) over the period preceding the EMS, and to use the estimates to forecast the endogenous variables during the EMS. Table 5.2 contains summary statistics of the model, estimated with quarterly data for Germany, Denmark, France, Italy, and the United Kingdom. The choice of these countries is mainly dictated by the availability of the data.[37] We include the United Kingdom to allow a comparison with a country that experienced a fall in inflation outside of the EMS. The equations were estimated with

37 We could not estimate the model for Belgium, since the wage series in that country follows a markedly different pattern before and after 1972. The real GNP series in Italy has been updated with the new national income accounts figures. The growth rate of real GNP from 1979:4 to 1980:1 has been computed using the old data. GNP numbers are available for France only after 1965. For this reason we used industrial production. The results with the GNP data, and a smaller sample, are very similar to the ones we report and, of course, are available on request.

Table 5.2
Summary statistics for the inflation-output model

Equation	d.o.f.	$\overline{R}^2$	Q	Neutrality test	Shift	
Germany 1960:2–1979:1 (sample ends 1987:2)					(79:2)	(81:4)
p	38	.642	.126	.811	.633	.528
w	38	.187	.820	.186	.962	.893
y	38	.238	.517	.700	.770	.697
Denmark 1968:2–1979:1 (sample ends 1984:4)					(79:2)	(82:4)
p	10	.490	.074	.462	.521	.636
w	10	.257	.423	.554	.899	.901
y	10	.193	.154	.636	.400	.976
France 1960:2–1979:1 (sample ends 1987:2)					(79:2)	(83:2)
p	40	.756	.806	.178	.015	.215
w	40	.698	.134	.389	.042	.771
y	40	.440	.021	.843	.820	.802
Italy 1960:2–1979:1 (sample ends 1986:4)					(79:2)	(82:1)
p	40	.663	.470	.561	.888	.995
w	40	.620	.889	.677	.810	.799
y	40	.117	.054	.789	.934	.917
United Kingdom 1963:2–1979:1 (sample ends 1987:1)					(79:2)	(81:4)
p	28	.779	.907	.200	.208	.982
w	28	.419	.981	.491	.951	.993
y	28	.861	.772	.939	.671	.976

ordinary least squares using four lags for all variables. In addition to seasonals and a linear time trend, we included dummy variables to capture the fall of the Bretton Woods regime and country-specific experiences that the model cannot explain.[38]

Long-run neutrality imposes restrictions on the coefficients of the equations in equation (5.27). The sum of the coefficients of lagged p and w and lagged money growth should be 1 in the p and w equations, and should equal zero in the y equation. These restrictions are tested, equation by equation, and are imposed when the test does not reject them. Tests of long-run neutrality in some sense are specification tests for the lag length. Table 5.2 also reports tests of zero autocorrelations of the residuals, which can provide evidence of misspecification. The table contains, country by country and equation by equation, the corrected R-square, the marginal significance level for the hypothesis of zero autocorrelation of residuals.[39] the marginal significance level for the F test of the neutrality restrictions, and the marginal significance levels for tests of subsample stability. We test the null hypothesis of no shift in the parameters of the equation after the EMS, and the hypothesis of no shift in the parameters in the mid-1980s.[40]

The table shows that the neutrality restrictions are not rejected at the 5 percent level, in all cases. Similarly, the hypothesis of zero autocorrelation of the residuals is not rejected at the 5 percent level, in all cases except for the output equation in France. The hypothesis of no change in the parameters of the equations after the beginning of the EMS is also not rejected, in all cases except for France, where we find that the parameters of both the price and wage equations shift significantly in 1979. By contrast, we were unable to detect any significant shift in parameters in correspondence with the policy turnaround of the spring of 1983. This result might suggest that the EMS has not brought about

---

38 The precise list of dummy variables is the following: For all countries, from 1971:3 to the end of the sample, fall of Bretton Woods. For Italy, 1969:2–1970:1, *Autunno Caldo*; and 1973:3–1974:1, price freeze. For France, 1963:4–1964:4, price freeze; 1969:1–1970:4, price freeze; 1968:2–1968:3, "May 1968"; 1974:1–1974:4, 1977:1– 1977:4, and 1982:3–1983:4, wage and price controls. For the United Kingdom, 1967:4, sterling devaluation, and 1973:4–1974:4, wage controls.

39 This is the probability that the Q statistic exceeds the computed value, under the null hypothesis. The Q statistic is distributed as a chi-square, with degrees of freedom that depend on the size of the sample.

40 This test statistic differs from the usual Chow test because the number of observations in the second subsample is smaller than the number of parameters in the equations. See Maddala [1977].

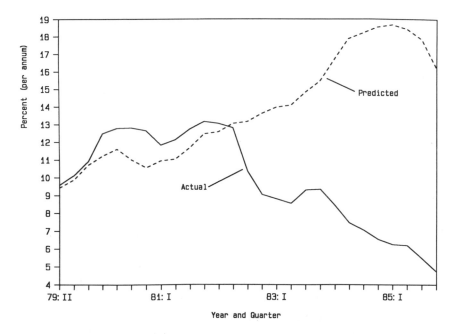

Figure 5.9 The effects of shifts in expectations—France: CPI inflation.

any of the changes in expectations we describe in the sections above, with the possible exception of France. The result should be interpreted with caution, however; as pointed out by Maddala (1977), the F-tests for shifts in the parameters constructed for the case where the second subsample does not contain enough degrees of freedom has much less power than the standard Chow test. Tests of shifts of parameters thus tend to be inconclusive.

We provide additional evidence on shifts of wage-price dynamics by simulating the estimated model after 1979. The results of the simulations are reported in figures 5.9 to 5.23.

For each country we report actual and forecast values of wage inflation, price inflation, and output growth during the EMS period. The forecasts are produced by estimating the model up to the first quarter of 1979 and using the estimates to obtain predictions on the vector Y, given the *actual* realizations of the variables in Z.[41]

---

41 This allows us to account for the selective wage and price guidelines imposed in France from the fall of 1983 to the end of 1984. We estimate the effects of price controls on wage, price, and output dynamics using dummy variables for the controls imposed in the 1960s and 1970s. See footnote 8 above.

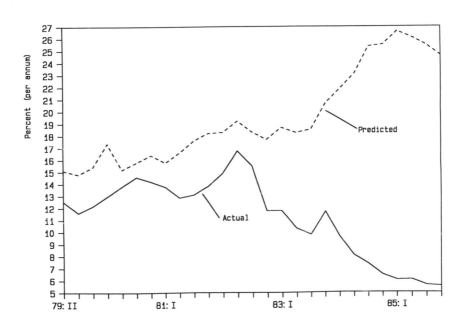

Figure 5.10 The effects of shifts in expectations—France: wage inflation.

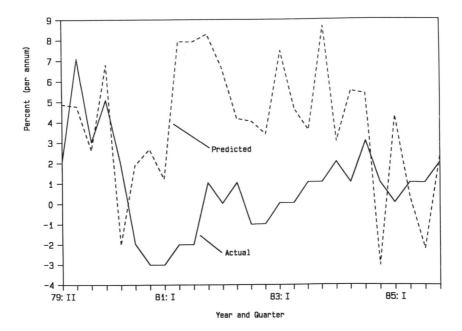

Figure 5.11 The effects of shifts in expectations—France: output growth.

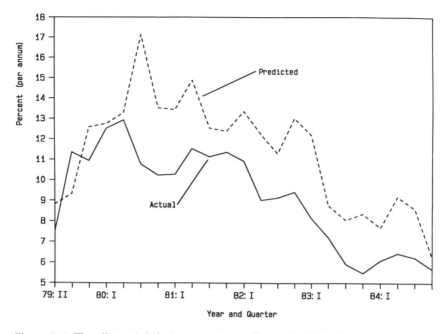

Figure 5.12 The effects of shifts in expectations—Denmark: CPI inflation.

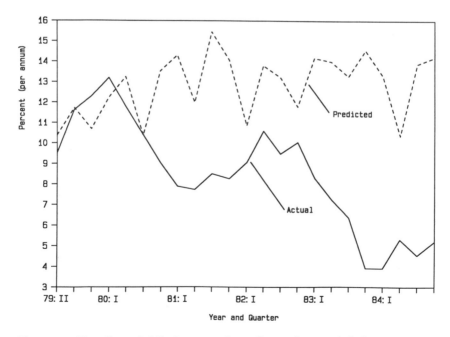

Figure 5.13 The effects of shifts in expectations—Denmark: wage inflation.

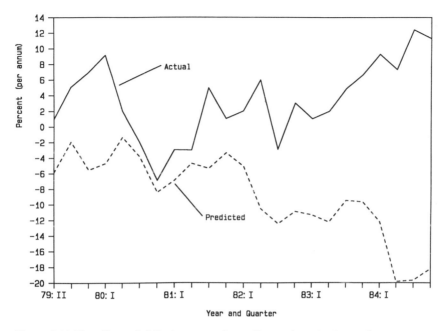

Figure 5.14 The effects of shifts in expectations—Denmark: output growth.

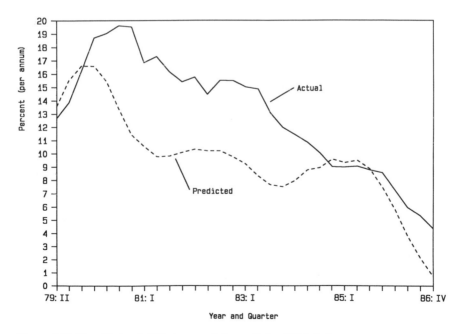

Figure 5.15 The effects of shifts in expectations—Italy: CPI inflation.

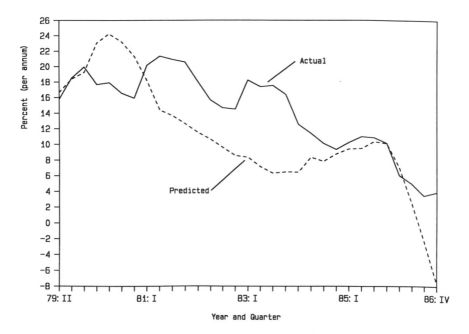

Figure 5.16 The effects of shifts in expectations—Italy: wage inflation.

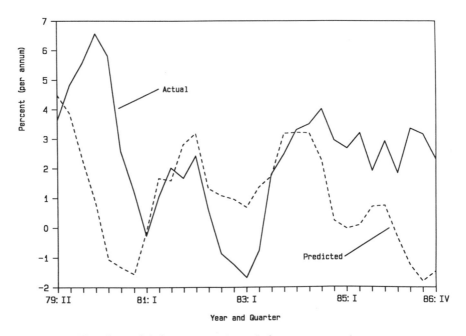

Figure 5.17 The effects of shifts in expectations—Italy: output growth.

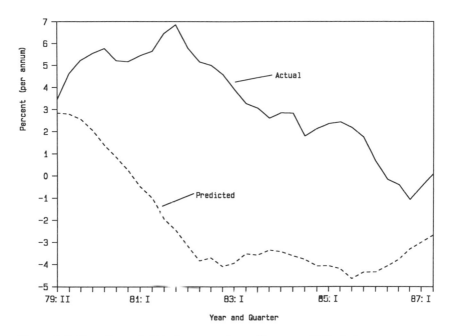

Figure 5.18 The effects of shifts in expectations—Germany: CPI inflation.

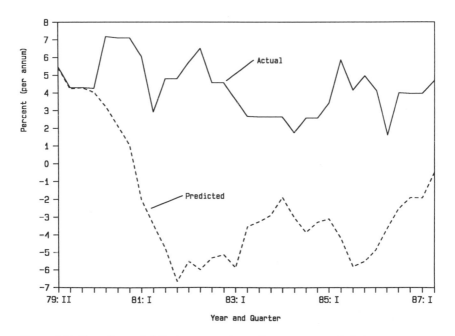

Figure 5.19 The effects of shifts in expectations—Germany: wage inflation.

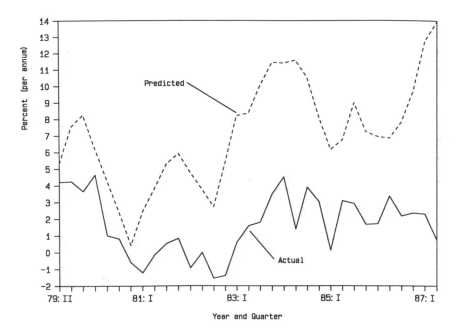

Figure 5.20 The effects of shifts in expectations—Germany: output growth.

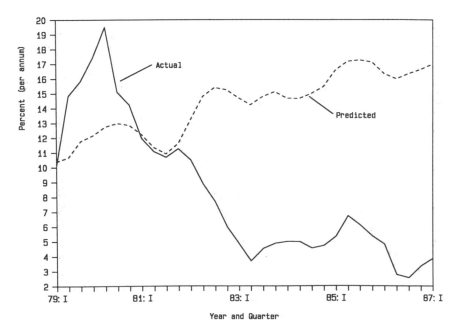

Figure 5.21 The effects of shifts in expectations—UK: CPI inflation.

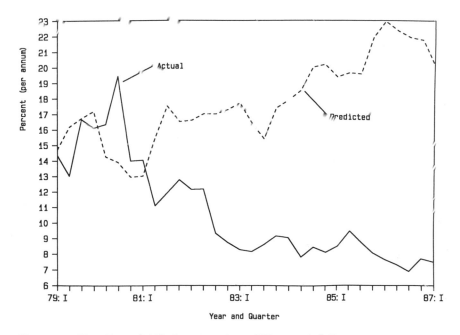

Figure 5.22 The effects of shifts in expectations—UK: wage inflation.

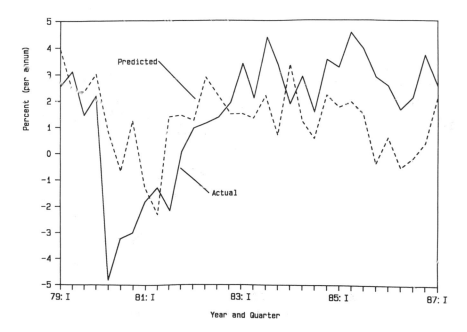

Figure 5.23 The effects of shifts in expectations—UK: output growth.

An interesting result from the figures is the asymmetry between Germany and the other countries in the EMS. In the case of Germany, the model underpredicts wage and price inflation, but overpredicts output growth. In the case of Denmark, exactly the opposite happens: The model overpredicts inflation but underpredicts output growth. The results of the simulations for France and Italy are slightly more difficult to describe. In France, actual inflation starts diverging clearly from the model's predictions from the third quarter of 1982. In the case of Italy, the model estimated up to 1979 underpredicts the inflation of the early 1980s, but overpredicts it in the recent past. Output growth also seems higher than predicted by the model after 1984.[42]

How should we interpret these experiments? The F-tests for parameter stability do not reject the null hypothesis for Italy, Denmark, and Germany. Thus wide divergences between actual and predicted values of the endogenous variables should not be taken as strong support for the hypothesis that the EMS has helped countries other than Germany in the disinflation of the 1980s, and—if anything—has hindered the Deutsche Bundesbank's monetary restraint. We cannot claim this because we do not compute the standard errors of the forecast and cannot perform a formal test of the difference between the model's predictions and actual experience. However, we find that the results of the simulations are suggestive with a shift in expectations. This shift in expectations is consistent with the theories discussed above. In the case of France, our statistical test also rejects the hypothesis of no shift in the parameters of both the price and wage equations in 1979.

The simulations seem to suggest that, if an adjustment of expectations similar to those described above has taken place, it has (except possibly in the case of Denmark) occurred well after the start of the EMS. This result is consistent with informal accounts of the EMS experience and the generally skeptical reactions of the public after its institution in 1979. Similarly, the figures for the United Kingdom would indicate a shift in expectations well after the change in regime. What could give rise to lagged adjustment of expectations? First, the large real depreciation of the lira and the French franc in 1978; this might have made the EMS rules less "binding" for those countries, at least during the first months. Sachs and Wyplosz (1986, pp. 294–95),

---

42 We have also found that, if the model is estimated for Italy up to the last quarter of 1981, inflation in the following years is systematically overpredicted and output growth is underpredicted. These results are not reported.

describing the events of 1981 and 1983, suggest that French authorities clearly signalled their intentions to abide by the EMS "discipline" well after the start of the system:

The role of external pressure was extremely important, since there is good reason to believe that French committments to the EMS tipped the balance towards austerity. Unlike the much looser committments under the European Snake in the 1970s, which France abandoned in two occasions, membership of the EMS has been invested with enormous political importance at the very highest levels of the government. That is why the debate over leaving the EMS was treated as synonymous with the debate over abandoning other spheres of cooperation in Europe, including participation in the Common Market. . .

. . .Economists have long debated whether international exchange rate agreements can really bind national policies, since the sanctions for breaking agreements are so small and diffuse. The example of the Socialist turnaround in March 1983 suggests that an international agreement can help to tip the balance towards domestic restraint.

In the case of Italy, the government signalled its strong stance against inflation well after the start of the EMS. Wage-indexation laws were repealed only in the summer of 1984. There is some evidence of an adjustment in expectations in the second quarter of 1985.

The second reason for a lagged reaction in expectations might have to do with learning. If price setters slowly adjust their views on the policymakers' intentions to remain in the EMS, the shift in expectations would be fully realized only well after the start of the EMS. The evidence of figures 5.9 to 5.23 could be consistent with a combination of these two factors.

5.6   Concluding Remarks

This chapter attempted to measure empirically the effects of the EMS on the dynamics of inflation in member countries. If the EMS can be thought of as an asymmetric system, where countries other than Germany passively peg their exchange rate to the DM and change the peg whenever inflation differentials force them to do so, then the low inflation propensity of Bundesbank should have shifted downward inflation expectations in the other countries. This is the model of "imported credibility" discussed in sections 5.3 and 5.4.

To measure the effects of the EMS, we exploit the predictions of the

Lucas critique. When there is a shift in regime, the public's expectations, as well as their behavioral rules, change. As a consequence, the observed shifts in well-specified reduced form equations provide a measure of the effects of the shifts in expectations.

Our empirical results appear to agree broadly with our theoretical presumption; however, there are a number of important caveats. The first regards the lack of statistical significance of the point estimates. Statistical tests indicate that the shifts in structural equations, although in the direction predicted by the theory, are not significant in the majority of cases. This is a well-known problem encountered by most empirical researchers applying vector autoregressions to macroeconomic time series. The second caveat concerns the timing, and the interpretation of the shifts in structural equations. In Italy and France, a downward adjustment of the inflation process—consistent with a downward adjustment of inflation expectations—occurs at least three years after the inception of the EMS. In both countries, the shift in the inflation process takes place in correspondence to an important reversal in government policies. This result has one of two causes. First, immediately after the beginning of the EMS, economic agents might have spent some time learning how the system works, and monetary authorities might have needed some time to convince the public of their intentions to stick to the rules of the new regime. Second, the 1982–83 policy turnaround in France, as well as the tough stance of the Italian government towards wage indexation in 1984, could both be motivated by the desire of the governments in the two countries to remain in the EMS and by their willingness to appeal to the EMS rules as an external justification for unpopular domestic policies.

Appendix A: Solution of the Model of Section 5.4

Substituting equation (5.16) into (5.23) the central bank problem in the pegged exchange rate regime becomes

$$\text{MIN } 0.5 \int_0^T \left\{ [\alpha \left(\pi_t - \pi_t^e \right) - \gamma z_t - k]^2 + a\pi_t^2 \right\} dt \qquad \text{(a1)}$$
$$\{\pi_t\}$$

subject to (5.22). The first-order conditions are

$$\alpha^2 \left(\pi_t - \pi_t^e \right) - \alpha\gamma z_t - \alpha k + a\pi_t - \lambda_t = 0 \qquad \text{(a2)}$$
$$\gamma^2 z_t - \alpha\gamma \left(\pi_t - \pi_t^e \right) + k\gamma = -\dot{\lambda}_t \qquad \text{(a3)}$$

where λ_t is the Lagrange multiplier associated with the dynamic constraint (5.22).

The optimal inflation path is obtained solving (a2) and (a3) subject to the boundary conditions

$$z_t = z_0 \qquad (\text{at } t = 0)$$
$$\lambda_t = 0 \qquad (\text{at } t = T)$$

The sustainability condition (10) imposes

$$z_0^* = (k/\gamma) \left(T/A - 1 \right) \qquad \text{(a4)}$$

where

$$A = \left\{ \left[exp \left(\mu_1 T \right) - 1 \right] / \mu_1 \right\} / (1 - \psi) - \left\{ \left[exp \left(\mu_2 T \right) - 1 \right] / \mu_2 \right\} / \left(1 - \Psi^{-1} \right)$$

and

$$\Psi = \left[(\mu_1 + \alpha\gamma/a) / (\mu_2 + \alpha\gamma/a) \right] exp \left[(\mu_1 - \mu_2) T \right]$$

The difference between the loss function in the pegged and flexible rate regimes reported in equation (11) is proportional to

$$F(T) = T\{ TB^{-1}/2[(\exp(2\mu_1 T) - 1) \left(1 + a(\mu_1/\gamma)^2 \right) (1 - \Psi)/\mu_1$$
$$+ (\exp(2\mu_2 T) - 1) \left(1 + a(\mu_2/\gamma)^2 \right) (1 - \Psi^{-1})/\mu_2]$$

$$- \left(1 - \alpha^2/a\right)\}$$ (a5)

where

$$B = \left(1 - \Psi^2\right)\left[\exp(\mu_2 T) - 1\right]/\mu_2^2 + \left(1 - \Psi^{-1}\right)^2$$
$$\cdot \left[\exp(\mu_1 T) - 1\right]/\mu_1^2$$

$F(t)$ is unambiguously negative in a neighbourhood of zero.

Appendix B: The Data

The two main sources are OECD *Main Economic Indicators*
(OECD) and IMF *International Financial Statistics* (IFS)

Price levels:
Consumer price indices, source: OECD

Wage rates:

Denmark	Index of hourly earnings in industry (OECD)
France	Index of hourly wage rates in manufacturing (OECD)
Germany	Index of hourly earnings in manufacturing (OECD)
Italy	Index of hourly wages in manufacturing (OECD)
UK	Index of weekly wages in manufacturing (OECD)

Imported materials:

Denmark	WPI industrial raw materials (OECD)
France	WPI raw materials (OECD)
Germany	1960–1967 WPI raw material prices (OECD), 1967–1987 basic material goods prices (OECD)
Italy	1960–1970 U.S. WPI raw materials (OECD) times lira\$ exchange rate (IFS) 1971–1987 *Indice Confindustria Materie Prime Non alimentari*
UK	WPI inputs of basic materials and fuels (OECD)

Exchange rates:
IFS line rf (quarterly averages)

Money stocks:
IFS line 34 (M1)

Output:
IFS lines 99 (real GNP or GDP)

Denmark	IFS line 66c (industrial production)
France	IFS line 66c (industrial production)

All variables are first differences of logs. Imported materials are relative to the CPI; imported final goods are obtained as a weighted average of the domestic-currency value of foreign CPIs, including all six countries plus the United States, and are relative to the domestic CPI. The weights for the indices, as well as the computer programs and the data sets used in the programs, are available on request.

6

The Dollar–Deutsche Mark Polarization

6.1 Introduction

So far in this book we have not addressed the relationship between European currencies and the dollar. Fluctuations of the dollar exchange rate have important effects in Europe, since they influence—other things equal—both the competitiveness of individual countries' exports, and the cost of imported intermediate goods, which are used heavily by all European countries.

Although the evidence in chapters 4 and 5 is largely consistent with the hypothesis that members of the EMS peg their currencies to the DM, the presence of target zones, and the possibility of realigning bilateral central rates, do not tie the DM to the other EMS currencies perfectly. In particular, there appears to be a tendency for currencies like the French franc and the lira to drift away from the DM, in relation to dollar fluctuations: It is often noted that when the dollar is strong in foreign exchange markets, the DM tends to be weak vis-à-vis other European currencies.[1] This observation typically is made in relation to day-to-day exchange rate movements, that occur within the bilateral target zones; sometimes, however, this phenomenon is considered to be some sort of structural feature of European currencies, which also characterizes their longer-term fluctuations. We call this the *dollar-DM polarization* view. This chapter investigates whether the data on exchange rate changes suggest the presence of dollar-DM polarization; we also assess potential explanations of the evidence.

---

1 See, among others, Masera (1981), Thygesen (1981), Baer (1982), Kaufman (1985), Russo (1984), Giavazzi and Giovannini (1985), Frankel (1985a, 1985b), Dennis and Nellis (1984), and Padoa Schioppa (1985b).

Before looking at the data, we should stress that the statement "when the dollar is strong, the DM weakens in the EMS" could be a tautology. If a depreciation of the dollar vis-à-vis the mark reflects a strenghtening of the mark, it is no surprise that the mark also appreciates relative to other European currencies. More precisely, if the variances of changes in the bilateral exchange rates of European currencies relative to the dollar are of comparable magnitude, then the covariance between changes in the dollar-DM rate and changes in the price of marks in terms of other European currencies has to be negative. Let $dln(\mathrm{DM}/\$)$ indicate the percent change of the price of one dollar in terms of marks. Consider the covariance between this variable and the percent change of the exchange rate between currency J and the mark:

$$\mathrm{COV}\left[dln(J/\mathrm{DM}), dln(\mathrm{DM}/\$)\right]$$
$$= \left\{\mathrm{VAR}\left[dln(J/\$)\right] - \mathrm{VAR}\left[dln(J/\mathrm{DM})\right] - \mathrm{VAR}\left[dln(\mathrm{DM}/\$)\right]\right\}/2 \quad (6.1)$$

There are no a priori restrictions on the variance-covariance matrix of exchange rate changes—implied by the definition of cross rates—that would determine the sign of the expression above. However, if the variability of bilateral exchange rates vis-à-vis the dollar is of comparable magnitude, we expect the expression above to be negative:[2] In this case, movements of the dollar-DM rate reflect changes in the value of the mark vis-à-vis all currencies. In the extreme case, where currency J is perfectly pegged to the Deustche mark, the covariance term in equation (6.1) equals 0. In summary, presumably the covariance between the dollar-DM exchange rate and the price of marks in terms of European currencies is always negative, simply because the dollar-mark rate is also the price of marks, and its movements should be mirrored by movements of other currencies' rates vis-à-vis the mark.

Negative values of equation (6.1) therefore are not surprising, because of the use of the DM as a common numeraire. The interesting question, however, is whether fluctuations in the value of the dollar, measured in terms of a *weighted average* of foreign currencies, are systematically associated with fluctuations of bilateral European rates. In the next sections we offer evidence of this issue.

---

2 This problem is mentioned in Frankel (1982).

6.2   European Bilateral Exchange Rates and the Dollar: 1973–87

In this section we report evidence on the comovement of the effective dollar exchange rate with bilateral exchange rates of the DM. We concentrate on seven European currencies (Dutch guilder, Belgian franc, Danish krone, French franc, Italian lira, pound sterling, and Swiss franc) plus the yen and the Canadian dollar. Our data set includes daily observations (New York noon time) of exchange rates. We compute daily percent changes in exchange rate (first differences of natural logarithms) and their averages over longer time periods (monthly and quarterly).

The choice of the weights to be used in computing the effective dollar index depends on the nature of the empirical phenomena we want to document. Shifts in international competitiveness are measured best by effective exchange rate indices constructed with trade weights, like the Multilateral Exchange Rate Model (MERM) weights of the International Monetary Fund. The correlations we want to analyze, most likely produced by disturbances in asset markets, need weights that represent the relative importance of each currency in the world financial market. We decided to compute GNP weights, because the more natural money (or broad money) weights in some cases reflect different definitions of the corresponding monetary aggregate adopted by different countries.[3] A comparison of our index with the MERM index shows, for example, that the 1980 MERM weight of the Canadian dollar in the U.S. dollar index is .185, whereas the weight of the DM is only .136; in contrast, those two currencies have weights equal to .075 and .192 respectively in our GNP index of the effective dollar rate.

Tables 6.1 to 6.3 report estimates of the percent changes in bilateral rates vis-à-vis the mark, associated with a percent change in the dollar effective rate using daily, monthly, and quarterly data, respectively. The sample runs from June 1, 1973 to July 20, 1987 and is divided into five subsamples: the EMS period; the years preceding it (1973–1979); the first long spell of depreciation of the dollar (May 1977 to October 1978); the uninterrupted appreciation of the effective dollar rate from November 1978 to August 1981; and the recent dollar slide from

---

3 See the data appendix for a detailed description of the index. We chose GNP weights after we noted discrepancies in the money weights that we could intepret only as suggested in the text.

Table 6.1
The effective dollar and bilateral DM exchange rates: daily data[a]

Dutch guilder	Belgian franc	Danish kroner	French franc	Italian lira	Pound sterling	Swiss franc	Japanese yen	Canadian dollar
Before EMS (1 June 1973 to 9 March 1979)								
−0.09	−0.23	−0.17	−0.16	−0.60	−0.56	0.32	−0.53	−1.38
EMS period (12 March 1979 to 20 July 1987)								
−0.07	−0.05	−0.10	−0.03	−0.10	−0.22	0.06	−0.25	−1.01
Dollar depreciating (13 May 1977 to 31 October 1978)								
−0.09	−0.10	−0.34	−0.26	−0.69	−0.34	0.72	−0.17	−1.28
Dollar appreciating (1 November 1978 to 5 August 1981)								
−0.02†	−0.07	−0.08	−0.08	−0.27	−0.29	0.23	−0.14	−1.08
Dollar depreciating (19 March 1985 to 20 July 1987)								
−0.08	−0.16	−0.09	−0.06	−0.02†	−0.16	0.05†	−0.37	−1.07

a. Regression coefficients of percent changes in each currency's price of the DM on percent changes of the effective dollar index. A negative sign indicates that a dollar depreciation is associated with a depreciation vis-à-vis the mark. Regressions include a constant term. The data is described in the data Appendix. A † indicates that the estimated coefficient is not significantly different from zero at the 5 percent confidence level. All unmarked coefficients are significant.

March 1985 to July 1987. The coefficients are obtained regressing the log-difference of each bilateral DM rate on the log-difference of the effective dollar rate. A minus sign indicates a depreciation of the given currency relative to the DM, in correspondence to a depreciation of the effective dollar index. For example, the figure for Belgium in the first row of table 6.1 (−0.23) means that a one percent depreciation of the effective dollar rate is associated—on average—with a 0.23 percent depreciation of the Belgian franc relative to the DM, in the same day.

The data confirm that fluctuations of bilateral exchange rates in Europe are associated in a systematic way with fluctuations of the dollar. The Dutch guilder and the Canadian dollar are at the two extremes of the spectrum: the guilder follows the DM most closely; the Canadian dollar follows the dollar effective rate most closely. The Swiss franc is the only currency which appreciates relative to the DM when the dollar falls: This phenomenon is most apparent—in the daily data—

during the early period of dollar depreciation. All other European currencies weaken vis-á-vis the DM when the dollar is weak, although by different magnitudes. Thus the perception that when the dollar is weak the DM tends to be strong vis-à-vis the EMS partners is clearly confirmed by the data on the Belgian franc, the French franc, the lira, and the Danish krone. However, the measured average responses of these bilateral rates to changes in the dollar effective rate are not uniform across currencies, and are by no means stable across subsamples.

In particular, there seems to be a dramatic change in the covariances of European exchange rates that corresponds to the beginning of the EMS. In both the daily and the monthly data, the negative comovements of the effective dollar rate and of the DM decrease substantially in terms of Belgian francs, French francs, Danish kroner and lire. The beginning of the EMS also represents a break in the data for countries outside the system. After March 1979 a change in the effective dollar rate is associated with smaller changes in the DM price of pounds, Swiss francs, yen, and Canadian dollars. However, the dampening of asymmetric movements vis-à-vis the DM has been much more pronounced *inside* than *outside* the EMS, for all currencies except the Swiss franc (which, since March 1979, has followed the DM very closely.)

Finally, the tables document the changes in covariances of exchange rates during periods of sustained dollar appreciation and depreciation. In the years preceding the EMS, the polarization between the dollar and the DM appears stronger when the effective dollar is depreciating: Table 6.1 shows that the negative covariation of the dollar index and bilateral DM rates is more pronounced in the 1977–8 period than during the whole pre-EMS era for all EMS currencies except the Belgian franc. During the recent dollar slide, however, the dollar-DM polarization has been much less pronounced. Conceivably, the EMS has limited the divergent behavior of weak currencies in the recent past: Our discussion of the disinflation experience in France, Italy, and Denmark in chapter 5 is consistent with this interpretation of the evidence.

Are the general patterns that we find in the daily data reproduced over longer frequencies? Tables 6.2 and 6.3 report the calculations of table 6.1 using monthly and quarterly data: Asymmetries in exchange rate movements do not characterize only the short run, but persist over longer horizons. Table 6.2 shows that the general patterns of correlations of daily data are reproduced by the monthly data, and

Table 6.2
The effective dollar and bilateral DM exchange rates: monthly data[a]

Dutch guilder	Belgian franc	Danish kroner	French franc	Italian lira	Pound sterling	Swiss franc	Japanese yen	Canadian dollar
Before EMS (June 1973 to February 1979)								
−0.14*	−0.12*	−0.23*	−0.20	−0.52*	−0.53*	0.05	−0.29	−1.45*
EMS period (March 1979 to July 1987)								
−0.01	−0.02	−0.02	−0.004	−0.10*	−0.30*	0.09	−0.05	−0.96*
Dollar depreciating (May 1977 to October 1978)								
−0.12	−0.11	−0.25	−0.26	−0.76*	−0.50	−0.02	0.37	−1.43*
Dollar appreciating (November 1978 to August 1981)								
0.01	0.006	−0.10	−0.002	−0.05	0.01	0.11	−0.07	−0.90*
Dollar depreciating (March 1985 to July 1987)								
−0.02*	−0.003	−0.02	−0.03	−0.13*	−0.26	0.19*	0.15	−0.95*

a. A * indicates that the coefficient is significantly different from zero at the 5 percent level.

Table 6.3
The effective dollar and bilateral DM exchange rates: quarterly data[a]

Dutch guilder	Belgian franc	Danish kroner	French franc	Italian lira	Pound sterling	Swiss franc	Japanese yen	Canadian dollar
Before EMS (1973:III to 1979:I)								
−0.15	−0.04	−0.18	−0.15	−0.23	−0.11	0.19	−0.02	−1.38
EMS period (1979:II to 1987:I)								
0.04	−0.05	0.006	0.009	−0.08	−0.26	0.06	−0.11	−1.03

a. None of the coefficients in this table is significantly different from zero at the 5 percent level.

in some cases accentuated. In the case of the Italian lira, for example, we find that the tendency to diverge from the DM during periods of dollar weakness is actually stronger in the monthly data than in the daily data. The point estimates of table 6.3, reporting the regressions results using quarterly data, seem to confirm the decrease in the dollar-DM polarization after 1979, although the standard errors are all very large.

6.3 The Behavior of Exchange Rates during Crises

Exchange rate dynamics are characterized by periods of quiescence followed by periods of turbulence, in which day-to-day movements are large and frequently in the same direction. As Mussa (1979) suggested, "crises" are unlikely to be simply a statistical artifact associated with the stochastic properties of exchange rates. Instead, they probably reflect instances of "the market changing its mind" in response to large shocks to the information set. Thus, crises should contain important information on the determinants of exchange rates.

In this section, we seek to determine whether the dollar-DM polarization that characterizes, on average, both the EMS experience and the years preceding the EMS is more evident during periods of foreign exchange markets' turbulence. In particular, we discuss evidence on the two questions: (1) To what extent are EMS crises associated with dollar crises? (2) How do exchange rates move during EMS realignments?

It is argued often that although "fundamentals" play the essential role in EMS realignments, dollar crises frequently determine the timing of a realignment. For example, the *Financial Times* of September 25, 1979, commenting on the events leading to the first EMS realignment of September 24, reported:

The main reason for the strains is the big difference in the economic performance of the EMS participants but the final twist has been provided by the renewed dollar crisis. Pressures were so intense that a meeting of EEC ministers had to be arranged hurriedly for Sunday.

Figure 6.1 shows the effective dollar index and highlights the dates of the realignments.In each realignment the mark has been revalued relative to (subsets of) the other EMS currencies. An interesting regularity is that all but one[4] EMS realignments took place after a fall in

4 On February 22, 1982 the Belgian franc and the Danish krone were devalued with re-

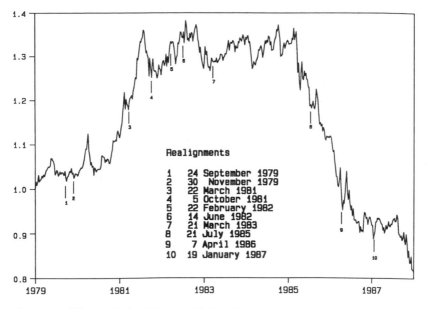

Figure 6.1 Effective dollar index and EMS realignments: 1979 = 1.

the dollar, and were followed by a dollar recovery. This is particularly evident in the 1983 and 1985 episodes, but is also present, though to a lesser degree, during the first half of the EMS experience.[5]

The financial press associates EMS crises with dollar movements almost as a matter of routine. Here is a small sampler from the *Financial Times*:

November 30, 1979 (the day of the second EMS realignment):

The crisis has crept up almost by stealth in the EMS over the past week—partly as a consequence of the sharp rise of the DM against the dollar in the wake of the monetary confrontation between the U.S. and Iran. ... The singling out of the DM once again as the main international target for currency speculation when the dollar gets into trouble is likely to remain a source of strain in the EMS.

spect to all other EMS currencies. The realignment was then attributed to "diminishing confidence in the future performance of the Belgian economy." (Ungerer et al., 1983).
5 Often the week which preceeds the realignment is characterized by a fall of the dollar and by a depreciation of some of the weak European currencies which move towards their maximum divergence limit relative to the DM.

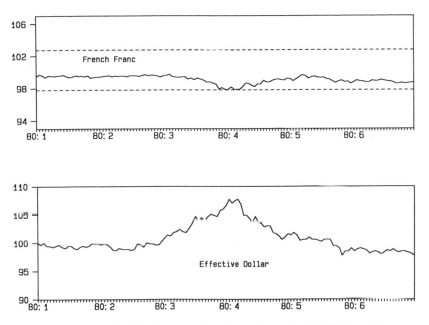

Figure 6.2 An episode of dollar strength and weakness: April 1980, French franc.

March 19, 1981:

The dollar lost ground rapidly in currency markets ... European currencies continued to show strains within the EMS. The lira eased to its divergence limit; the system suffered further pressure as the Belgian franc stood resolute outside its divergence limit.

March 20, 1981 (the Friday before the lira devaluation):

The time is ripe for the long overdue, carefully rehearsed piece of theater of DM revaluation ... especially if it is accompanied by more signs from across the Atlantic that President Reagan's dollar levitation act is starting to lose its magic.

Figures 6.2–6.4 show a sharp, and soon reversed, dollar *appreciation* in April 1980, accompanied by a sudden strengthening of the French franc, the Italian lira, and the Belgian franc with respect to the DM, which fell to the bottom of its fluctuation band. The following two quotes from the *Financial Times* are from that period:

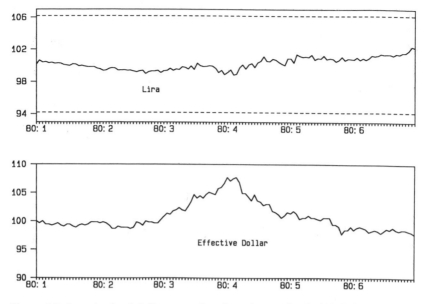

Figure 6.3 An episode of dollar strength and weakness: April 1980, Italian lira.

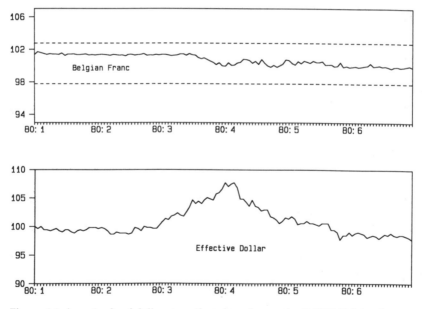

Figure 6.4 An episode of dollar strength and weakness: April 1980, Belgian franc.

April 1, 1980:

Dollar rises to two-year peak. .... The DM weakens in the EMS. .... The lira, recently weak in the EMS, is now firmer against most EMS currencies. .... The French franc, firmer at the top of the EMS, improved again against the DM.

April 4, 1980:

The DM required support against the French franc last week to keep it within the agreed EMS limits. The French franc at the top of the EMS gave assistance to its weakest partner.

When the dollar surge reversed itself, the lira and the French franc suffered sharp losses relative to the DM. This episode is of special interest, since it is a case where a dollar movement appeared to strengthen the lira and the French franc at a time when no significant change in fundamentals was observable. In summary, the dollar-DM polarization seems more noticeable during well-known episodes of sharp fluctuations of the dollar effective rate.

This evidence raises the question of the behavior of exchange rates during realignments. All EMS realignments resulted in some appreciation of the DM relative to other EMS currencies. The dollar–DM polarization view would imply that, in correspondence to realignments, the DM also appreciates vis-à-vis currencies outside of Europe. The greater DM area model of chapter 4, on the other hand, suggests that realignments should not systematically affect the value of the DM outside of Europe. Clearly, the two views cannot be rigorously tested with these data because we have too few observations of EMS realignments and because there is a need to distinguish anticipated from unanticipated exchange rate changes. Nevertheless, it is useful to observe the movements of the DM within and outside the EMS in correspondence to the realignments. Table 6.4 reports: the percent changes in the price of a DM in terms of French francs, liras, Belgian francs, Dutch guilder, and Danish kroner from the Friday preceding to the Monday immediately following EMS realignments; their weighted average; a weighted average percent change of the DM in terms of currencies outside of the EMS; and, for reference, the changes of bilateral central rates decreed by the EMS realignments (in parentheses).

The table shows that, in the majority of cases, changes in market rates are much smaller than the changes in central rates, and in some cases even of the opposite sign. The change in the value of the DM

Table 6.4
Changes in the DM rate around EMS realignments (percent changes of the value of the DM from Friday to Monday)[a]

Date	FF	LIT	BF	HFL	DKR	DM inside	DM outside
9/24/79	0.00 (2.00)	−0.22 (2.00)	0.00 (2.00)	0.00 (2.00)	0.78 (4.90)	−0.02	−0.01
3/23/81	0.43 (0.00)	1.84 (6.00)	0.00 (0.00)	0.00 (0.00)	0.77 (0.00)	0.31	−0.36
10/5/81	4.58 (8.50)	3.11 (8.50)	1.28 (5.50)	0.00 (0.00)	−1.10 (5.50)	1.27	0.69
2/22/82	0.55 (0.00)	0.47 (0.00)	6.44 (8.50)	0.00 (0.00)	1.16 (3.00)	0.50	0.16
6/14/82	4.92 (10.00)	1.16 (7.00)	1.93 (4.25)	0.00 (0.00)	2.33 (4.25)	0.10	−0.23
3/21/83	3.85 (8.00)	−0.33 (8.00)	−0.05 (4.00)	0.91 (2.00)	0.46 (3.00)	0.66	−0.63
7/22/85	−0.16 (0.00)	3.87 (8.00)	0.50 (0.00)	0.00 (0.00)	0.39 (0.00)	0.49	−0.04
4/7/86	−0.06 (6.00)	−1.72 (3.00)	−1.26 (2.00)	−0.27 (0.00)	−0.23 (2.00)	−0.32	0.09
1/12/87	−0.36 (3.00)	−0.24 (3.00)	−0.14 (1.00)	0.00 (0.00)	−1.10 (3.00)	−0.10	0.39

a. A positive number indicates a DM appreciation relative to the currency in the given column. Numbers in parentheses indicate the changes in the EMS bilateral central rates of the DM. The weights for the DM inside the EMS are: French franc, 0.3993; lira, 0.299; Belgian franc, 0.1164; Dutch guilder, 0.146; Danish krone, 0.039. The weights for the DM outside the EMS are: U.S. dollar, 0.4655; Sterling, 0.1026; Yen, 0.27; Swedish krone, 0.0858; Swiss franc, 0.0758.

is of the same sign inside and outside of the EMS in only three out of nine cases: EMS realignments most of the time have brought about a correction of the value of European currencies other than the mark, rather than a change in the value of the mark both vis-à-vis EMS currencies and the rest of the world. The realignment data does not support the polarization view.

6.4 Summary of the Empirical Regularities: What Needs to Be Explained

We conclude our survey of empirical regularities with a short summary of the most important findings:

• We find that the Belgian franc, the French franc, the lira, and the Danish krone tend to appreciate or depreciate relative to the DM as the dollar exchange rate appreciates or depreciates relative to a basket of representative currencies. These exchange rate movements suggest that the weakness of the dollar is mirrored by the strength of the DM, and vice versa, with the other EMS currencies "sitting on the fence."

• The comovements of spot exchange rates differ across currencies. Among EMS currencies, the guilder is most tightly linked to the mark; the lira, the French franc, and the krone more clearly display a tendency to diverge from the DM in correspondence with dollar fluctuations. Outside of the EMS, the Swiss franc seems to represent another important pole for short-term capital flows: It tends to appreciate relative to the DM when the dollar depreciates.

• The comovements of spot exchange rates differ across time periods. The DM-dollar polarization is much more evident in the years preceding the EMS than during the 1979–87 period. It is also more evident during the dollar slide of 1977–8. The period of dollar weakness after 1985, however, has not so far had serious disruptive effects within the EMS.

• Although the data on average show that the dollar-DM polarization is weaker during the EMS years, almost all EMS realignments (which resulted in an appreciation of the mark vis-à-vis the European partners) are preceded by a large fall in the effective dollar index and are followed by a recovery of the dollar. Other specific episodes of strain in the EMS, also identified by the financial press, are associated with large swings of the dollar exchange rate.

• The data on exchange rate movements around EMS realignments show that market rates are not strongly affected by changes in central parities: EMS realignments might—at least to some extent—accommodate existing trends in market rates. Furthermore, in the majority of cases the DM value vis-à-vis EMS partners has not changed as has its value outside of the EMS: EMS realignments, to the extent that they affect spot exchange rates, appear to be centered around the DM.

6.5   Explanations of the Dollar–DM Polarization

One intuitive interpretation of the evidence discussed above relies on some concept of international asset market equilibrium: Exchange rate movements could behave asymmetrically if international portfolios tend to polarize around the DM, the dollar, and other major currencies.   As an illustration, consider a hypothetical case where assets denominated in U.S. dollars and pounds are very close substitutes in investors' portfolios, while assets denominated in U.S. dollars and DMs are less close substitutes.   In this world, an exogenous shock which affects relative prices gives rise to an incipiently large portfolio reallocation between U.S. dollars and pounds, whereas the relative demands for U.S. dollars and DMs change less. Exchange rate movements will have to reflect these portfolio reallocations accordingly.

To determine whether this explanation of the evidence is valid, we need to select a model not statistically rejected by the data, and then to identify those fundamentals that give rise to the observed asymmetric behavior of exchange rates.   Clearly this is too ambitious a task for this chapter, for a number of reasons. While the empirical literature testing international asset pricing models has grown considerably in the recent years, the results so far are not supportive of any theoretical model: Thus, there is no "off-the-shelf" model we can use to interpret the empirical evidence.   Failure of recent empirical tests, however, does not always suggest the inadequacy of the theoretical models, but can be caused by specification problems, data problems, and general limitations of the tests performed.[6]

The existing empirical studies concentrate on two different versions of the portfolio model.   The linear-quadratic asset pricing model of

---

6 Adler and Dumas (1983) provide a useful survey of portfolio models in international finance.   Empirical evidence on foreign exchange risk premia is reported by Cumby (1988), Cumby and Obstfeld (1984), Giovannini and Jorion (1987), and Frankel and Meese (1987).

Kouri (1977) and Dornbusch (1982) has been tested recently by Frankel and Engel (1984), who used data for six currencies (DM, pound sterling, yen, French franc, Canadian dollar, and U.S. dollar). The dynamic asset pricing model of Lucas (1982) has been tested by Hansen and Hodrick (1983) and Hodrick and Srivastava (1984), also using data for six currencies; the only difference is that their sample includes the Swiss franc and excludes the Canadian dollar. All of these authors report rejections. Their tests are based on two assumptions: (1) that expected rates of return are time varying and (2) that variances and covariances of rates of return are constant over time. The first assumption is confirmed by the large body of empirical work on the stochastic properties of the deviations from uncovered interest rate parity. There is increasing empirical evidence, however, that the second assumption might be violated by the data. Parameter instability could be a source of the failure of the empirical tests cited above: Not only do expected rates of return vary over time, but the subjective *uncertainty* about rates of return is also time-varying. In response to these results, very recent attempts have been made to test capital asset pricing models taking into account the joint variation of conditional expected returns and conditional variances of returns. Engel and Rodrigues (1987) and Giovannini and Jorion (1988) estimate the static CAPM on two different data sets and with different specifications of the time-variation of conditional variances. Their results indicate that the fluctuations of conditional variances cannot explain in any way fluctuations in rates of return. Hodrick (1987) implements a version of Svensson's (1985) dynamic asset pricing model with money that allows for persistent changes in the volatility of returns, but he too reports negative results.

While this preliminary evidence is surely discouraging, it might be too early to dismiss the heuristic value of these models. In particular, the models are useful for identifying the fundamentals that should affect the exchange rate movements we observed earlier. For this reason, we carry out a more detailed analysis of the predictions of current portfolio models in the following sections, to identify the factors that most likely account for our empirical regularities.

6.6   Evidence from Dynamic Portfolio Models

The task of explaining correlations among exchange rates, the balance of payments, and prices in a stochastic, general equilibrium dynamic model has been undertaken only very recently, with the work of Lucas

(1982), Svensson (1985), and Stockman and Svensson (1985) among others.[7]

The essential building blocks of these models are the following: There are N countries $i = 1,2, \ldots ,N$ inhabited by risk averse, infinitely lived families. Tastes are identical across countries. In each period, each family receives dividends from holdings of titles of productive capital in the home and foreign country, and a lump-sum monetary transfer. In the asset markets monetary transfers, dividends, stocks, and any other assets are traded before goods market trading occurs. Trading in the goods market is subject to a constraint: A country's goods have to be bought with that country's currency. Money growth and output follow a joint first-order Markov process. Each family maximizes the following time-separable utility function:

$$V = \sum_{t=0}^{\infty} \delta^t U (c_{1t}, c_{2t}, \ldots, c_{Nt}) \tag{6.2}$$

where δ is the utility discount rate and c_i is consumption of the output of country i. Money is the only outside financial asset. In this model, money is held because of the transactions constraint that we have mentioned earlier. This transactions constraint implies a constant-velocity demand for each country's money.[8] Since money is the only outside asset and is held only for transaction purposes, velocity is constant and unitary and the exchange rate is determined by the simple expression below:

$$E_j^{jk} = \frac{M_t^k \, y_t^j \, U_j \left(y_t^1/N, \ldots, y_t^N/N \right)}{M_t^j \, y_t^k \, U_k \left(y_t^1/N, \ldots, y_t^N/N \right)} \tag{6.3}$$

Where E^{jk} is the nominal exchange rate expressed as units of currency k per one unit of currency j, M^i is the stock of country i's money, y^i is country i's GDP, and U_i is the partial derivative of U with respect to good i. In equilibrium, the rate of exchange of country j goods and country k goods equals the marginal rate of substitution between countries j and k's goods. The nominal exchange rate is such that the purchasing power of the two currencies in terms of the same goods

---

7 A survey of this work is in Obstfeld and Stockman (1985).

8 Svensson (1985), and Stockman and Svensson (1985) use versions of this model which allow for interest-elastic money demand functions.

is equalized. (The law of one price holds, eliminating international goods arbitrage opportunities).

Not surprisingly, equation (6.3) is very similar to Frenkel's (1976) traditional monetarist equation; the main difference is that real exchange rates are allowed to fluctuate here if changes in any country's GDP affect the marginal rate of substitution. The similarity is caused by the role of money in this model; the unit-velocity money demand prevents future money stocks in the two countries from affecting the current exchange rate.

The correlation of exchange rate changes is determined by the co-movements of money growth and output in the different countries and by the degree of substitutability of the N goods in consumption. For example, a higher correlation of monetary policy between Italy and the United States than between Germany and the United States would, other things equal, produce correlations among the effective rates of the dollar, the lira, and the DM which are akin to the ones reported in tables 6.1, 6.2, and 6.3.

Using monthly data for money (M1) and industrial production as a proxy for GDP, we generate "theoretical" time series with which we compute the same regression coefficients as in table 6.2. In order to construct the theoretical exchange rates, we need assumptions about the utility function. We assume the following two-level CES function:

$$U^\rho = \left[\left(c_1^\alpha + \ldots + c_7^\alpha\right)^{1/\alpha} \right]^\rho + \left[\left(c_8^\beta + c_9^\beta\right)^{1/\beta} \right]^\rho \tag{6.4}$$

which implies a constant elasticity of substitution among European goods, c_1 to c_7, a constant elasticity of substitution between American (U.S. and Canadian) and Japanese goods, c_8 and c_9, and a constant elasticity of substitution between the two groups. Weighted averages of theoretical bilateral rates are computed using GNP weights.

Table 6.5 shows both the regression coefficients computed with the theoretical exchange rate series and (in parentheses) the same coefficients computed with the actual data. The numbers we are most interested in are those of France, Belgium, and Italy, which show the tendencies of these currencies to diverge from the DM in correspondence with dollar fluctuations. The difference between theoretical and actual regression coefficients is striking in all subsamples. Indeed, in most cases theoretical regression coefficients suggest that a deprecia-

Table 6.5
The effective dollar and bilateral DM exchange rates—monthly data:
theoretical correlations produced by the dynamic CAPM with unit velocity[a]

Dutch guilder	Belgian franc	French franc	Italian lira	Pound sterling	Swiss franc	Japanese yen	Canadian dollar
Before EMS (June 1973 to February 1979)							
−0.20	0.21	0.12	0.75	−0.19	0.15	−1.25	−1.41
(−0.14)	(−0.12)	(−0.20)	(−0.52)	(−0.53)	(0.05)	(−0.29)	(−1.45)
EMS period (March 1979 to July 1987)							
−0.24	0.51	0.030	−0.26	0.14	−0.31	−0.44	−0.59
(−0.01)	(−0.02)	(−0.004)	(−0.10)	(−0.30)	(0.09)	(−0.05)	(−0.96)
Dollar depreciating (May 1977 to October 1978)							
−0.34	2.51	0.41	5.32	−0.55	0.25	0.01	−0.54
(−0.12)	(−0.11)	(−0.26)	(−0.76)	(−0.50)	(−0.02)	(0.37)	(−1.43)
Dollar appreciating (November 1978 to August 1981)							
−0.26	0.91	0.13	0.16	0.44	−0.27	1.04	0.07
(0.01)	(0.006)	(−0.002)	(−0.05)	(0.01)	(0.11)	(−0.07)	(−0.90)
Dollar depreciating (March 1985 to July 1987)							
−1.53	−1.18	0.88	−1.11	0.76	−0.79	1.26	−0.85
(−0.02)	(−0.003)	(−0.03)	(−0.13)	(−0.26)	(0.19)	(0.15)	(−0.95)

a. Elasticity of substitution among European goods equal to 2 (α = .5); elasticity of substitution between European goods and goods produced by the rest of the world, and between American and Japanese goods, equal to 1.25 ($\beta = \rho$ = .2). Numbers in parentheses are the sample regression coefficients from table 6.2.

tion of the effective dollar exchange rate is associated with a depreciation of the DM vis-à-vis these three currencies, which is just the opposite of the phenomenon we want to explain.

Since the assumption of unit velocity on which equation (6.3) relies is questionable, we compute in table 6.6 the same regression coefficients using actual nominal price levels rather than those implied by the quantity theory. The table shows that relaxing the assumption of constant unit velocity of circulation of money does not help the model to reproduce the empirical findings in any appreciable way. In only three out of fifteen cases do the coefficients computed using the model match the signs of the empirical regression coefficients for the lira, the Belgian franc, and the French franc. These results are not affected in any important way by the assumptions we make about the marginal rate of substitution between European goods and goods in the rest of the world. We have experimented with several different values of the parameters in the utility function (equation (6.4)) without noticing any improvement in the ability of the model to reproduce the data. The results are also inconsistent in the case of Cobb-Douglas utility functions when relative output levels drop out of equation (6.3). Thus money supply covariances by themselves are insufficient to explain the observed covariances of exchange rates.

6.7   Exchange Controls

Differences in the degree of financial integration often are offered as an explanation of the observed correlations. For example, the *Federal Reserve Bulletin*, September 1984, commenting on the EMS experience in the early months of that year, reported

The joint float came under some pressure in the early part of the period, as the dollar fell from its January highs. Flows out of dollar assets were attracted to the German mark to a far greater extent than to any other EMS currencies— reflecting sanguine assessments of the investment climate in Germany as well as the wider opportunities for inflows afforded by its relatively open financial system.

Gaston Thorn, former president of the European Commission, refers to "large scale flows of short-term speculative capital between the U.S. dollar and the German mark" as a specific cause of strains within the

Table 6.6
The effective dollar and bilateral DM exchange rates—monthly data:
theoretical correlations produced by the dynamic CAPM (actual price levels)[a]

Dutch guilder	Belgian franc	French franc	Italian lira	Pound sterling	Swiss franc	Japanese yen	Canadian dollar
Before EMS (June 1973 to February 1979)							
0.11	0.27	0.48	2.18	0.23	0.06	0.09	−0.36
(−0.14)	(−0.12)	(−0.20)	(−0.52)	(−0.53)	(0.05)	(−0.29)	(−1.45)
EMS period (March 1979 to July 1987)							
−0.19	1.46	−0.03	−0.04	−0.38	−0.50	−1.15	−1.29
(−0.01)	(−0.02)	(−0.004)	(−0.10)	(−0.30)	(0.09)	(−0.05)	(−0.96)
Dollar depreciating (May 1977 to October 1978)							
−0.09	0.48	0.08	8.22	0.04	−0.04	−0.11	−0.17
(−0.12)	(−0.11)	(−0.26)	(−0.76)	(−0.50)	(−0.02)	(0.37)	(−1.43)
Dollar appreciating (November 1978 to August 1981)							
0.43	0.23	0.25	0.76	0.38	−0.12	−0.30	−0.96
(0.01)	(0.006)	(−0.002)	(−0.05)	(0.01)	(0.11)	(−0.07)	(−0.90)
Dollar depreciating (March 1985 to July 1987)							
1.29	2.86	0.17	0.25	−0.03	−0.16	−0.22	−0.81
(−0.02)	(−0.003)	(−0.03)	(−0.13)	(−0.26)	(0.19)	(0.15)	(−0.95)

a. Elasticity of substitution among European goods equal to 2 ($\alpha = .5$); elasticity of substitution between European goods and goods produced by the rest of the world, and between American and Japanese goods, equal to 1.25 ($\beta = \rho = .2$). Numbers in parentheses are the sample regression coefficients from Table 6.2.

EMS.[9] In the period preceding the EMS capital controls were most stringent in Italy, the United Kingdom, and Japan, and their exchange rates vis-à-vis the DM appear to have had the largest negative correlations with the dollar. This is what one would observe if shifts out of dollars had only a small effect on the demand for assets denominated in lire, pounds, and yen. The systematic appreciations of the Swiss franc in terms of marks in correspondence of dollar depreciations are also suggestive of the important role of Swiss franc assets—which can be freely traded in international financial markets—as an alternative to dollar assets in international portfolios.

In this section we address the question of the effects of exchange controls on international transactions and international portfolio diversification, and of their role in explaining the exchange rate movements that we observe. To this end we employ an extension of the dynamic portfolio model that accounts explicitly for exchange controls. The model is due to Stockman and Hernandez (1988).

International capital markets are perfect, but they are subject to the constraint that all purchases of goods and assets have to be made with currency. Exchange controls are imposed as a tax on currency transactions. This is the simplest form of restriction to study, and the one most likely to be enforced by monetary authorities: All financial transactions ultimately have to be cleared in the countries of the two parties involved, and in most countries monetary authorities control the clearing of payments that involve the domestic banking system directly.

A tax on all exchanges of domestic currency with the rest of the world ultimately has the same effect as a tax on the purchase of foreign goods (a tariff), since domestic currency is exchanged for foreign currency for the ultimate purpose of consuming foreign goods. As Stockman and Hernandez [1988] show, the equilibrium exchange rate in this case is:

$$E_t^{jk} = \frac{P_t^k}{P_t^j} \frac{U_j\left(y_t^1/N, \ldots, y_t^N/N\right)}{U_k\left(y_t^1/N, \ldots, y_t^N/N\right)} \frac{1}{(1+\tau)} \tag{6.5}$$

The marginal rate of substitution between domestic and foreign goods is determined by the relative endowments of all goods. Given domestic and foreign prices, an increase in the tax on foreign exchange pur-

---

9 In *International Herald Tribune*, May 18, 1983, quoted in Marston (1985). See also Frankel (1985b) and Ungerer et al. (1983).

chases *appreciates* the domestic currency, because the given marginal rate of substitution between domestic and foreign goods has to equal the aftertax cost of purchasing foreign goods with domestic goods.

To simulate the predictions of the dynamic portfolio model with capital controls, we need an estimate of the tax on foreign exchange purchases. A natural proxy for this tax is the differential between onshore and offshore interest rates, which we study in detail in the next chapter. As we will show in chapter 7, the differential between offshore and onshore interest rates is equal to the shadow price for acquiring short term financial assets outside national boundaries.[10] Table 6.7 reports estimates of the statistics in table 6.6, corrected by the offshore-onshore interest rate differential as a proxy for τ in equation (6.5). We obtain data for the differential between Euro and domestic interbank one-month interest rates for the United Kingdom, France, and Italy. We compute the actual price levels and the log-differences of bilateral dollar rates for all countries using equation (6.5).[11]

From the table it appears that the effects of exchange controls on international portfolio equilibrium studied by Stockman and Hernandez do not improve the performance of the dynamic portfolio model, at least given our own measure of the tax on foreign exchange transactions. For the French franc, the lira, and the Belgian franc, the covariance between the effective dollar rate and the bilateral DM rate is still positive, contrary to the findings. Alternatively, the results could indicate that when the dollar is weak the offshore-onshore interest differential in Italy and France increases as a result of the selling pressure on those currencies; the increase in the offshore-onshore differential, however, tends to cause the lira and French franc exchange rate to appreciate in the model.

6.8   Transaction Costs and International Portfolio Allocation

The model by Stockman and Hernandez does not satisfactorily explain the empirical regularities, most likely because it does not not fit the type of capital controls prevailing in Europe. Since in their model

---

10 In the model of chapter 7, it is easy to verify that the ratio of offshore to onshore interest rates is equal to the value of the constraint associated with the purchase of foreign assets by firms, relative to the marginal utility of wealth.

11 Of course, for countries other than France, Italy, and the United Kingdom, the formula applies with $\tau = 0$.

Table 6.7
The effective dollar and bilateral DM exchange rates—monthly data:
theoretical correlations produced by the dynamic CAPM
with exchange controls[a]

Dutch guilder	Belgian franc	French franc	Italian lira	Pound sterling	Swiss franc	Japanese yen	Canadian dollar
Before EMS (January 1974 to February 1979)							
−0.04	0.05	0.31	2.63	0.33	−0.22	−0.27	−0.55
(−0.13)	(−0.07)	(−0.12)	(−0.34)	(−0.29)	(0.14)	(−0.04)	(−1.30)
EMS period (March 1979 to February 1987)							
−0.14	1.56	0.08	0.14	−0.39	−0.42	−0.99	−1.14
(−0.01)	(0.02)	(0.004)	(−0.10)	(−0.30)	(0.09)	(−0.05)	(−0.96)
Dollar depreciating (May 1977 to October 1978)							
−0.08	0.61	0.08	7.90	0.02	−0.03	−0.08	−0.16
(−0.12)	(−0.11)	(−0.26)	(−0.76)	(−0.50)	(−0.02)	(0.37)	(−1.43)
Dollar appreciating (November 1978 to August 1981)							
0.42	0.75	0.27	0.99	0.35	−0.04	−0.09	−0.78
(0.01)	(0.006)	(−0.002)	(−0.05)	(0.01)	(0.11)	(−0.07)	(−0.90)
Dollar depreciating (March 1985 to February 1987)							
1.09	2.61	0.22	0.24	−0.05	−0.17	−0.07	−0.75
(−0.08)	(−0.11)	(−0.09)	(0.007)	(−0.68)	(−0.24)	(−0.96)	(−1.38)

a. Elasticity of substitution among European goods equal to 2 (α = .5); elasticity of substitution between European goods and goods produced by the rest of the world, and between American and Japanese goods, equal to 1.25 ($\beta = \rho = .2$). Foreign exchange tax computed for the French franc, lira and sterling using the differential between one-month Euro interest rates and domestic interbank rates. Numbers in parentheses are the sample regression coefficients computed as in table 6.2.

money is demanded only for the purpose of purchasing goods, taxes on the purchase of foreign moneys are a tax on the purchase of foreign goods. In most European countries, while there are taxes on the purchase of foreign moneys for the purpose of transactions in financial assets, these taxes are waived when foreign moneys are purchased for the purpose of transactions in goods with other European countries.

In this section we explore an alternative model of the effects of regulations on the diversification of international portfolios and, as a result, on the comovements of exchange rates. According to this model capital controls result in increased transaction costs in the exchange of assets denominated in the currencies subject to capital controls. These costs represent the obstacles imposed by controls on free exchange of a country's financial assets for the purpose of international portfolio diversification.[12] The first important effect of these costs is the limitation of the number of agents who actively trade for portfolio purposes in currencies subject to capital controls. The second effect of capital controls as modelled in this section is to make a country's financial assets less substitutable for assets denominated in other currencies. Finally, transaction costs make price responses to exogenous shocks asymmetric between assets that are costly to trade and assets that are not.

These effects are obtained by introducing transactions costs in a two-period capital asset pricing model. We follow the analysis of Mayshar (1983).[13] There are $N + 2$ assets: N risky assets, a riskless bond, and a "market" asset,[14] with which all rates of return on risky assets are correlated. Every asset j's payoff is made up of three components

$$x_j = \bar{x}_j + b_j z + \zeta_j \tag{6.6}$$

where z is the market rate of return, with

$$COV(\bar{x}_j, \zeta_j) = E(\zeta_j) + COV(z, \zeta_j) = 0$$

---

12 Discussing capital controls in Italy, Baffi (1978) suggests that one of their effects is to increase transaction costs in the foreign exchange market. See Black (1974) and Stulz (1981) for yet other models of international capital controls, based on the assumption that residents of different countries are subject to different tax rates on foreign asset incomes.

13 Pagano (1985) illustrates a rational expectations version of that model.

14 The latter two assets are assumed for analytical simplicity. Their elimination would not affect the main results presented below.

$E()$ is the expectations operator, b_j measures the "systematic risk" of asset j, and ζ is the nondiversifiable component in the return on asset j. Let there be L investors who maximize the utility of final wealth, a function of its expected value and its variance. Investors' demands for the N risky assets are set equal to their (fixed) supplies, to determine the standard equilibrium asset pricing equations

$$q_j (1 + r) = E\left(x_j\right) - b_j\pi_z - (A/L)\, F_j \mathrm{VAR}\left(\zeta_j\right) \tag{6.7}$$

where q_j is the price of asset j, r is the riskless rate of interest, A is the coefficient of risk aversion, and the market risk premium π_z is equal, in equilibrium, to

$$\pi_z = (a/L)\left(\sum_{j=1}^{N} b_j F_j\right) \mathrm{VAR}\,(z) \tag{6.8}$$

What is the effect of transaction costs? Investors have to decide whether the cost of trading in assets with transaction costs is worth the expected return on these assets, given their market price.[15] Transactions costs are made up of two components: a lump sum component and a component proportional to the value of the trade. We assume that lump sum costs differ across investors. Investors are ordered by increasing cost of trading.[16] In equilibrium, for every asset k with transaction costs the following condition has to hold

$$E\left(x_k\right) - b_k\pi_k - q_k\,(1 + r + t_k) = \Phi_k\,(\ell_k) \tag{6.9}$$

where Φ_k is the lump-sum transaction cost function for asset k,[17] $\Phi_k'>0$, ℓ_k is the number of active traders, and t_k is the proportional cost. As shown in Mayshar [1983], equation (6.9) together with

$$q_k\,(1 + r + t_k) = E\,(x_k) - b_k\pi_z - (A/\ell_k)\, F_k \mathrm{VAR}\left(\zeta_k\right) \tag{6.10}$$

---

15 We assume for simplicity that investors demand positive quantities of each asset. Mayshar (1983) shows that the analysis can be extended to the case where asset holdings can be negative.

16 Differential trading costs in the Euromarkets for example can be observed between banks and nonbanks.

17 That is $\Phi_k(\ell_k)$ is the transaction cost associated with asset k, incurred by the ℓ_k-th investor. We assume a continuum of investors for analytical tractability.

Table 6.8
Offshore market size by currency of denomination
(percentage share of total market size, December 1984)

	U.S.$	DM	SF	YEN	UK	FF	DG	LIT	ECU
Mkt. share	77.0	10.0	5.0	2.0	1.3	0.9	0.9	0.4	1.3
GNP share	50.0	10.0	1.5	16.2	6.9	7.9	2.1	5.4	–

Source: Bank of International Settlements, *International Banking Developments,*
for the Euromarket shares. GNP shares from World Bank, *World Development
Report 1985.* They are computed as the ratio of each country GNP in U.S.
dollars to the total U.S. dollar value of all eight countries' GNP.

determine the number of traders in the market for the kth asset, and its
equilibrium price. Assets which have no transactions costs are priced
according to equation (6.7).

Equations (6.9) and (6.10) can be used to show that the number of
active traders ℓ_k decreases when transaction costs are significant. Table 6.8 reports the offshore market size for a number of currencies,
and compares the size of the offshore market with the economic importance of the country as measured by GNP: The table is consistent
with the hypothesis that countries imposing capital controls, like Italy
and France, limit the size of financial markets in their own currency.

More important, in the presence of transaction costs, assets become
less substitutable: That is a change in their outstanding supply has
a larger effect on their price. By differentiating equations (6.9) and
(6.10), the effect of changes in the supply of asset k on its price is

$$\frac{dq_k}{dF_k} = -(1 + r + t_k)^{-1} \left[\frac{(A/\ell_k)\, \text{VAR}\,(\zeta_k)}{\left[1 + \frac{A}{\ell_k^2} \text{VAR}\,(\zeta_k)\, F_k \Psi'_k \right]} + b_k \frac{\partial \pi_z}{\partial F_k} \right] \tag{6.11}$$

where Ψ'_k is the first derivative of the inverse of the function Φ_k, and
measures the potential number of entrants in the market when q_k decreases.

Notice that, in the absence of costs,

$$\frac{dq_k}{dF_k} = -(1 + r)^{-1} \left[(A/L)\, \text{VAR}\,(\zeta_k) + b_k \frac{\partial \pi_z}{\partial F_k} \right] \tag{6.12}$$

A comparison of equations (6.11) and (6.12) shows that transactions costs affect the response of prices to a change in asset supplies in two ways. Lump-sum costs, by decreasing the number of market participants, tend to make prices more sensitive to changes in asset supplies. If lump sum costs are such that ℓ_k is small relative to L, and if the potential number of entrants in the market is small (Ψ'_k small), then changes in F_k have a larger effect on q_k compared with a situation where asset k can be traded without costs. The presence of proportional transaction costs dampens this effect, but is unlikely to reverse it if the number of active traders is very small.

Equation (6.11) sheds light on an important effect of capital controls. The traditional literature on capital controls—for example Aliber (1973), Claassen and Wyplosz (1982), and Obstfeld (1982b)—suggests that their presence makes assets less substitutable because the uncertainty about imposition of future controls increases the variance of the rate of return. We show here that even if the probability of tighter capital controls in the future is zero, assets are less substitutable because of market thinness endogenously generated by capital controls. As a consequence, foreign exchange market operations affecting the supply of assets are likely to be more effective in the presence of capital controls.

Can this model of capital controls help to explain the observed correlations of exchange rates? Consider two assets which have identical systematic risk but differ in transaction costs. Equations (6.9) and (6.10) show that an identical increase in their expected rate of return, or a change in the market risk premium, has a larger effect on the asset which is more freely tradeable, that is the asset with smaller proportional transaction costs t.[18] This model has no direct implications for the movements of exchange rates. Typically, asset demand models are closed by assuming that exchange rates are the relative prices of assets denominated in different currencies. Under this assumption we could use the market thinness model to interpret our data.

Consider an exogenous and identical increase in expected returns on DM and French franc assets. Equations (6.9) and (6.10) imply that the incipient portfolio shift into DMs and francs has different effects on exchange rates if transactions costs differ. If they were higher for French francs, we would observe the effective dollar exchange rate depreci-

---

18 Notice that differences in lump-sum costs do not affect the responses of prices to changes in expected return, because changes in expected return do not affect the number of active traders in each asset.

ate and the DM appreciate in terms of francs. The market thinness model would reproduce exactly the empirical regularity described in this chapter.

This model, however, is ill-suited to computing the implied second moments of exchange rates as we did using the general equilibrium dynamic models in sections 6.6 and 6.7. It needs to be extended to a dynamic version and to be closed with equations specifying goods market equilibrium. In chapter 7 we present a first attempt in this direction with a model that, for simplicity, assumes away all uncertainty but at the same time makes explicit the sources of the transaction costs implied by capital controls.

Appendix: The Data

Effective exchange rates weights

The effective dollar exchange rates used in tables 6.1 to 6.7 are constructed with weights equal to the ratio of the dollar value of GNP in each country to the dollar value of GNP of all nine countries included in the set. GNP and exchange rates are averages over the period 1973 to 1984. They are obtained from *International Financial Statistics*. The result is reported below:

BE	.027
CA	.075
FR	.150
GY	.192
IT	.091
JP	.282
NL	.039
SW	.027
UK	.118

Tables 6.1 to 6.7: exchange rates are noon-time New York bid rates for the dollar from Data Resources Inc., FACS Databank.

Tables 6.4 to 6.7: money stocks (M1) from IMF, *Int.Fin.Stat.*, line 34. Industrial production (line 66c) was used as a proxy for monthly GDP.

7   Capital Controls

7.1   Capital Controls in Regimes of Controlled Floating

Despite the general aversion of economists and at least some policy-makers to controls on international trade in goods, controls on financial transactions are by far the most common feature of international capital markets. The large majority of countries regulate international asset trade.[1] Furthermore, as we already noted in chapter 2, even the Articles of Agreement of the International Monetary Fund contain provisions allowing capital controls to be imposed in order to stem short-run speculative pressures. By contrast, both the 1961 OECD Code of Liberalization of Capital Movements and the Single European Act of 1986, which lays the foundations for the liberalization of 1992, advocate the progressive removal of restrictions to international trade in assets.

The widespread use of capital controls is not clearly justified by any widely agreed-upon economic theory; indeed, to our knowledge, there have only been a very few attempts to study capital controls using explicit second-best arguments.[2] The policymakers' justifications for capital controls are: first, that they help to stabilize domestic interest rates in a regime of controlled floating, and, second, that they avoid speculative attacks—which might or might not be justified by

---

1 See, for instance, IMF *Annual Report on Exchange Arrangements and Exchange Restrictions.*
2 See Krugman (1987) and Tornell (1986). For a survey of the standard macroeconomics arguments for capital controls, see Dornbusch (1986b). Adams and Greenwood (1985), Greenwood and Kimbrough (1984), and van Wijnbergen (1987) study the effects of capital controls using choice-theoretic models. Giovannini (1988b, 1988c) assesses second-best arguments for capital controls related to the presence of distortionary taxation.

fundamental disequilibria—against the central bank's reserves.[3]

We review the interest rate stability argument first. The main thrust of the argument is that, with perfect capital mobility, the discrete exchange rate realignments occurring in an adjustable peg regime can cause extremely high interest rate differentials. Large discrete devaluations are not unusual in adjustable peg regimes. The experience of the Bretton Woods years has shown several instances where currencies were devalued by more than 5 percent; the table of EMS realignments that we report in chapter 6 (table 6.4) also shows more than one case where realignments resulted in non-negligible jumps in the level of the exchange rate.[4]

Whenever large exchange rate changes are expected, equilibrium interest rate differentials widen deeply. To illustrate this fact, assume that uncovered interest rate parity between domestic and foreign assets holds, so that the (continuously compounded) interest rate on domestic assets equals the (continuously compounded) interest rate on foreign assets, plus the expected rate of change of the price of foreign currency in terms of domestic currency. Suppose a 5 percent devaluation of the domestic currency is expected to occur in the next month but no changes in the exchange rate are expected to take place afterwards. The expected devaluation twists the term structure of interest rate differentials: The differential between domestic and foreign rates on comparable 1-year instruments in equilibrium is equal to 5 percent; but it increases to 10, 20, and 60 percent on assets of 6, 3, and one-month maturity, respectively. In proximity of a devaluation equilibrium interest rates on overnight assets can easily exceed 100 percent! In general, fluctuations in expected exchange rate devaluations increase the volatility of short-term nominal interest rates to levels that are considered unacceptable by most central banks. While there is no widely agreed-upon welfare justification for the desirability of targeting nominal interest rates, many economists argue that nominal interest rate targeting seems a reasonable description of central banks' activities.[5]

Controls on international capital flows can protect domestic interest

---

3 Stockman (1988) argues that the desire of central banks to defend their foreign exchange reserves against speculative attacks makes the use of capital controls more common during regimes of controlled floating than under flexible exchange rates.

4 Williamson (1985) stresses the potential disruptive effects of large parity realignments in the EMS.

5 See Barro (1988) for a recent appraisal of that argument.

rates from the fluctuations associated with expectations of discrete exchange rate realignments. They do so by prohibiting domestic and foreign residents from borrowing at the domestic interest rate in order to lend abroad, in the expectation of the capital gains accruing after the exchange rate realignment.[6]

However, when a devaluation is expected, accepting the fluctuations of domestic interest rates required to prevent the reallocation of international financial portfolios does not avoid a speculative attack on the reserves of the central bank. A large enough increase in domestic interest rates can compensate portfolio-holders for the capital loss expected on the day of the devaluation, but does not help holders of domestic *high-powered money*. Since the purchasing power of the domestic money stock falls after a devaluation, holders of high-powered money will try to avoid the loss by selling the domestic currency to the central bank in exchange for foreign currency just before the devaluation, then buying it back after the devaluation. Speculative attacks on central banks' reserves thus can occur even when domestic interest rates are allowed to jump to equilibrate financial portfolios.[7] This problem could be especially bothersome to central banks, since the magnitude of the expected devaluation does not affect the size of the speculative attack: If buying and selling the reserves of the central bank were costless, the central bank would end up losing all of its reserves before the devaluation, no matter how small. The reluctance of central banks to suffer large swings in their foreign exchange reserves is an additional motive for prohibiting the purchase of foreign exchange by domestic residents, for reasons that are not related to the the financing of international trade.[8]

Finally, capital controls are often said to eliminate the possibility of multiple equilibria, which may occur in financial markets where asset

6 In section 7.2 below we describe in detail the techniques that exporters and importers can use, even in the presence of capital controls, to manage their working capital with the objective of gaining the maximum advantage from discrete exchange rate changes.
7 See Krugman (1979) for a model of speculative attacks in the presence of interest rate arbitrage.
8 If, on the other hand, the central bank was willing to allow its foreign exchange reserves to become sufficiently negative, so that the post-attack domestic money stock would be sufficiently low, then the speculative attack would not occur, since the post-attack equilibrium value of the domestic currency would be sufficiently high. See Alesina and Grilli (1987). International monetary policy interactions with capital controls are studied by Begg and Wyplosz (1987).

prices are determined by expectations. Obstfeld (1986) has demonstrated the possibility of self-fulfilling speculative attacks under fixed exchange rates.

7.2   Capital Controls in Europe

Speculative capital flows in anticipation of a realignment occur through two main channels: trade credits and portfolio movements. Trade credits are important because the management of foreign trade financing allows domestic residents to acquire foreign assets and is thus a perfect substitute for portfolio investment. For this reason, both channels—portfolio movements and trade credits—have been regulated by EMS central banks. The incentive to use exchange controls to stabilize domestic interest rates in principle should be symmetric. Weak currency countries have an incentive to impose exchange controls to avoid the large interest rate hikes that accompany the anticipation of a *devaluation*. Strong currency countries have an incentive to use exchange controls to set domestic interest rates independently while limiting the inflow of reserves associated with the anticipation of a *revaluation*. In Europe, however, foreign exchange regulations are very asymmetric: Weak currency countries (France, Italy, Belgium, and Denmark) have sealed off the domestic financial market from the international financial market. Exchange controls, in contrast, are almost nonexistent in strong-currency countries (Germany and the Netherlands.) These asymmetric regulations mirror the asymmetric functioning of the EMS. As discussed at length in chapter 4, the interest rate pressures that precede an EMS realignment are very different in strong and weak currency countries, because the asymmetric nature of the system shelters interest rates in strong currency countries and shifts the pressure onto the weak currencies. Thus, strong currency countries have a much smaller incentive to use capital controls to stabilize domestic interest rates: the asymmetry of controls on international capital flows mirrors the asymmetry of monetary policy roles across countries.[9] This is confirmed by the observation that Ger-

---

9 The following quote from J. W. Birch, governor of the Bank of England, complaining about capital controls in France and Germany during the classical gold standard (when England was the central country), provides a striking analogy to the current situation: "In the Banks of France and Germany the money box seems to have two slits, the one, a tolerably broad one, and if you turn the box on a certain corner, the gold comes out; this slit is marked 'For Home Use;' but the other is an uncommonly narrow one, and

many imposed regulations on capital inflows in the 1960s, since the country that enjoyed monetary policy independence in the early years of Bretton Woods was clearly not Germany but the United States.

This section describes foreign exchange regulations in the EMS.[10] We deal first with the regulations on portfolio transactions by households and banks, and then with the financing of foreign trade.

7.2.1 Controls on Portfolio Investment

• *France*: Exchange controls in France date back to the law of September 9, 1939.[11] In the postwar period, administrative controls had been relaxed gradually following the return to convertibility in 1958; convertibility had been accompanied by a devaluation which helped to eliminate the pressure on the franc, thus allowing a higher degree of capital mobility. Liberalization proceeded throughout the 1960s and reached its peak in 1971, when the French government abolished the *devise titre* system. Until that time a French resident could only purchase foreign assets from another French resident[12]—a regulation that effectively froze the stock of foreign assets held by domestic residents. From 1971 to 1981, the purchase of foreign financial assets was unrestricted; domestic lending abroad remained restricted, however, and residents were forbidden to lend French francs to non-residents.[13] The *devise titre* was reintroduced in 1981, and not abolished until the liberalization of 1986.

• *Italy*: As in the French case, Italy's foreign exchange regulations date back to the 1930s and had been relaxed progressively in the 1960s. A new tightening occurred in 1972, when portfolio investment was de facto prohibited by the introduction of a tax on the purchase of foreign securities: Residents were subject to a zero-interest deposit requirement equal to 50 percent of the value of their foreign investment.

---

that is marked 'For Export,' and very difficult it is to get the gold out through this slit." From the *Journal of the Institute of Bankers* 1887, pp. 509–510, quoted in Ford (1962).

10 For a recent review of exchange controls in the EMS see *European Economy*, 36, May 1988.

11 For an analysis of French exchange controls in the postwar period see Neme (1986), Claasen and Wyplosz (1982), and Wyplosz (1988b).

12 The *devise titre* was the exchange rate that cleared the market for financial transactions among residents.

13 The liberalization also excluded foreign direct investment in France, which always remained subject to authorization.

This regulation lasted until May 1987 and for a period of 15 years made it virtually impossible for an Italian resident to acquire foreign assets. Foreign lending has also been prohibited since 1972.[14]

Thus throughout most of the EMS period portfolio movements were ruled out in France and Italy, since domestic residents of either country were forbidden from borrowing and lending abroad.

• *Belgium*: While France and Italy impose a quota or a prohibitive tax on the purchase of foreign assets, Belgium has a dual exchange market. Belgian residents are free to purchase foreign assets, but the foreign exchange required for such purchases must be bought in a special market. There are two parallel exchange markets in Belgium: Current account transactions go through the official market, in which the Belgian central bank is committed to follow EMS rules; capital account transactions go through the financial market, where the price of foreign exchange is freely floating. Capital outflows are strictly assigned to the financial market; capital inflows may enter through either market. The repatriation of dividends also may go through either market.[15]

• *Germany*: Unlike residents of the weak currency countries, German residents have not been subject to restrictions on the purchase of foreign assets since the late 1950s. The German monetary authorities, however, have resorted repeatedly to administrative controls on capital inflows.[16] During the Bretton Woods years, these measures were introduced regularly when a revaluation of the DM was expected, or at times when the volume of Bundesbank intervention in the foreign exchange market was endangering monetary stability. For example, in the run-up to the revaluation of 1961 the purchase of domestic money market instruments by nonresidents was subjected to an authorization requirement; that measure was accompanied by a ban on the payment of interest on non-residents' deposits with German banks. Both restrictions remained in force throughout the 1960s, and were

---

14 On two occasions the Italian authorities also imposed a ceiling on foreign borrowing by domestic banks: in 1975, and then again from July 1984 to December 1985. As we shall discuss below, these episodes are important because they help to explain why, in a system generally designed to prevent capital outflows, we sometimes observe a covered interest rate differential in favor of the domestic market.

15 The Belgian two-tier market is described in Decaluwe (1977). The analytical properties of dual exchange systems are discussed in Dornbusch (1986b), Delbeque (1987), Obstfeld (1984), Bacchetta (1988).

16 For a review of German exchange controls in the 1970s see Bundesbank, (1985).

removed only after the DM revaluation of October 1969. When the Bretton Woods system collapsed, the ban on the payment of interest, as well as the authorization requirement for the purchase of domestic money-market paper by non-residents, were reintroduced. The administrative measures directed at limiting capital inflows were tightened as the pressure on the DM mounted. In March 1972, a 40 percent cash deposit on foreign borrowings was introduced; in July, the purchase of domestic bonds by nonresidents was subject to authorization; in February 1973, the authorization requirement was extended to all foreign borrowings. The controls were gradually phased out in 1974–75, but the purchase of domestic money market instruments, and of bonds with remaining maturities up to four years, continued to require an authorization. To further limit capital inflows, a reserve ratio on banks' foreign liabilities, higher than the reserve ratio on domestic liabilities, was introduced; the differential was abolished in 1978. In the early years of the EMS (1979–81), Germany still bore the signs of this long tradition of administrative controls on capital inflows. By 1981, however, capital inflows into Germany were completely liberalized; since then Germany can be characterized as a country with free capital mobility.

7.2.2   Controls on Foreign Trade Financing

In countries like France and Italy, where portfolio investment by households is ruled out, the only way for domesic residents to trade in foreign assets is through the financing of foreign trade. By extending or shortening the maturity of trade credits, exporters and importers can increase or reduce their holdings of foreign assets: claims against their foreign customers and with their suppliers. In anticipation of a devaluation, for example, exporters can lengthen the maturity of their credits: increase the "lags." Similarly, importers can pre-pay the goods that they plan to purchase—increase the "leads"—thus effectively granting a credit to their foreign suppliers. In either case the effect is a capital outflow, similar to what would be observed if firms had been able to diversify their financial portfolio in anticipation of a devaluation. The possibility of playing with leads and lags provides a channel through which the anticipation of a realignment may pressure the reserves of the central bank. However, such pressure is limited by the volume of foreign trade itself—which puts an upward bound on

Table 7.1a
Regulations concerning trade credits: France

Exporters:

1974–81:   no compulsory financing up to 6 months following delivery
           of the goods
           100 percent financing thereafter
1981–82:   100 percent compulsory financing applies after 1 month
1982–86:   100 percent compulsory financing applies after 15 days

Importers:

(a) Possibility to anticipate payments:
              1974–76:   1 month before delivery
              1976–81:   8 days before delivery
              1981–86:   2 days before delivery
(b) Possibility to buy foreign currency forward:
              1974–76:   3 months before delivery
              1976–81:   2 months before delivery
              1981–86:   prohibited

the volume of trade credits at each point in time—and by foreign exchange regulations. A central bank can protect itself against the runs on reserves that can take place through trade credits in two ways. First, it can regulate leads and lags. For example, if it is worried about a capital outflow, it may shorten the maturity of export credits and limit the possibility of pre-paying imports. Second, the central bank can ask exporters to match trade credits with corresponding foreign currency liabilities, forcing them to borrow foreign currency whenever they grant a trade credit to a foreign customer. By raising the foreign currency borrowing requirement to 100 percent of the trade credit, the central bank can effectively seal off this channel for capital flows. In section 7.5 we present a model of capital flows based on trade credits that makes explicit the role of compulsory financing.

Tables 7.1a and 7.1b summarize the regulations on trade credits in France and Italy. In France, following the tightening of exchange controls in 1981, export credits not subject to compulsory financing could not extend beyond one month; the period was shortened to 15 days in 1982. Exporters willing to extend a trade credit beyond this period must finance the total value of the credit in foreign currency and thus are prevented from using trade financing as a vehicle for increasing their *net* holdings of foreign assets. Credit to foreign suppliers is also restricted. Table 7.1b documents the Italian experience. The timing of

Table 7.1b
Italy

Exporters:

1973–75: trade credits cannot extend beyond 3 months;
          over that period there is no compulsory financing

1975–76: maximum length of trade credits is increased to 4 months;
          still no compulsory financing

1976:   maximum length remains 4 months, but compulsory financing
          is introduced in the amount of 30 percent of the total credit

1977:   compulsory financing is increased to 50 percent

1978:   compulsory financing is reduced to 25 percent

1980:   compulsory financing is abolished in September,
          and raised back to 50 percent in December

1982:   maximum length of trade credits is reduced to 2 months,
          but compulsory financing is abolished

1983:   maximum length of trade credits is raised to 5 years;
          compulsory financing is raised to 70 percent

1984–88: in various steps, compulsory financing is lowered to 50 percent,
          than raised to 75 percent, and finally completely abolished

Importers:

1973–75: advanced payments of imports limited to 1 month, and subject to a
          100 percent compulsory financing in foreign currency

1975–78: advanced payments of imports extended to 2 months;
          compulsory financing in foreign currency unchanged

1978–80: advanced payments of imports extended to 4 months;
          compulsory financing in foreign currency unchanged

1980:   possibility to prepay imports is temporarily suspended
          (September to December)

1982:   possibility to prepay imports is suspended

1984:   all limits to advanced payments of imports are removed,
          but compulsory financing in foreign currency continues

1987:   compulsory financing is abolished

Sources: France, Neme (1986); Italy, Banca Commerciale Italiana, *Tendenze Monetarie*, 41, 1982, with updates.

export credits was lengthened substantially in 1983, but at the same time compulsory financing began to be used more actively. When the central bank lost the power to affect the timing of leads and lags—which were regulated by the EEC—the Italian authorities used forced financing of trade credits to control short-term capital flows.

How important are trade credits as a vehicle for moving capital in and out of a country? In table 7.2 we report some evidence on their importance in terms of total short-term capital movements. We compare France and Italy, where trade credits were the only way to acquire net foreign assets in the years we consider, with Germany, where portfolio movements were completely free. Notice that even in Germany trade credits in many years are by far the largest item among private short-term capital inflows and outflows: These are years when the volume of total short-term capital flows is relatively small. In 1983, for example, when short-term capital inflows and outflows amounted to less than one half of one percent of total trade (imports plus exports), trade credits accounted for 44 percent of total short-term capital inflows by the private non-bank sector and 95 percent of capital outflows.[17] But when the pressure mounts—as in 1986—the bulk of short-term capital flows in and out through the financial market, and the share of trade credits, becomes negligible.[18] The numbers for France are different in two respects. Exchange controls make private capital inflows and outflows much more stable over time: There is nothing like the swings we observed in Germany, from less than one percent to almost 10 percent of total trade. Moreover, the bulk of short-term capital movements by the private non-bank sector occurs through trade credits.[19] In the case of Italy, where we do not have separate data on short-term capital flows, trade credits account for more than 50 percent of total capital

17 These figures are 70 percent and 27 percent respectively, if we consider trade credits as a share of private short-term capital flows *inclusive* of the banking sector.

18 These numbers are obviously even smaller if we include the banking sector: 5 percent for outflows, and almost zero for inflows.

19 If we consider the share of French trade credits over private short-term capital movements *inclusive* of the banking sector, the numbers are much smaller:

	1981	1982	1983	1984	1985	1986
Inflows	4	20	4	10	35	7
Outflows	30	13	48	25	5	4

This occurs because *net* portfolio transactions of French banks with the rest of the world are constrained, but gross positions are not. The numbers also show the effects of the liberalization of 1986.

Table 7.2
Short-term trade credits as a percent of total short-term capital transactions
by the private non-bank sector

	1980	1981	1982	1983	1984	1985	1986
Germany:							
Capital inflows	19	36	32	44	53	23	0
Capital outflows	65	79	68	95	60	3	12
Pro-memoria:							
Short-term private capital							
Flows, as a share of total trade							
(import plus exports)							
Capital inflows	2.6	3.1	1.6	−0.3	2.5	0.8	−1.2
Capital outflows	3.1	3.6	0.3	0.4	4.2	4.5	9.8
France:							
Capital inflows	—	62	70	1	48	81	31
Capital outflows	—	58	56	100	80	100	100
Pro-memoria:							
Short-term private capital							
Flows, as a share of total trade							
(import plus exports)							
Capital inflows	—	6.7	4.8	2.5	4.1	2.4	4.8
Capital outflows	—	2.5	2.0	2.2	75.0	2.8	2.7
Italy[a]:							
Capital inflows	69	59	59	60	58	49	43
Capital outflows	69	63	64	58	58	49	41

a. In the case of Italy, the share of short-term trade credits is underestimated,
because the data show the share over *all* capital transactions by the private
non-bank sector, both short and long term. Separate data for short term capital
transactions are not available.

Sources: Germany: Statistical Supplements of the *Monthly Reports of the Deutsche
Bundesbank*, Series 3, Balance of Payments Statistics, Table 6; France: Banque
de France, *La balance des payments de la France*; Italy: Banca d'Italia, *Relazione
Annuale*, Appendice.

flows, both short and long.

7.3   Onshore and Offshore Interest Rates

To what extent have the regulations described in the previous section
been effective in severing the link between the domestic and international financial markets, and thus at insulating domestic interest rates
in the wake of parity realignments? Again we look at France and Italy.
For comparison we also consider the case of the Netherlands, an EMS
member where, as in Germany, there are almost no impediments to
international capital flows.

We study the degree of insulation of the domestic financial market from the international market by looking at the onshore-offshore
differential: that is at the differential between the return on a deposit
issued in the domestic money market and the return on a deposit of
the same maturity issued in the Euromarket and also denominated in
domestic currency. Onshore-offshore differentials signal the presence
of unexploited profit opportunities that can be attributed only to the
active enforcement of exchange controls. In the case of the lira, however, the market for Eurolire deposits is extremely thin; often no price
is quoted. As an alternative to the onshore-offshore differential, we
use the deviations from the condition of covered arbitrage between
the return on a deposit issued in Milan and denominated in lire and
the covered return on a Eurodollar deposit of the same maturity.[20]

In order to detect the presence of unexploited profit opportunities,
we must use data to compute the onshore-offshore differential that
reflects the prices at which an investor could actually have carried
out the transactions involved in the arbitrage operation, if it had been
allowed. This requires two conditions: (1) that the observations be
simultaneous; and (2) that the prices account for all transaction costs.
The data set we used nearly satisfies both conditions: The data con-
sist of weekly observations—last business day of each week—from
the fall of 1980 to December 1987.[21] Onshore and offshore interest
rates are collected with a three-hour difference: mid-morning London
prices for Eurorates and closing prices for domestic rates in Paris,

---

20 Under the assumption that covered interest rate parity holds on the Euromarket, the
two differentials are identical.
21 Similar analyses have been carried out by Ito (1985), using Japanese data, and by
Giavazzi and Pagano (1988a), using daily data in the EMS during the 1980–84 period.

Amsterdam, and Milan. When the differential is constructed using the covered Eurodollar rate, the spot and forward exchange rates are opening New York prices and are therefore almost simultaneous with domestic interest rates. All interest rates are on three-months loans. The domestic rate used for Italy is the interest rate on Repurchase Agreements (*pronti-contro-termine*); this is better than the interbank rate because interbank deposits are taxed, and the rates quoted are not net of tax. Repurchase Agreements are tax-free and subject to no other fee, so that by using bid and offer prices we measure the full cost of carrying out the transaction. Comparable rates are used for France and the Netherlands.[22]

Two arbitrage operations between the domestic money market and the Euromarket are possible: either borrowing on the domestic market to buy a Eurodeposit, or borrowing on the Euromarket to invest at home. Assuming that there are no transaction costs beyond the bid-offer spread, the profit to be earned in the first operation is

$$\pi = r_B^E - r_A \tag{7.1}$$

where r and r^E are the onshore and the offshore rates—respectively, the domestic interest rate and the interest rate on a Eurodeposit denominated in domestic currency; the subscript A denotes the rate at which one can borrow (asked, or offer rate); and the subscript B is the rate at which one can lend (bid rate). The profit to be earned borrowing in the Euromarket to invest at home is instead

$$\pi_2 = r_B - r_A^E$$
$$= -\pi_1 + (r_B - r_A) + \left(r_B^E - r_A^E\right) \tag{7.2}$$

i.e. it is equal to the negative of π_1 plus the sum of the bid-offer spreads in the domestic and in the Euromarket. If the arbitrage operation instead requires borrowing or lending dollars, then the arbitrage profits are:

$$\pi_1' = \left(1 + r_B^\$\right) F_B / S_A - (1 + r_A) \tag{7.1'}$$
$$\pi_2' = (1 + r_B) S_B / F_A - \left(1 + r_A^\$\right) \tag{7.2'}$$

---

22 All rates are as quoted by the branches of Bank of America in the various countries. *Source*: Data Resources Inc., FACS Databank.

where S is the spot exchange rate (the price of one dollar in units of domestic currency) and F is the forward rate; here the subscript A denotes the price at which one can buy dollars (spot or forward) and the subscript B is the price at which one can sell dollars (spot or forward). Equation (7.1$'$) is the arbitrage profit from borrowing at home to buy a covered Eurodollar deposit; equation (7.2$'$) is the arbitrage profit in the opposite direction.

Notice that although π_1 and π_2 (π_1' and π_2' respectively)[23] have the dimension of a rate of return (for example 5 percent), they represent the instantaneous profit to be earned on each (costless and riskless) arbitrage operation. In the absence of exchange controls these profits are potentially infinite, and prices would move so as to eliminate such profit opportunities: In this case we should observe $\pi_1 \leq 0, \pi_2 \leq 0$. If controls are effective at preventing capital *outflows* we should observe $\pi_1 > 0$, $\pi_2 \leq 0$: It would be profitable to borrow at home to buy a Eurodeposit. If controls are effective at preventing capital *inflows* instead we should observe $\pi_1 \leq 0, \pi_2 > 0$.[24]

We compute weekly series of π_1 and π_2 over a sample that runs from October 1980 to December 1987; the results are reported in table 7.3. The mean of the positive realizations of π_1 measures the extent to which exchange controls on average have kept the rate on domestic loans below what it would have been in the absence of controls (the offshore bid rate) in the weeks when such controls were binding. Similarly, the mean of the positive realizations of π_2 measures the extent to which the offshore offer rate was below the domestic bid rate in periods when the controls were effective in preventing capital inflows. Finally, the frequency of the observations in which both $\pi_1 \leq 0$ and $\pi_2 \leq 0$ indicates how often there were no profit opportunities in either direction.[25]

The interest rate data show that capital controls do not keep a constant wedge between onshore and offshore rates. Instead they allow central banks to shield domestic interest rates from fluctuations associated with exchange rate realignments. Consider the data for Italy: Between 1980 and 1987 we observe an incentive for arbitrage, in one

23 In the paragraphs that follow we refer to π_1 and π_2, with the understanding that the same is also true for π_1' and π_2'.

24 Neither $\pi_1 = \pi_2 = 0$, nor $\pi_1 > 0, \pi_2 > 0$ can ever be observed because of the transaction costs reflected in the bid-offer spread.

25 Covered interest rate differentials for a group of 24 countries—including the three European countries we study here—are analyzed in Frankel and MacArthur (1988).

Table 7.3
Onshore-offshore differentials (November 1980–December 1987)[a]

Sample	1980:11–1987:12			1982:10–1983:3			1983:4–1985:11		
Number of observations	(372)			(27)			(138)		
Direction	Out	In	Neither	Out	In	Neither	Out	In	Neither
France									
No. of weeks	309	8	55	27	—	—	115	—	23
Frequency (%)	83	2	15	100	—	—	83	—	17
Mean rate of return (%)	2.2	0.3		7.2			1		
Italy									
No. of weeks	112	75	185	25	1	1	1	58	79
Frequency (%)	30	20	50	92	4	4	1	42	57
Mean rate of return (%)	2.7	0.6		3.2			0.1	0.6	
Netherlands									
No. of weeks	2	1	369	0	0	27	1	0	137
Frequency (%)	.005	.003	99.9	—	—	100	—	—	100
Mean rate of return (%)	.03	—		—	—		—		

a. *Direction* indicates the direction in which unexploited arbitrage profits are observed. The *mean rate of return* represents the instantaneous profit that could have been earned on each riskless and costless arbitrage operation, if there had been no exchange controls. *Out* refers to observations for which π_1 is positive; *in* to observations for which π_2 is positive, and *neither* refers to observations for which $\pi_1 \leq 0$, and $\pi_2 \leq 0$. π_1 and π_2 are defined in equations (7.1) and (7.2) in the text. In the case of France and of the Netherlands the data refer to the differentials between onshore and offshore rates, that is to equations (7.1) and (7.2). In the case of Italy they refer to the covered interest rate differentials described in equations (7.1') and (7.2).

direction or the other, only half of the time: 50 percent of all weeks in the sample. When a profit opportunity is observed, 30 percent of the time it signals a differential in favor of the Euromarket, but 20 percent of the time the differential goes in the opposite direction. That is to say, onshore rates were higher than the corresponding Eurorates. The results are similar for France, except that the frequency of weeks when we observe a differential in favor of the domestic market is much lower: only 8 weeks out of 372. The results for the Netherlands show that in the absence of exchange controls, covered interest parity between the onshore and the offshore market always holds.

To highlight the role of exchange controls at times of realignments, we have divided the whole sample into two sub-periods. The first, which runs from October 1982 to March 1983, includes 27 weeks of turbulence in the EMS: the months preceding the realignment of 21 March 1983, when the central parities of the lira and the French franc were both devalued by 8 percent relative to the DM. The second sub-sample, April 1983 to November 1985, is characterized instead by a long period of calm in the system: the two-and-a-half years from the 1983 realignment up to the fall of 1985, when the market started to anticipate the realignment that eventually took place on April 6, 1986 (and which also implied a devaluation of the lira and the French franc relative to the DM.) The comparison is interesting because, as discussed in section 7.2, there were no big changes in the French and Italian exchange-control regulations between the two periods. The results for both France and Italy indicate that deviations from covered interest rate parity are larger and more frequent before the dates of realignment. Almost every week in the months preceding the 1983 realignment is characterized by a positive value of π_1, signalling that the controls were effective at decoupling domestic and foreign interest rates in the anticipation of a realignment. The difference between the domestic offer rate and the covered Eurodollar bid rate on average was 3.2 percent in Italy and 7.2 percent in France, expressed in annualized percentage rates of return. Looking at the period of EMS calm, the most interesting finding is the frequency of weeks characterized by the absence of arbitrage opportunities: 57 percent of the time in the case of Italy, and almost 20 percent of the time in the case of France. For the Netherlands, throughout both sub-periods, most observations keep revealing the absence of potential arbitrage profits.

A visual summary of these results appears in figures 7.1 through

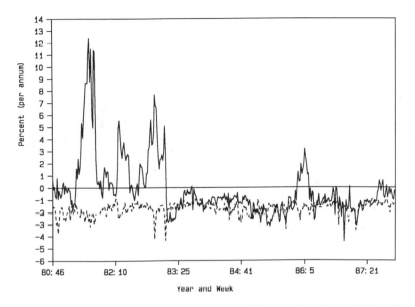

Figure 7.1 Incentives for inward and outward arbitrage—Italy: 3-month Euro-domestic rate differentials.

7.3, which plot the onshore-offshore differential at 3-month maturity over the entire sample. The continuous line is the difference between the offshore bid rate and the onshore ask rate, i.e. π_1; the dotted line is (minus) the sum of the bid-ask spreads in the domestic market and the Euromarket. When the continuous line lies above zero, capital controls prevent outward arbitrage: It would be profitable to borrow at home to invest offshore. There is an incentive for inward arbitrage whenever the continuous line lies below the dotted line, that is when π_2, as defined in equation (7.2), is positive. In the wake of EMS realignments—for example in March and October 1981, in March 1983, and in April 1986—the differential between offshore and onshore rates widens dramatically. In periods of EMS calm, however, onshore rates are not very different from offshore rates. The model we discuss in section 7.5 explores the determinants of these *temporary* deviations of onshore from offshore rates.

As mentioned above, an intriguing aspect of the data for Italy is the frequency of observations when the continuous line falls below the dotted line, signalling an incentive for inward arbitrage: On these occasions it would have been profitable to borrow on the Euromarket to invest at home. This is surprising, since exchange controls are

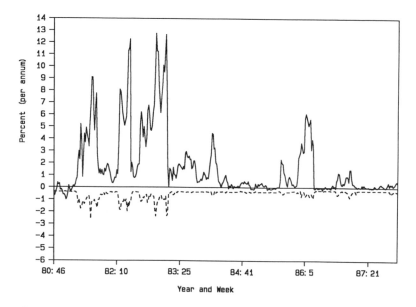

Figure 7.2 Incentives for inward and outward arbitrage—France: 3-month Euro-domestic rate differentials.

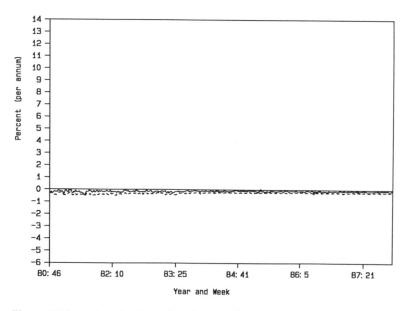

Figure 7.3 Incentives for inward and outward arbitrage—The Netherlands: 3-month Euro-domestic rate differentials.

generally designed to prevent capital outflows. The timing of the observations where the differential is negative suggests however that what we observe may be the product of a temporary regulation, introduced in the summer of 1984[26] and lasting until the beginning of 1985, which prevented foreign borrowing by domestic commercial banks.[27]

7.4 Are Interest Rate Fluctuations around Realignments "Excessive"?

Figures 7.1 and 7.2 show that EMS realignments are accompanied by dramatic swings in offshore interest rates: When the market starts anticipating a realignment, the return on one-month Eurodeposits may jump as much as 30–40 percent. What gives rise to such large interest rate fluctuations? Do they simply reflect exchange rate expectations, or do they imply an increase in risk premia? If the observed interest rate swings were simply the product of the expected exchange rate jump on the day of the realignment, we would expect the volatility of offshore rates to fall as the maturity increases. An expected devaluation of 1 percent raises the interest rate on one-week deposits above 50 percent, but has a small effect on one-year rates. Fluctuations in risk premia are more likely to affect interest rates at all maturities by similar amounts. Figures 7.4 through 7.7 show the behavior of the forward premium on French francs at different maturities around two realignments: March 21, 1983, and April 7, 1987. Figures 7.4 and 7.6 plot the *annualized* forward discount on French francs, which corresponds to the differential between the *annualized* interest rates on Eurodeposits denominated in French francs and DMs. Figure 7.4 seems consistent with the expectations' view. The one-month differential jumps to 100 percent, but the effect is much smaller on 12-month deposits. The 1986 realignment tells a similar story.[28]

Figures 7.5 and 7.7 show how exchange rate expectations at differ-

26 See footnote 14 above.

27 The negative differentials for Italy could alternatively depend on the absence of a secondary market for government bills and, in general, on the low degree of liquidity of the Italian money market. This should explain the reluctance of foreign investors to buy Italian assets even in the presence of arbitrage opportunities. However this cannot be the explanation for the negative differentials we observe in our data, since we use interest rates on deposits.

28 On that occasion, however, interest rates jumped twice: the first time the realignment was expected, but did not take place.

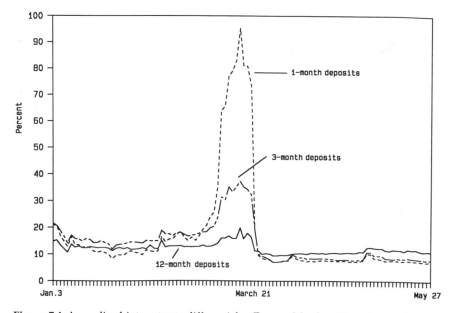

Figure 7.4 Annualized interest rate differentials—France: March 1983 realignment.

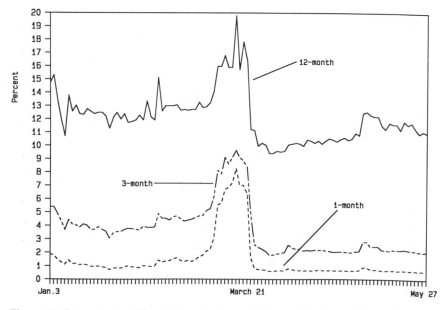

Figure 7.5 Interest rate differentials at 1-, 3-, and 12-month horizon—France: March 1983 realignment.

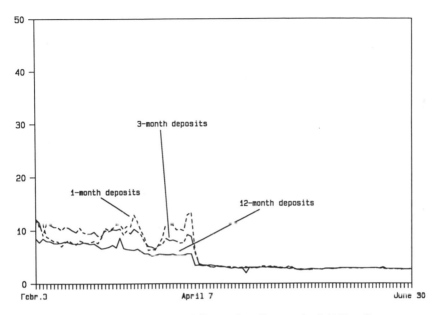

Figure 7.6 Annualized interest rate differentials—France: April 1986 realignment.

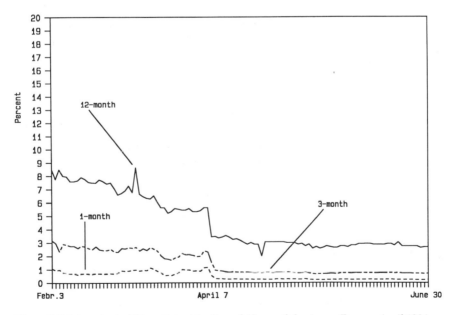

Figure 7.7 Interest rate differentials at 1-, 3-, and 12-month horizon—France: April 1986 realignment.

Table 7.4
Realized returns on one-month investments on the day preceding
a realignment: percent return over one month on a long position in[a]

	DM	French francs	DM	Lire
March 1981	.34	−.66	.92	−1.37
October 1981	2.29	−3.15	1.88	−2.38
Febrary 1982	1.89	−2.30	1.40	−1.76
June 1982	3.19	−3.69	−.21	−.18
March 1983	−4.41	2.54	−3.34	2.32
July 1985	−.22	−.62	3.17	−1.18
April 1986	.62	−1.65	−2.45	1.82
January 1987	−.70	.04	−.25	.29

a. Returns are expressed in percent per month. They are defined as the difference betwen the one-month forward rate prevailing on the Friday preceding the realignment and the spot rate 30 days hence. Transaction costs are accounted for by applying the appropriate bid-ask quotes.

ent horizons move around a realignment. The figures plot the forward discount on French francs at one-month, three-months, and 12-months horizons: the 12-month premium is always above the one- and three-months premia indicating that the market expects the pending realignment to be followed by another one within the following 12 months. One way to verify the expectations view is to look at the ex-post rates of return on one-month positions in French francs, lire, and DM taken on the day preceeding the realignment, when most of the uncertainty regarding its timing has vanished. If interest rate fluctuations reflect an increase in risk premia, we should observe positive returns from long positions in lire and French francs. Our results are summarized in table 7.4. A long position in lire and French francs would have been ex-post profitable in March 1983 and (to a limited extent) in January 1987. The same was true for the lira in April 1988. On those occasions one-month interest rates on lire and French franc deposits were higher than warranted by exchange rate movements during the following month, including the jump on the date of realignment. In all other cases, ex-post returns are either zero or negative, indicating that one-month interest rates on French franc- and lire-denominated deposits were *lower* than what would have been required to account for the ensuing exchange rate changes.[29]

---

29 The term structure of forward premia around the 1983 realignment is studied in

We conclude that the fluctuations of offshore interest rates which we observe around EMS realignments usually are consistent with the exchange rate changes that take place on the day of the realignment and on the following weeks; if anything, they tend to be too small, i.e. to underestimate exchange rate devaluations.

7.5   Interest-Rate Differentials and Controls on International Capital Flows

As we pointed out in section 7.2, capital controls in France and Italy usually prohibit trade in foreign assets for portfolio purposes. Expectations of exchange rate changes affect domestic portfolios only to the extent that firms engaging in international trade can choose the allocation of their assets and liabilities in domestic and foreign currency. As a result, the volume of financial flows in response to exchange rate expectations is limited by the volume of trade flows. In this section we illustrate the determinants of capital flows and international interest rate differentials using a stylized equilibrium model of a small country trading in goods and assets with the rest of the world and subject to constraints resembling the institutional features described above. Dooley and Isard (1980) offer an alternative model of international interest rate differentials, based on political risk. Bhandari and Decaluwe (1987) also study the circumvention of capital controls through the use of trade credits.

We consider an economy populated by a representative, infinitely lived consumer, maximizing the following utility function:

$$\sum_{j=0}^{\infty} \frac{\beta^j}{1-\theta} c_{t+j}^{1-\theta} \tag{7.3}$$

where β is the utility discount factor and $1/\theta$ represents the elasticity of intertemporal substitution. Assuming an infinite horizon in the consumer problem compels us to pin down steady states: We require that the foreign interest rate converges to $1/\beta - 1$, i.e. that the utility discount rate equals the foreign interest rate in the long run. The foreign interest rate in this small-country model fluctuates exogenously. In order to highlight the basic effects of capital controls as clearly as

---

Collins (1986). See also Collins (1987).

possible, we assume that domestic residents are completely prevented from trading in assets with the rest of the world. Since there are no domestic investment technologies available, domestic residents only consume the profits of the firms. This reduces the consumers' budget constraint to

$$C_{t+j} \leq z_{t+j} \quad \text{for all } j\text{'s} \tag{7.4}$$

where z_{t+j} is the net cash flow of firms at time $t + j$. Firms do not reinvest profits, but always distribute them to domestic shareholders in full. The firms' technology is

$$Y_{t+j} + Y_{t+j}^* \leq y \tag{7.5}$$

Firms are endowed with resources y (from nondepreciable and nonre-producible capital) every period. These resources can be used for sale to the domestic market, Y, or for export, Y^*.

   Trade in financial assets with the rest of the world can only be carried out by firms. They acquire foreign assets by granting credit to their foreign customers at the foreign interest rate. These trade credits are one-period securities, with unit price, and coupon rate equal to r_{t+j}^{*t} (the foreign real interest rate). Of the current sales to the rest of the world, a fraction $(1 - \phi)$ is settled with cash, while the rest is exchanged for the one-period foreign securities. The allocation of the given endowment from the domestic to the foreign market, however, is done at a cost that increases (at the margin) with the size of the production reallocation.[30] All domestic sales are settled with cash. The firms' net cash flow at time $t + j$ is

$$z_{t+j} \leq Y_{t+j} + (1 - \phi)Y_{t+j}^* + f_{t+j-1}(1 + r_{t+j-1}^*) - (c/2)(Y_{t+j} - Y_{t+j-1})^2 \tag{7.6}$$

where

$$\phi Y_{t+j}^* \geq f_{t+j} \tag{7.7}$$

We consider a competitive equilibrium, where firms maximize the

---

30 See Blanchard (1983) for evidence on the relevance of adjustment costs in production. Gagnon (1987) provides empirical evidence on the importance of adjustment costs in international trade flows.

present discounted value of future cash flows (using the domestic shareholders' discount factor) and domestic residents maximize utility. In this competitive equilibrium, since there is no net outstanding stock of a domestic asset, the domestic interest rate is defined as the rate at which domestic residents would be indifferent between current and future consumption. From the consumer's maximization problem we have the usual Euler equation

$$C_{t+j+1} = C_{t+j} \left[\beta \left(1 + r_{t+j} \right) \right]^{1/\theta} \tag{7.8}$$

where

$$\left(1 + r_{t+j} \right) = \lambda_{t+j} / \lambda_{t+j+1}$$

and λ is the Lagrange multiplier associated with the constraint in equation (7.4) and, of course, equation (7.6). Notice that, if firms could maximize value also by choosing ϕ, they would be free to trade in international financial markets, and take positions many times the volume of their sales abroad. From the first-order conditions with respect to ϕ it is easy to obtain the following result:

$$\left(1 + r^* \right) = \lambda_{t+j} / \lambda_{t+j+1} \tag{7.9}$$

which implies interest rate parity. In this model, where there is only one good and no money, the equality between the domestic and foreign interest rates is the same as the equality between the onshore and offshore domestic interest rates, which we studied in the previous sections. Therefore, preventing domestic consumers from trading in assets with the rest of the world is not sufficient to shelter domestic interest rates when domestic financial markets are perfect:[31] By reallocating production, firms can carry out all portfolio diversification for private consumers. The implication is that in order to be effective, capital controls must impose constraints *both* on consumers' and on firms' portfolio choices.

Following our analysis of the existing institutions, we explore the case where ϕ is exogenously given by current regulations. From the

---

31 This assumption, implicit in our analysis, amounts to the absence of bankruptcy costs and distortionary taxation.

firms' optimal production and working capital choice, we obtain

$$f_t - f_{t-1} = (1 + r_t)^{-1} \left[(\phi^2/c) \, (r_t^* - r_t) + ({}_t f_{t+1} - f_t) \right] \tag{7.10}$$

where $f_t - f_{t-1}$ describes the accumulation of foreign assets. The parameters ϕ and c play analogous roles in the equilibrium dynamics of international capital flows. While high values of ϕ allow faster adjustment of portfolios to interest rate changes, low values of c permit a fast adjustment of production. In the limiting case where production reallocation is costless, we fall back again on interest rate parity: firms's intertemporal terms of trade are equal to the foreign interest rate.[32] Solving equation (7.10) recursively, and given our assumptions on the convergence of r^* to $1/\beta - 1$, we have

$$(f_t - f_{t-1}) = \sum_{j=0}^{\infty} \left[\prod_{k=0}^{j} \frac{1}{(1 + r_{t+k})} \right] \frac{\phi^2}{c} \left(r_{t+j}^* - r_{t+j} \right) \tag{7.11}$$

Thus equilibrium capital flows are determined by the present discounted value of interest rate differentials, computed using the firms' discount factor, that is the domestic interest rate. Equations (7.10) and (7.11) provide a description of the dynamics of international capital flows in clear contrast to the standard models, based on the assumption of perfect international capital mobility, like those discussed by Branson and Hill (1971). With perfect international capital mobility, stock equilibrium holds at all times; therefore, international capital flows need to be a function of the first differences of interest rates on various financial assets. By contrast, our model implies that capital flows are a function of the *levels* of interest rate differentials, and that these differentials do not disappear instantaneously.[33] This latter implication is clearly consistent with the empirical evidence described in the previous sections. In addition, equation (7.10) naturally lends itself to empirical testing, and provides an alternative framework to

---

32 In this model, Y could actually be negative: In this case firms buy the good from the rest of the world for cash and sell it back abroad for credit, in order to carry out interest arbitrage. The firms' cash flow is positive and allows consumers to purchase the consumption good in the world market.

33 Notice also that the stock of foreign assets follows a second-order difference equation and, in equilibrium, is a function of its lagged value and of expected future interest rate differentials.

equations based on perfect and costless international portfolio diversification.[34] Finally, our model differs in an important way from ad hoc specifications of international capital flows, like that of Gros (1987). In Gros's model, international arbitrage is *assumed* to cost real resources. In our model, the absence of costless financial stock adjustment is grounded in the specifics of capital flow regulations, which prevent private residents from diversifying portfolios internationally but allow firms to diversify, provided that their acquisition of foreign assets does not exceed the fraction of foreign trade established by law.

Do these regulations shelter domestic financial markets from international interest rate fluctuations? This question requires study of the dynamic system of equations (7.8) and (7.10) together with the national accounts identity from equations (7.4), (7.6), and (7.7). In that system the capital flows equation has non-constant coefficients and therefore cannot be solved with the standard techniques. Hence we limit ourselves to some numerical simulations. These simulations were obtained by solving a finite-horizon equivalent of the model, and by studying the effects of an unanticipated increase in the foreign interest rate (from 10 to 50 percent, to match the values observed in figures 7.1–7.3), followed by a perfectly-anticipated gradual decrease back to the long-run value of 10 percent.

In the initial steady state the home-country interest rate also equals 10 percent, and 50 percent of domestic production is devoted to the export market. To explore the role of capital controls, and their effectiveness at decoupling domestic and foreign interest rates, we study the response of domestic rates assuming different values for ϕ. Since ϕ represents the fraction of exports that can be sold in exchange for foreign securities, $(1 - \phi)$ can be thought of as the compulsive foreign-currency financing of export credits that we described above: In this case, all exports are sold for credit but $(1 - \phi)$ of these credits have to be financed by borrowing abroad. Hence the net increase in foreign assets equals ϕ times the value of exports.

In the simulations, we assume that the intertemporal elasticity of substitution in consumption equals $1/2$ ($\theta = 2$) and the adjustment-cost parameter c equals 10. The results are reported in figure 7.8. The figure shows that tightening capital controls—decreasing the value of

34 This framework seems to be more appropriate in countries that impose international capital controls. However, a fully fledged empirical testing of the models we outline in this chapter goes well beyond the scope of this book, and is left for future research.

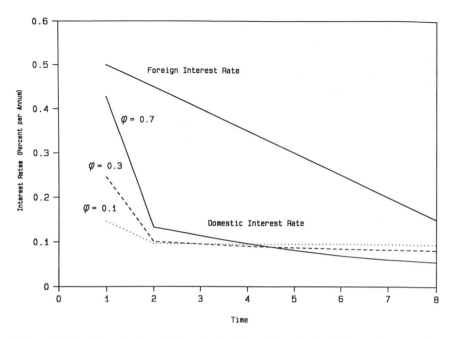

Figure 7.8 Capital controls and interest rate differentials: effects of changes in compulsory foreign-currency financing of export credits.

ϕ, or increasing the compulsory foreign-currency financing of export credits—decreases the response of the domestic rate to the foreign interest rate shock. If net export credits can reach only 10 percent of export sales, the increase of the foreign rate from 10 to 50 percent only increases the domestic rate from 10 to about 15 percent. The initial jump in the domestic rate increases to 25 percent and 43 percent, approximately, when export credits can reach 30 and 70 percent of export sales, respectively.

The sensitivity of domestic interest rates to ϕ appears to be a general result, since it can be obtained under a number of different combinations of taste and technology parameters. However, domestic interest rates are not always more stable than foreign rates under all values of ϕ from 0 to 1. The impact response of domestic rates depends on two parameters. The parameter θ affects the change in domestic rates needed to induce savings and the increase in foreign asset holdings after the increase in the foreign interest rate. A low value of θ implies high intertemporal substitution of consumption and a small equilibrium response of domestic interest rates to an increase in the foreign rate. On the other hand, low intertemporal substitution requires large equilibrium changes in domestic interest rates. Similarly, high values of the parameter c reduce the profitability of international portfolio readjustments and imply that only a small amount of domestic savings has to be mobilized to increase foreign asset holdings: The equilibrium response of domestic rates is—*ceteris paribus*—small. On the other hand, if adjustment costs are low, the large production reallocation requires large domestic savings, which can be mobilized only by high domestic interest rates.

In conclusion, the highly stylized general equilibrium model we used in this section has helped to highlight a few fundamental factors that determine the effectiveness of controls on international asset transactions. We have found how controls on consumers' transactions are complementary to controls on firms' transactions, and we have identified the firms' incentives to use trade credits as a means of international diversification. One important result is that controls on trade credits are completely ineffective if firms can adjust their trade and production patterns costlessly and instantaneously to match their desired portfolio compositions: This implies that any divergences between domestic and offshore rates are bound to disappear over time, as domestic production and savings adjust to international rate-of-return differentials.

An interesting extension of the analysis would be to include nominal variables in the model. This extension, however, highlights once again the importance of the assumptions about aggregate price level behavior. If prices are perfectly flexible, it can easily be shown that expected nominal exchange rate devaluations would be reflected immediately in domestic interest rates.

8   What Do We Learn from the EMS Experience?

8.1 Introduction

When the EMS was launched in 1978, the new plan for exchange rate stability in Europe was accepted with much skepticism. Economists and policymakers still were influenced by the collapse of Bretton Woods, and concentrated on learning how to live with flexible exchange rates. Because professionals were also attempting to understand the working of flexible exchange rates, there was no analysis of the EMS until the mid-1980s. Now, the situation is quite different. According to the conventional wisdom the EMS has been a success: The current debate in Europe has moved on to the issue of monetary unification and the European central bank. Outside Europe, the reform of the international monetary system is no longer an unfashionable topic: "Target zones" and the simple return to fixed exchange rates have taken centerstage in policy discussions and, to some extent, in economic analysis.[1]

There are three views on the future of the international monetary system. Two of them advocate reforms which would limit the degree of exchange rate flexibility; a third concentrates on fundamentals, and rules out the active management of exchange rates. Ronald McKinnon (see for example McKinnon 1988) is responsible for the first set of proposals. He argues for fixed nominal exchange rates. The system he envisages is very similar to a symmetric gold standard: Central banks would use domestic credit policies to peg the price of a common basket of internationally traded goods. Fiscal policy would target external balance: Deficits and surpluses could be corrected by changes in the

---

1 See for instance Krugman (1988a).

level of spending in the various countries, at given relative prices.

The second proposal, target zones, was originally formulated by John Williamson (1985) and later elaborated in Miller and Williamson (1988) and Croham Committee (1988). The central point of the plan is the assignment of monetary policy to a real exchange rate target: Interest rate differences among countries keep the real effective exchange rate of each country within a preassigned band. Nominal variables (nominal GDP) can be controlled by the average level of world real interest rates, and by domestic fiscal policy in each country.

A radically different view seems to be favored by the staff of the International Monetary Fund. It begins with the premise that "a reform of the international monetary system should be viewed as a constitutional change that should not be taken lightly, ... [and] not viewed as an instrument for crisis management." (Frenkel 1987, p. 11.) Policymakers should concentrate on eliminating the fundamental sources of imbalance in the world economy: "The use of monetary policy to sustain exchange rate stability has definite drawbacks as a longer term strategy: monetary policy is no more than a temporary substitute for changes in underlying fiscal positions." (IMF 1987, p. 17.)

In the debate surrounding these proposals, the EMS experience is often referred to. Some—McKinnon, for instance—point to the success of the system at limiting exchange rate volatility. Others—Miller and Williamson—point to the evidence indicating that the EMS has operated as a DM zone, demonstrating how difficult it is to build symmetric exchange rate regimes. Still others—Fischer (1988b)—point to the apparently crucial role played by capital controls in keeping the system together. These frequent references to the EMS have lacked, so far, the rigor of a thorough review of the system, aimed at identifying which lessons—if any—one can draw from this experiment at limiting exchange rate flexibility. Analyses of the EMS have been limited to Europe, and have never been brought to bear on the wider issues of world monetary arrangements. This is the aim of the present chapter.

Two issues seem particularly relevant. The first is the formal resolution of the so-called $N-1$ problem—that is the issue of "symmetry." Mundell (1968, p.195) pointed out the importance of this problem in any plan for the reform of the international monetary system, and Frenkel (1987) has recently reminded us: "It is essential to ask how the various proposals, including those for target zones, deal with the extra degree of freedom." The second is the extent to which the exchange rate system imposes constraints upon domestic policies, and upon inflation in particular—that is the issue of "discipline." The discipline question was central in discussions over the reform of the Bretton Woods system in the 1960s,[2] and has been raised recently by Fischer (1988b).

This chapter draws on lessons learned from our analysis of the EMS experience. The material is organized in five sections. Section 8.2 discusses symmetry. Section 8.3 discusses discipline: that is, can the exchange rate regime affect inflation expectations? In section 8.4 we discuss the effects of the exchange rate regime on public finance. Finally, in sections 8.5 and 8.6 we ask what the policy options in Europe are, and whether the EMS experience is "exportable."

8.2 Symmetric and Asymmetric International Monetary Arrangements: The Historical Experience, the Current Proposals, and the Evidence from the EMS

A central feature of any operational monetary system must be a solution of the $N-1$ problem—namely a solution for the problem that in a system of N interdependent countries (and N currencies), only $N-1$ policies can be set independently, and therefore one policy instrument is redundant. The problem has a symmetric and an asymmetric solution. The symmetric solution "par excellence" is flexible exchange rates: Each country sets its own monetary policy independently, and exchange rates are endogenous. Whenever countries actively manage their exchange rates, the consistency between the $N-1$ targets and the N instruments can be achieved symmetrically or asymmetrically. In the symmetric solution, each central bank uses domestic credit policies to peg the price of a basket of goods in units of domestic currency, and it abstains from sterilizing reserve flows. If exchange rates are fixed, central banks must peg similar baskets, ideally to the price of a single good—for example gold.

In an asymmetric system, the center country pegs the price of a good (or a basket) in units of its own currency: all other countries peg the bilateral exchange rate vis-à-vis the center country. If exchange rates are fixed, the peripheral countries relinquish all monetary autonomy. In a managed exchange rate system, the possibility of changing the bilateral exchange rate vis-à-vis the central country gives the others

---

2 See for example Johnson (1965), p.28.

some leeway in the pursuit of independent monetary policy.[3]

The current proposals for reform of international monetary arrangements all envisage symmetric solutions to the $N-1$ problem. The McKinnon plan resembles a symmetric gold standard. The target zone proposal also calls for symmetry in the management of world monetary policy: "We reject the idea that any one country should in effect use the level of world interest rates solely for its own purposes." (Croham Committee 1988, p. 50.) These blueprints of symmetric exchange rate systems contrast sharply with the historical experience.

In *the Bretton Woods system*, as discussed in chapters 1 and 2, the $N-1$ problem was solved asymmetrically. Although the numeraire of the system was gold, and thus it was theoretically possible to affect all countries' exchange rates independently by changing their gold price, the *dollar* price of gold was very much regarded as the cornerstone of the system. A change in the dollar/gold parity was considered a de facto abandonment of the system. The role of the dollar contrasted with the ability that countries other than the United States had to change their exchange rates. After the abandonment of the "gold pool," in 1968, the Bretton Woods system evolved into a *dollar standard*: a system in which the United States would choose domestic policies with a view to domestic objectives, while the other countries pegged to the dollar, retaining the right to change their peg.

The international gold standard that operated from the late 1870s to World War I also worked asymmetrically. Triffin (1947, pp. 58–64) argues that the system was less similar to the classical gold standard than it was to a sterling-exchange standard managed by the Bank of England. The Committee on Finance and Industry (1931) concluded that Britain could "by operation of her bank rate almost immediately adjust her reserve position. Other countries had, therefore, in the main to adjust their conditions to hers."[4]

---

3 If countries retain some policy independence, as in the case of flexible and managed rates, the shortage of independent instruments gives rise to policy conflicts. In the managed exchange rate regime the possibility of international conflicts can make the regime unstable, because managed rates give the peripheral countries the ability to control the exchange rate in their own interest and thus against the interest of the central country. This problem does not arise under fixed rates, since international conflicts are ruled out by construction.

4 Quoted in Yaeger (1976), p. 304. Giovannini (1986) shows that the data are not consistent with the hypothesis that the Bank of England followed the rules of the game by using domestic credit policies to minimize the volatility of international gold flows. In

The EMS provides one more example of a managed exchange rate regime that has worked asymmetrically. Although "symmetry" was the word most frequently pronounced at the Bremen and Brussels summits where the EMS was created, and notwithstanding rules designed with the explicit purpose of "sharing the burden of adjustment," the system has worked effectively as a DM-zone. Germany by and large has retained the ability to set monetary policy independently; the other countries have pegged to the DM. Our conclusion that the EMS has worked as a DM zone is supported by the following three empirical observations:

• The institutional features designed to achieve symmetry in the EMS did not work. The divergence indicator does not bind central banks to take action, and de facto has disappeared from the management of the system. The burden of EMS-related intervention is shared very unevenly among EMS central banks. (This evidence is discussed in chapters 2 and 4).
• The evidence on interest rate movements around EMS realignments, presented in chapter 4, also suggests that the $N-1$ problem is solved asymmetrically in the EMS. When the market anticipates a revaluation of the DM relative to other EMS currencies, interest rates increase sharply in the countries whose currencies are expected to devalue. German interest rates, in contrast, are almost unaffected by the anticipation of a realignment.
• The data on exchange rate movements around EMS realignments, discussed in chapter 6, show that at the time of a realignment the DM appreciates vis-à-vis its EMS partners in the majority of cases. However, the DM value outside of the EMS is hardly affected by what happens within Europe. This is consistent with the view that EMS realignments—to the extent that they affect spot exchange rates—are centered around the DM.

8.3   Inflation and the Exchange Rate Regime

An international monetary system may work asymmetrically because of the efficiency of solving the overdeterminacy associated with the $N-1$ problem by allocating the task of providing the "nominal anchor" for the whole system to one country. The center country should be

---

the case of the Reichsbank, on the contrary, the hypothesis could not be rejected.

chosen from those whose monetary authorities have the highest "anti-inflationary reputation." This often is referred to as the discipline argument for fixed exchange rates.

The discipline argument dates back to Mundell's (1968) "optimal burden of adjustment" argument.[5] More recently, it has acquired new fame—along with the emergence of a new and influential view of the inflation process. Inflation is seen simply as the inefficient outcome of a non-cooperative "game" between the public and the monetary authorities. If inflation is just a source of inefficiency, then the inflation standard in an international monetary system should be set by the country where the game produces the least inefficiency; that is the lowest equilibrium rate of inflation. Thus there is an incentive to build monetary areas centered around low inflation countries.

This view rests on the assumption that the exchange rate system can influence inflationary expectation because exchange rate targets are more credible than monetary targets. As we argued in chapter 5, this remains an empirical question. What is the evidence from the EMS?

The EMS has worked as a DM zone: According to the discipline view we would expect the low inflation propensity of the Bundesbank to have shifted inflation expectations downward in the other countries. We found very weak evidence of a shift in expectations associated with the institution of the EMS. Inflationary expectations seem to have adjusted with a long lag: 4–5 years. One explanation might be that learning takes time. Another and more appealing explanation is that some European governments might have used the EMS to justify unpopular domestic policies. These policies, in turn, shifted expectations.

Using the exchange rate regime to justify being tough is an indirect, albeit effective, way to impose discipline. If it worked in Europe—and our evidence suggests that it might have—then it did so under two *very special* circumstances. First, the EMS is just one element of a much richer set of agreements among European countries in the trade, industrial, and agricultural areas. As discussed in chapter 1, these agreements rest on exchange rate stability in Europe. Leaving the EMS is perceived as a move that would endanger other spheres of cooperation as well.

---

5 There is also an influential view (see Johnson 1973 and Yeager 1976, p. 643) maintaining that the Bretton Woods system collapsed when the United States stopped providing price stability to the world economy.

The other reason why the EMS may have shifted inflationary expectations is capital controls. By allowing "weak-currency" countries to fend off speculative attacks against the reserves of the central bank, capital controls have performed two important functions in the EMS. They have avoided realignments during periods of crisis in the system—for example, when the dollar falls. As we discussed in chapter 6, episodes of dollar weakness are often associated with a crisis in the EMS: in the absence of capital controls, it would be difficult to sustain existing parities. Second, capital controls have enabled central banks to delay parity realignments during the disinflation. This has been a crucial factor in forcing inflation convergence, because the discipline imposed by the EMS upon its high inflation members depends crucially on the interval between successive realignments being sufficiently long. If high inflation countries had been forced to realign as soon as higher-than-average inflation (combined with the rigidity of the nominal exchange rate) started hurting competitiveness, then the system would have been indistinguishable from a crawling peg. all discipline gains would have vanished.

In conclusion, despite its popularity,[6] the view that European countries may have joined the EMS simply to buy the anti-inflationary reputation of the Bundesbank is quite narrow. First of all, the discipline argument certainly was not prominent when the EMS was designed. By neglecting the incentives to stabilize intra-European exchange rates, the reputation view overlooks the main motivations that brought about the establishment of the EMS. As we argued in chapter 1, failure to understand the importance of intra-European agreements and institutions may result in a very misleading assessment of the role of the exchange rate regime in Europe.

Moreover, the reputation view fails to explain Germany's incentives. What did Germany gain from the discipline it provided to the rest of Europe? The simulations in chapter 5 suggest that German inflation if anything has been negatively affected by the EMS. We have no general explanation for the incentives of the central country. As discussed in chapter 5, models of credibility and reputation do not provide an answer. A tentative explanation for why Germany might have accepted this role is suggested by the evidence discussed in chapter 3. By joining the EMS, Germany seems to have achieved more stability

---

6 See, for example, the quote from the *Economist* reported in the Introduction of chapter 5.

in its real effective exchange rate. EMS membership has dampened
the effects on the German economy of extreme dollar-DM fluctuations.
This has happened because, since the beginning of the EMS, European
currencies on average have kept closer to the DM, thus contributing
to stabilization of Germany's global competitiveness. This is the opposite of what happened in the early 1970s, when the fall of Bretton
Woods was accompanied by an appreciation of the DM *both* in Europe
and vis-à-vis the United States.

8.4 Public Finance and the Exchange Rate Regime

The model of imported reputation, and the discipline argument for
fixed exchange rates[7], rely on the assumption that inflation is only a
source of inefficiency, arising from the information costs of nominal
price volatility. However, there are other important aspects of the
cost-benefit analysis of inflation. One is the role of inflation in public
finance, which might be particularly relevant for European countries.[8]

Inflation is an important source of government revenue. It should
thus be thought of as just one element in an optimal tax problem,
namely the problem of raising a given amount of revenue at the lowest cost in terms of welfare. In solving this problem, the distortions
induced by inflation should be traded off with those induced by regu-
lar taxes.[9] The extent to which governments generate revenue through
the seignorage attached to money creation varies across Europe. Table 8.1 documents the importance of seignorage among the sources of
government revenue in the EEC. The data show clearly that countries
where seignorage revenue is highest are also countries where revenue
from other forms of taxation is lowest. Seignorage accounts for 10 percent of total government revenue in Portugal and Greece, 9 percent in
Spain, and 6 percent in Italy; these are also the countries where the
share of tax revenue (net of seignorage) in GDP is the lowest. In the
rest of Europe, seignorage accounts for one percent at most of total
revenue (2 percent in Ireland).

Low tax revenues often reflect the structure of the economy; it is not

---

7 For a recent restatement of this argument, see Obstfeld (1985).
8 Dornbusch (1988a,b) points to the public finance role of inflation as an important
factor in choosing an exchange rate regime for Europe.
9 The role of seignorage in the design of optimal exchange rate regimes is discussed in
Fischer (1983).

Table 8.1
The importance of seignorage among total tax revenues in Europe

	Tax revenues excluding seignorage (% GDP)	Seignorage		
		(% GDP)		(% of total tax revenues)
	1984–86	1971–78	1979–87	1979–87
Portugal	32.0	4.2	3.4	10.0
Greece	35.6	3.0	3.5	9.6
Spain	29.5	2.1	3.2	9.3
Italy	35.3	3.4	2.1	6.4
Ireland	39.5	n.a.	0.9	2.3
France	44.4	0.8	0.5	1.3
Germany	37.6	0.9	0.3	0.7
Belgium	46.1	1.0	0.2	0.4
Netherlands	45.2	0.5	0.5	0.9
Denmark	49.0	0.3	0.3	0.9
U. K.	38.5	0.8	0.1	0.3

Sources and definitions:
Seignorage is the change in the monetary base (line 14 from: International Monetary Fund, *International Financial Statistics*), as in Fischer (1983).
Tax revenues are from OECD: *Revenue Statistics of OECD Member Countries*, Paris, OECD, 1987. They refer to total tax revenues, including taxes on personal and corporation income, employers' and employees' Social Security contributions, property taxes, consumption taxes, and excises.

clear whether they could be raised very fast. They are often associated with a narrow tax base, rather than with lower-than-average tax rates.[10] In some countries a substitution of seignorage for other forms of taxation may not be possible without further adding to the distor-

---

10 In discussing the Greek economy, for example, the OECD writes: "There is [in Greece] a relatively heavy tax burden on incomes and transactions that are easily taxable (wages and salaries, purchases of cars and some consumer durables, real estate and inheritance transactions.) Tax evasion and avoidance are partly responsible, but the most important factor is the structure of the economy characterized by a large share of agriculture in GDP (18 percent), and of self-employment in the non-agricultural labour force (33 percent)." (OECD, *Economic Survey of Greece*, 1987.) The case of Portugal is similar: "Low tax yield is attributable to the narrowness of the tax-base, which is not unrelated to the high marginal tax-rates." (OECD, *Economic Survey of Portugal*, 1986.) Barro (1988) points out that inflation may be the only way of taxing economic activity in the underground economy.

tions of the tax system. Differences in fiscal structures thus justify differences in the "optimal" revenue from seignorage. In all likelihood the "optimal" inflation rate is not the same across Europe; it is therefore surprising that European countries may have passively accepted the inflation rate autonomously chosen by the Bundesbank. As we show in the next section, countries other than Germany have accepted the inflation targets of the Bundesbank, but, at the same time, have used administrative controls as a substitute for the possibility of choosing their own preferred long run rate of inflation.

8.4.1 Seignorage and the Reserve Requirements of Commercial Banks

The surprising fact in table 8.1 is that disinflation does not seem to be accompanied by a corresponding cut in seignorage revenue. Since the time when Italy joined the EMS, the Italian inflation rate has fallen from 20 to 5 percent. The cut in seignorage was much smaller: from 2.7 percent of GDP in 1979–80, to 1.3 percent in 1986–87. Spain and Portugal have also experienced large disinflations with small cuts in seignorage revenue. In the case of Italy, the ability to keep seignorage revenue high when inflation was falling is explained by the *increase* in the marginal reserve requirements of commercial banks: from 15.75 percent in 1976, to 20 percent in 1981, to 25 percent in 1982. The reserves of commercial banks are an important source of seignorage revenue. As documented in table 8.2, intra-European differences in the revenue from seignorage stem more from differences in bank reserves than from differences in the ratio of currency to GDP. The reserves of commercial banks, as a share of GDP, are as high as 12 percent in Spain and Italy, but 1.5 percent on average in the other EMS countries.

Why are bank reserves so much higher in southern Europe? The degree of financial intermediation by commercial banks—as measured by the ratio of bank deposits to GDP, for example—could be higher, or reserve requirements could be higher for given deposits. Table 8.2 shows that reserve requirements are the explanation for the large intra-European differences in the seignorage that accrues from bank reserves. Average reserve requirements are as high as 20 percent in Spain, and 18 percent in Italy and Greece: This compares with 5 percent on average in the rest of Europe. By contrast, the ratio of bank deposits to GDP is similar in Germany, Spain, and Italy.[11]

---

11 The role of reserve requirements in generating seignorage revenue is analyzed in

Table 8.2
Seignorage and the reserve requirements of commercial banks (1986)[a]

	Monetary base (percent GDP)		Commercial banks		
	Total of which	Currency	Bank reserves	Deposits (percent GDP)	Reserves (ratio to deposits)
Portugal	14.8	9.0	5.8	99.2	5.9
Greece	18.3	9.8	8.4	48.6	17.4
Spain	19.8	7.8	12.3	60.0	20.4
Italy	17.5	6.8	11.8	63.2	18.0
France	6.3	4.3	2.0	38.5	4.9
Germany	9.4	5.8	3.6	53.2	6.9
U.K.	3.7	3.6	0.2	45.1	0.4
Belgium	8.2	7.8	0.4	35.1	0.8
pro memoria:					
U.S.	6.1	4.4	1.7	34.3	4.7

a. All data for Portugal are from Bank of Portugal, *Quarterly Bulletin.*

Sources and definitions:
Monetary base: line 14 from: IMF *International Financial Statistics.*
Currency: line 14a from: *IFS.*
Bank reserves: line 20 from *IFS.*
Deposits: demand deposits, time and saving deposits, and foreign currency deposits: lines 25+26 of *IFS.*
Seignorage: from table 8.1.

Thus reserve requirements were instrumental in reconciling lower inflation rates in southern Europe with a relatively higher seigniorage revenue, as is evident in the case of Italy. The ability to control seigniorage revenue through commercial banks' reserve requirements would be lost if common banking regulations applied throughout Europe.

8.5   What Next for Europe?

There have been two important developments in Europe since the EMS began. One was the decision—made in 1985—to "complete the internal market": that is, to eliminate by 1992 a variety of practices

---

Drazen (1989) and Grilli (1989). The Italian experience is studied in Bruni et al. [1988].

that still cause frontiers to matter in the EEC. The plan would create a truly unified market, comparable to the United States.

The second important development was the entry into the EEC of three southern European countries: Greece, Portugal, and Spain. These two events confront Europe with choices that are apparently incompatible: flexibility to accomodate the new entrants and an acceleration of the integration process to complete the internal market. Parallel to these choices, two views have emerged on the future of the EEC. One calls for *widening* the integration process; another for making it *deeper*.[12] In this section we discuss these views and ask what lies ahead for Europe.

The entry of Greece, Portugal, and Spain has made the EEC much less homogeneous. Over the next fifteen years the labor force will be essentially stationary in the nine original members (+0.09 percent per year), but will grow by three-quarters of one percent per year in the three southern countries. Starting conditions are also quite different: the average unemployment rate is 11 percent in the nine original members and 18 percent on average in the three southern countries.[13] Regional imbalances also have become wider as a result of the enlargement of the Community. The dispersion of unemployment rates has increased by 50 percent: the standard deviation of regional unemployment rates was twice as large in Europe as in the United States before the enlargement—now it is three times as large.[14] Unemployment is just one side of the picture. Fiscal structures, as documented in section 8.4, also differ widely across Europe. Tax systems are less efficient in the southern countries: as a consequence, governments there optimally rely more on the inflation tax than northern countries do.

The plan to complete the internal market raises very different issues. As set out in the *Single European Act* of 1986, it is motivated by the widespread impression that, notwithstanding the EEC, European markets remain less than fully integrated, sometimes because of less than visible obstacles.[15] Market segmentation is particularly evident

12 This choice is discussed in Dornbusch (1988a).
13 All averages are weighted by GDP shares. Data are from *European Economy*, November 1987.
14 Regional unemployment rates are weighted by regional labor force shares. Data are from the 1988 *Economic Report of the President*, p. 85, and from *European Economy*, July 1987, p. 36.
15 For a discussion of market segmentation in the EEC, see Krugman (1988c) and Smith and Venables (1988).

in the banking and insurance industries: In fact, the high point of the Single European Act is the establishment of a common market for financial services. The plan for integrating European financial markets comes up against the inconsistency between full financial integration and the current working of the EMS. As discussed in chapter 7, the survival of the current system of fixed but adjustable parities must be ascribed to the operation of capital controls. However, capital controls prevent financial integration. Thus, financial integration requires that European countries give up realignments altogether, moving toward a system of credible, and thus irrevocably fixed, exchange rates. That is a monetary union.[16]

The enlargement of the EEC and the Single European Act suggest different priorities for Europe. Dornbusch (1988a) advocates one set of priorities calling for concentrating European initiatives on *widening* the integration process and extending the gains achieved so far to a larger area that includes the new entrants. Speeding up the integration of the new entrants is in the interest of the original members. Since the average level of protection of the center countries relative to the periphery is small, integration amounts to opening up markets for goods and services. An example is the recent explosion of Spanish imports from the rest of the EEC: from 37.9 percent of total imports in 1985, to 55 percent in 1987.[17] The integration of the new members requires the extension of the area of exchange rate stability to include the three southern European countries: At the same time the degree of financial integration must be limited. As discussed in chapter 1, exchange rate stability is a necessary condition for being part of the EEC.[18] On the other hand, a low degree of financial integration may

---

16 There exists a time-honored tradition of debates and analyses of monetary unification in Europe. The high point of this tradition is the 1975 "All Saints' Day Manifesto" (*The Economist*, November 1, 1975) by G. Basevi, M. Fratianni, H. Giersch, P. Korteweg, D. O'Mahony, M. Parkin, T. Peeters, P. Salin, and N. Thygesen, The manifesto recommended that European central banks issue a parallel currency, Europa, against national moneys. Europa's exchange rate would be determined so that the new currency would maintain a constant purchasing power in terms of a European basket of goods. The purpose of this parallel currency was to substitute national moneys with a single money of stable value. Currency substitution would have taken place spontaneously in the market, because Europa would have offered a more stable store of value and unit of account.

17 This compares with a much smaller redirection of exports: In the same years Spain's exports to the EEC increased from 53.6 to 60.6 percent of the total.

18 This is recognized by Spain and Portugal, who are seriously considering joining the

be necessary to accomodate different fiscal structures, and to reconcile different levels of seigniorage revenue with similar inflation rates.

The priorities set forth by the Single European Act are very different: a *deepening* of the integration process, concentrated on financial markets. Are the two strategies really incompatible? One way out would be a "two-speed Europe": Financial integration cum monetary unification should be limited to the current members of the EMS. Agreements with the new entrants should not extend beyond the trade area: They should be limited to removing trade barriers. Two problems arise with this compromise strategy. Integration of Spain, Greece, and Portugal into the EEC would be more difficult outside the EMS. The drachma is already part of the ECU, the escudo and the peseta will join the basket in January 1989. As discussed in chapter 2, operation of the EMS is complicated by the presence in the basket of some currencies that do not belong to the exchange rate agreement. Membership in the Common Agricultural Policy also would be complicated outside of a system that guarantees exchange rate stability. That is, it would be difficult for the original members, after having accepted the new entrants, to effectively refuse their membership in the exchange rate mechanism by creating conditions that Spain, Greece, and Portugal could not accept for a long time: membership in a monetary union centered around the northern European countries.

A note of caution on the "financial integration strategy" is also suggested by the situation of some *current* members of the EMS. The three OECD countries characterized by the highest ratio of public debt-to-GDP are also members of the EMS. In these countries, the debt problem has emerged during the EMS years and is far from being solved. From 1981 to 1988, the ratio of public sector debt-to-GDP has increased from 61 to 97 percent in Italy, from 88 to 130 percent in Belgium, and from 90 to 145 percent in Ireland. While Belgium and Ireland have a primary budget surplus—and thus have gone some way toward stabilizing the budget—Italy still has a primary deficit equal to 3 percent of GDP. When fiscal policy turns around, will the optimal inflation rate still be the same in Italy, Belgium, and the Netherlands? Further steps toward financial integration and monetary unification in Europe are closely linked to the issue of fiscal reform.

EMS.

8.6   Is the EMS Exportable?

This chapter began with the observation that the EMS experience is often referred to in the discussions over the reform of the international monetary system. Policy coordination, and the successful attempt at making exchange rate targets credible, are sometimes hailed as important European achievements and examples for experiments outside of Europe as well. By contrast, the logical conclusion of our analysis is that the EMS experience is not directly exportable. A few items should be carefully considered.

• The degree of *policy coordination* probably has been higher in the EMS than under Bretton Woods, particularly during realignments. However, coordination has never been extended to the area of monetary policy targets. As a result, the EMS is essentially a DM zone, and has worked similarly to other regimes of fixed exchange rates.
• The *credibility of exchange rate targets* has been enhanced under very special conditions, unlikely to be reproduced outside Europe. Intra-European agreements, and the EEC Common Agricultural Policy in particular, rely on the stability of intra-European exchange rates. Leaving the EMS is perceived in Europe as a move that would threaten the survival of other EEC institutions as well. Capital controls also have played a major role in making exchange rate targets credible. As we discussed in chapter 7, the European experience shows that in order to be effective, capital controls must be "waterproof": In particular, the ability of firms to acquire foreign assets through trade credits must be curtailed. As the Italian experience shows, small leakages in foreign trade financing are enough to allow large speculative attacks.
• The effects of the recent liberalization in France and Italy confirm the importance of *capital controls*. The old rules—monetary policy set by Germany, the other countries left with the option of either going along with German monetary targets or realigning—are inconsistent with integrated financial markets. No sooner had the Italian monetary authorities removed the administrative controls on export credits (in May 1987) than they were faced with a severe speculative attack. The choice was either giving in and accepting a realignment they viewed as unwarranted by fundamentals, or reintroducing administrative controls. So went (temporarily) the attempted liberalization of leads and lags. Irrevocably fixed exchange rates, reserve pooling, and the setting of monetary targets by a supranational institution—the European

Central Bank—have become urgent issues on the agenda.[19]
• Finally, the EMS experience provides more evidence in favor of the view that exchange rate targets may be effective at forcing the convergence of monetary policies but have no power to force the convergence of *fiscal policies*. If fiscal divergencies are the fundamental source of imbalance in the world economy, then target zones are not a good idea.

---

19 The issue of a European central bank is discussed in Cohen (1989), Thygesen (1987), and Gros and Thygesen (1988). The new prospects of the EMS after financial liberalization in France and Italy are discussed in Padoa Schioppa (1988).

References

Adams, C., and Greenwood, J. "Dual Exchange Rate Systems and Capital Controls: An Investigation." *Journal of International Economics* 18 (1985): 43–64.

Adler, M. and Dumas, B. "International Portfolio Choice and Corporate Finance: A Synthesis. " *Journal of Finance* 38 (1983): 925–984.

Alesina, A., and Grilli, V. "Avoiding Speculative Attacks on EMS Currencies: A Proposal." *Economic Growth Center Discussion Paper 547*, Yale University, 1987.

Aliber, R. Z. "The Interest Rate Parity Theorem: A Reinterpretation. " *Journal of Political Economy* 81 (1973): 1451–1459.

Anderson, T. A., and Risager, O. "The Role of Credibility for the Effects of a Change in the Exchange-Rate Policy." *Institute for International Economic Studies Discussion Paper 377*, University of Stockholm, 1987.

Aoki, M. "A Note on the Stability of the Interaction of Monetary Policy." *Journal of International Economics* 7 (1977): 81–94.

Argy, V. *The Postwar International Monetary Crisis: An Analysis.* London: George Allen & Unwin, 1981.

Artis, M. J., and Taylor, M. P. "Exchange Rates and the EMS: Assessing the Track Record." *CEPR Discussion Paper 250*, 1988.

Bacchetta, P. *Restrictions on International Capital Flows.* Unpublished Ph.D. dissertation. Harvard University, 1988.

Backus, D., and Driffill, J. "Inflation and Reputation." *American Economic Review* 75 (1985): 530–38.

Baer, G. U. "Some Reflections on a Co-ordinated Dollar Policy: The Pivotal Role of Germany in the EMS." *Aussenwirtschaft* 37 (1982)

Baffi, P. "I Cambi: Ieri, Oggi, Domani." *Bancaria* 8 (1978).

Balassa, B. "Trade Creation and Trade Diversion in the European Common

Market: An Appraisal of the Evidence." *Manchester School* XLII (1974): 93–135.

Baldwin, R. "Hysteresis in Trade." Columbia University. Mimeo, 1986.

Barro, R. J. "Reputation in a Model of Monetary Policy with Incomplete Information." *Journal of Monetary Economics* 17 (1986): 3–20.

Barro, R. "Interest Rate Smoothing." *NBER Working Paper 2581*, 1988.

Barro, R. J., and Gordon, D. "Rules, Discretion, and Reputation in a Model of Monetary Policy." *Journal of Monetary Ecqnomics* 12 (1983a): 101–121.

Barro, R. J., and Gordon, D. "A Positive Theory of Monetary Policy in a Natural-Rate Model." *Journal of Political Economy* 91 (1983b): 589–610.

Baxter, M., and Stockman, A. C. "Business Cycles and the Exchange Rate Regime: An Empirical Investigation." University of Rochester. Mimeo, 1987.

Bean, C. R. "Sterling Misalignment and British Trade Performance." Paper presented at the NBER Conference on Exchange Rate Misalignment, May 1987.

Bean, C. R., Layard, P. R. G., and Nickell, S. J. "The Rise in Unemployment: A Multi-Country Study." *Economica* 53 (1986): S1–S22.

Begg, D. and Wyplosz, C. "Why the EMS? Dynamic Games and the Equilibrium Policy Regime." in R. C. Bryant and R. Portes (eds.) *Global Macroeconomics*. London: Macmillan, 1987.

Bhandari, J. S., and Decaluwe, B. "A Stochastic Model of Incomplete Separation between Commercial and Financial Exchange Markets." *Journal of International Economics* 18 (1987): 25–55.

Black, F. "International Capital Market Equilibrium with Investment Barriers." *Journal of Financial Economics* 1 (1974): 337–52.

Blanchard, O. J. "The Production and Inventory Behavior of the American Automobile Industry." *Journal of Political Economy* 91 (1983): 365–400.

Blanchard, O. J. "The Lucas Critique and The Volker Deflation." *American Economic Review-Papers and Proceedings* 74 (1984): 211–15.

Blanchard, O. J. "Empirical Structural Evidence on Wages, Prices and Employment in the United States." *NBER Working Paper 2044*, 1986.

Blanchard, O. J. "Why Does Money Affect Output: A Survey." *NBER Working Paper 2614*, 1988.

Blanchard, O. J., and Summers, L. H. "Hysteresis and the European Unemployment," in S. Fischer (ed.) *NBER Macroeconomics Annual*. Chicago: University of Chicago Press, 1986.

Bollerslev, T. "A Multivariate Generalized ARCH Model with Constant Correlations for a Set of Exchange Rates." Northwestern University. Mimeo, 1987.

Boyd, C. "The EMS and the New Arrangements for MCA Dismantling." EC Commission, Directorate General for Economic and Financial Affairs. Mimeo, 1987.

Branson, W. H. "Exchange Rate Policy After a Decade of 'Floating,'" in J. F. O. Bilson and R. C. Marston (eds.) *Exchange Rate Theory and Practice*. Chicago: University of Chicago Press, 1984.

Branson, W., and Hill, R. "Capital Mobility in the OECD Area: An Econometric Analysis." *OECD Economic Outlook, Occasional Study* 1971.

Branson, W. H., and Love, J. P. "Dollar Appreciation, Manufacturing Employment and Output." *NBER Working Paper No. 1972*, 1986.

Branson, W. H. and Love, J. P. "The Real Exchange Rate and Employment in U. S. Manufacturing: State and Regional Results," NBER Working Paper No. 2435, 1987.

Bruni, F., A. Penati and A. Porta, "Financial Regulation, Implicit Taxes and Fiscal Adustment in Italy," Milan: Bocconi University. Mimeo, 1988.

Bruno, M. "Sharp Disinflation Strategy: Israel 1985." *Economic Policy* 2 (1986): 379–408.

Bundesbank "Monetary Policy Aspects of the Revision of Agricultural Monetary Compensatory Amounts in the EC." *Monthly Report of the Deutsche Bundesbank* 36,5 (1984): 37–43.

Bundesbank "Freedom of Germany's Capital Transactions with Foreign Countries," *Monthly Report of the Deutsche Bundesbank* 37, 7 (1985): 13–23.

Caesar, R. "German Monetary Policy and the EMS." Ruhr-University of Bochum. Mimeo, 1986.

Calvo, G. A. "On the Time Consistency of Optimal Policy in a Monetary Economy." *Econometrica* 46 (1978): 1411–1428.

Canzoneri, M. B. "Exchange Intervention Policy in A Multiple Country World." *Journal of International Economics* 13 (1982): 267–289.

Canzoneri, M. B. "Monetary Policy Games and the Role of Private Information." *American Economic Review* 75 (1985): 1056–1070.

Canzoneri, M. B., and Henderson, D. W. *Noncooperative Policies in an Interdependent World*. Unpublished Manuscript, 1988a.

Canzoneri, M. B., and Henderson, D. W. "Is Sovereign Policymaking Bad?" *Carnegie-Rochester Conference Series on Public Policy* 1988b.

Claasen, E. M., and Wyplosz, C. "Capital Controls: Some Principles and the French Experience." *Annales de l'INSEE* 47–48 (1982): 237–267.

Cohen, B. J. "The European Monetary System: An Outsider's View." *Essays in International Finance 142*, International Finance Section, Princeton University, 1981.

Cohen, D. "Problems of a European Central Bank," in M. De Cecco and A. Giovannini (eds.), *A European Central Bank?* Cambridge (UK). Cambridge University Press, 1989.

Collins, S. "Exchange Rate Expectations and Interest Parity During Credibility Crisis: The French Franc, March 1983." Harvard University. Mimeo, 1984.

Collins, S. "The Expected Timing of Devaluation: A Model of Realignment in the European Monetary System." Harvard University. Mimeo, 1986.

Collins, S. "PPP and the Peso Problem: Exchange Rates in the EMS." Harvard University. Mimeo, 1987.

Collins, S. "Inflation and the EMS." *NBER Working Paper 2599*, 1988.

Committee on Finance and Industry *Report*. London: H. M. S. O., 1931.

Cooley, T. F., and LeRoy, S. F. "Atheoretical Macroeconometrics." *Journal of Monetary Economics* 16 (1985): 283–308.

Croham Committee *After the Louvre: Promoting Exchange Rate Stability*. London: Public Policy Center, 1988.

Cukierman, A. "The End of the High Israeli Inflation: An Experiment in Heterodox Stabilization," in R. Dornbusch and S. Fischer (eds.) *Inflation Stabilization: The Experience of Israel, Argentina, Brasil, Bolivia, and Mexico*. Cambridge, Mass. MIT Press.

Cumby, R. E. "Is It Risk?" *Journal of Monetary Economics* 22 (1988): 279–299.

Cumby, R. E. and Obstfeld, M. "A Note on Exchange-Rate Expectations and Nominal Interest Differentials: A Test of the Fisher Hypothesis." *Journal of Finance* 36 (1981): 697–704.

Cumby, R. E., and Obstfeld, M. "International Interest Rate and Price Level Linkages under Flexible Exchange Rates: A Review of Recent Evidence," in J. F. O. Bilson and R. C. Marston (eds.) *Exchange Rate Theory and Practice*. Chicago: University of Chicago Press, 1984.

De Cecco, M. "The Italian Payments Crisis of 1963–64," in R. A. Mundell and A. Swoboda (eds.) *Monetary Problems of the International Economy*. Chicago: University of Chicago Press, 1969.

De Grauwe, P. "The Interaction of Monetary Policy in a Group of European Countries." *Journal of International Economics* 5 (1975a): 207–228.

De Grauwe, P. "International Capital Flows and Portfolio Equilibrium: Comment." *Journal of Political Economy* 83 (1975b): 1077–1080.

De Grauwe, P. "International Trade and Economic Growth in the European Monetary System." University of Leuven. Mimeo, 1986.

De Grauwe, P., and Bellefroid, B. "Long-Run Exchange Rate Variability and International Trade." Paper prepared for the NBER/AEI Conference on Real Financial Linkages in Open Economies, January 1986.

De Grauwe, P., and Verfaille, G. "Exchange Rate Variability, Misalignment, and the European Monetary System." Paper prepared for the NBER Conference on Exchange Rate Misalignment, May 1987.

de Vries, M. G. "The Par Value System: An Overview," in J. K. Horsefield (ed.) *The IMF, 1946–65*, Vol. II. Washington D.C.: International Monetary Fund, 1969.

Decaluwe, B. "The Two Tier Exchange Market in Belgium." *Kredit und Kapital Beihefte* 3 (1977).

Delbeque, B. "A Model of Dual Exchange Rates." University of Pennsylvania. Mimeo, 1987.

Dennis, G., and Nellis, J. "The EMS and UK Membership: Five Years On." *Lloyds Bank Review* (1984)

Dixit, A. "Entry and Exit Decisions of Firms under Fluctuating Real Exchange Rates." Princeton University. Mimeo, 1987.

Dooley, M., and Isard, P. "Capital Controls, Political Risk, and Deviations from Interest Rate Parity." *Journal of Political Economy* 88 (1980): 370–384.

Dornbusch, R. "Stabilization Policies in Developing Countries: What Have We Learned?" *World Development* 10 (1982a): 701–708.

Dornbusch, R. "Exchange Risk and the Macroeconomics of Exchange Rate Determination," in R. Hawkins, R. Levich and C. Wihlborg (eds.) *The Internationalization of Financial Markets and National Economic Policy*. Greenwich, Connecticut: JAI Press, 1982b.

Dornbusch, R. "Inflation, Exchange Rates, and Stabilization." *Essays in International Finance* 165, International Finance Section, Princeton University, 1986a.

Dornbusch, R. "Special Exchange Rates for Capital Account Transactions." *The World Bank Economic Review* 1 (1986b): 3–33.

Dornbusch, R. "Money and Finance in European Integration," in *Money and Finance in European Integration*. Geneva: EFTA, 1988a.

Dornbusch, R. "The EMS, the Dollar and the Yen," in F. Giavazzi, S. Micossi and M. Miller (eds.) *The European Monetary System*. Cambridge (UK): Cambridge University Press, 1988b.

Dornbusch, R., and Giovannini, A. "Monetary Policy in an Open Economy." MIT. Mimeo, 1988.

Drazen, A. "Inflation-Tax Revenue in Open Economies." in M. De Cecco and A. Giovannini (eds.), *A European Central Bank?* Cambridge (UK). Cambridge University Press, 1989.

Dutton, J. "The Bank of England and the Rules of the Game under the International Gold Standard: New Evidence," in M. D. Bordo and A. J. Schwarz (eds.) *A Retrospective on the Classical Gold Standard, 1891–1931*. Chicago: University of Chicago Press, 1984.

Edison, H. J., and Fisher, E. "A Long-Run View of the European Monetary System." Federal Reserve Board, Washington, D.C. Mimeo, 1988.

Eichengreen, B. "Real Exchange Rate Behavior under Alternative International Monetary Regime: Interwar Evidence." *European Economic Review Papers and Proceedings* 1988.

Emminger, O. "The D-Mark in the Conflict Between Internal and External Equilibrium, 1948–75." Essays in International Finance 122, *International Finance Section*, Princeton University, 1977.

Engel, C., and Rodrigues, A. P., "Tests of International CAPM with Time-Varying Covariances." *NEBR Working Paper 2303*, 1987.

European Community, Monetary Committee *Compendium of Community Monetary Texts*. Brussels, 1986.

European Community, Monetary Committee *Guide to Agri-Monetary Matters*. Mimeo, 1987.

European Community Commission "Completing the Internal Market." *White Paper from the Commission of the European Council*, COM(85) 310 Final, 1985.

European Community Commission "Second Report on the Implementation of the White Paper on the Completion of the Internal Market." COM(87) 203 Final, 1987.

Fischer, S. "Dynamic Inconsistency, Cooperation, and the Behavior of the Benevolent Dissembling Government." *Journal of Economics Dynamics and Control* 2 (1980): 93–107.

Fischer, S., "Seignorage and Fixed Exchange Rates," in P. Aspe, R. Dornbusch and M. Obstfelf (eds.) *Developing Countries in the World Financial Market*. Chicago: University of Chicago Press, 1983.

Fischer, S. "British Monetary Policy," in R. Dornbusch and R. Layard (eds.) *The Performance of the British Economy*. Oxford: Oxford University Press, 1987.

Fischer, S. "Real Balances, the Exchange Rate and Indexation: Real Variables in Disinflation." *Quarterly Journal of Economics* 103 (1988a): 27–50.

Fischer, S. "Comments to Miller and Williamson." *European Economic Review* 32 (1988b): 1048–1051.

Flood, R. P. "Explanations of Exchange-Rate Volatility and Other Empirical Regularities in Some Popular Models of the Foreign Exchange Market." *Carnegie-Rochester Conference Series on Public Policy* 15 (1981): 219–250.

Ford, A. G. *The Gold Standard: 1880–1914: Britain and Argentina*. Oxford: Clarendon, 1962.

Frankel, J. "Tests of Rational Expectations in the Forward Exchange Market." *Southern Economic Journal* 46 (1982): 1083–1101.

Frankel, J. "Comments on Williamson and Giavazzi and Giovannini," in A.

Giovannini and R. Dornbusch (eds.) *Europe and the Dollar*. Torino: Istituto Bancario San Paolo di Torino, 1985a.

Frankel, J. "The Implications of Mean-Variance Optimization For Four Questions in International Finance." University of California, Berkeley. Mimeo, 1985b.

Frankel, J., and Engel, C. "Do Asset-Demand Functions Optimize Over the Mean and the Variance of Real Returns? A Six-Currency Test." *Journal of International Economics* 17 (1984): 309–324.

Frankel, J. A., and MacArthur, A. T. "Political vs. Currency Premia in International Real Interest Rate Differentials: A Study of Forward Rates for 24 Countries." *European Economic Review* 32 (1988): 1083–1114.

Frankel J., and Moose, R "Are Exchange Rates Excessively Variable?" in S. Fischer (ed.) *NEBR Macroeconomics Annual*. Chicago: Chicago University Press, 1987.

Frenkel, J. "A Model of the Exchange Rate: Doctrinal Aspects and Empirical Evidence." *Scandinavian Journal of Economics* 78 (1976): 200–224.

Frenkel, J. "The International Monetary System: Should it be Reformed?" *NBER Working Paper 2163*, 1987.

Gagnon, J. E. "Adjustment Costs and International Trade Dynamics." Federal Reserve Board, Washington, D.C. Mimeo, 1987.

Giavazzi, F., and Giovannini, A. "Asymmetries in Europe, the Dollar and the European Monetary System," in A. Giovannini and R. Dornbusch (eds.) Europe and the Dollar. Torino: Istituto Bancario San Paolo di Torino, 1985.

Giavazzi, F., and Giovannini, A. "Models of the EMS: Is Europe a Greater Deutsche-Mark Area?" in R. Bryant and R. Portes (eds.) Global Macroeconomics: Policy Conflicts and Cooperation. London: McMillan 1987a.

Giavazzi, F., and Giovannini, A. "Exchange Rates and Prices in Europe." *Weltwirtschafliches Archiv* 183 (1987b): 592–605.

Giavazzi, F., and Giovannini, A. "Monetary Policy Interaction under Managed Exchange Rates." *Economica* 1989.

Giavazzi, F., and Pagano, M. "Capital Controls in the EMS" in Fair, D. E., and de Boissieu, C. (eds.) *International Monetary and Financial Integration—The European Dimension*. Dordrecht (NL): Martinus Nijhoff Publishers, 1988a.

Giavazzi, F., and Pagano, M. "The Advantage of Tying One's Hand: EMS Discipline and Central Bank Credibility." *European Economic Review* 32 (1988b): 1055–1075.

Giovannini, A. "Rules of the Game during the International Gold Standard: England and Germany." *Journal of International Money and Finance* 5 (1986): 467–483.

Giovannini, A. "Prices and Exchange Rates: What Theory Needs to Explain."

Paper prepared for the 1987 ASSA Meetings, Chicago, December 1987.

Giovannini, A. "The Macroeconomics of Exchange-Rate and Price-Level Interactions: Empirical Evidence for West Germany." *NBER Working Paper* 2544, 1988a.

Giovannini, A. "International Capital Mobility and Tax Evasion." *Working Paper*, 1988b.

Giovannini, A. "Capital Controls and Public Finance: The Experience in Italy," in Giavazzi, F., and Spaventa, L., (eds.) *High Public Debt: The Italian Experience.* Cambridge (UK): Cambridge University Press, 1988c.

Giovannini, A., and Jorion, P. "Interest Rates and Risk Premia in the Stock Market and in the Foreign Exchange Market." *Journal of International Money and Finance* 6 (1987): 107–123.

Giovannini, A., and Jorion, P. "The Time-Variation of Risk and Return in the Foreign Exchange and Stock Markets." *NBER Working Paper 2573,* 1988.

Girton, L., and Henderson, D. "Financial Capital Movements and Central Bank Behaviour in a Two-Country, Short-Run Portfolio Balance Model." *Journal of Monetary Economics* 2 1976: 33–36.

Giscard d'Estaing, V. "The International Monetary Order," in R. A. Mundell and A. K. Swoboda (eds.) *Monetary Problems of the International Economy.* Chicago: University of Chicago Press, 1969.

Gold, J. "The Standby Arrangements of the International Monetary Fund." Washington: International Monetary Fund, 1970.

Goodhart, C. A. E. *The Business of Banking: 1891–1914.* London: Weidenfeld, 1972.

Greenwood, J., and Kimbrough, K. P. "Capital Controls and International Transmission of Fiscal Policies." *Centre for the Study of International Economic Relations Discussion Paper 8432*, University of Western Ontario, 1984.

Grilli, V. "Seignorage in Europe." in M. De Cecco and A. Giovanni (eds.), *A European Central Bank?* Cambridge (UK). Cambridge University Press, 1989.

Gros, D. "Capital Controls in the EMS: A Model with Incomplete Market Separation." *CEPS Working Paper 32*, 1987.

Gros, D. and Thygesen, N. "The EMS: Achievements, Current Issues and Directions for the Future" *CEPS Paper 35*, 1988.

Gylfason, T., and Lindbeck, A. "Wages, Money, and Exchange Rates: With Endogenous Unions and Governments." *Institute for International Economic Studies Discussion Paper 370*, University of Stockholm, 1986.

Gylfason, T., and Lindbeck, A. "Money, Exchange Rates, Wages, and Games." *Institute for International Economic Studies Discussion Paper 383*, University of Stockholm, 1987.

Haas, E. *Beyond the Nation-State*. Stanford: Stanford University Press, 1964.

Hajek, J., and Sidak, Z. *Theory of Rank Tests*. New York: Academic Press, 1967.

Halm, G. N. "Toward Limited Exchange-Rate Flexibility." *Essays in International Finance 73*, International Finance Section, Princeton University, 1969.

Hansen, L. P., and Hodrick, R. J. "Forward Exchange Rates as Optimal Predictors of Future Spot Rates: An Econometric Analysis." *Journal of Political Economy* 88 (1980): 829–853.

Hansen, L. P., and Hodrick, R. J. "Risk Averse Speculation in the Forward Exchange Market: An Econometric Analysis of Linear Models," in J. A. Frenkel (ed.) *Exchange Rate and International Macroeconomics*. Chicago: University of Chicago Press, 1983.

Helpman, E. "An Exploration of the Theory of Exchange Rate Regimes." *Journal of Political Economy* 89 (1981): 865–890.

Helpman, E., and Razin, A. "Towards a Consistent Comparison of Alternative Exchange Rate Systems." *Canadian Journal of Economics* 12 (1979): 394–409.

Helpman, E., and Razin, A. "A Comparison of Exchange Rate Regimes in the Presence of Imperfect Capital Markets." *International Economic Review* 23 (1982): 365–388.

Helpman, E., and Razin, A. "The Role of Saving and Investment in Exchange Rate Determination under Alternative Monetary Mechanisms." *Journal of Monetary Economics* 11 (1984): 307–325.

Helpman, E. and Razin, A. "Exchange Rate Management: Intertemporal Trade-offs." *American Economic Review* 77 (1987): 107–123.

Herring, R. J., and Marston, R. C. "Sterilization Policy: The Trade-Off Between Monetary Autonomy and Control over Foreign Exchange Reserves." *European Economic Review* 10 (1977): 325–343.

Hodrick, R. J. "Risk, Uncertainty and Exchange Rates." *NBER Working Paper 2429*, November 1987.

Hodrick, R., and Srivastava, S. "An Investigation of Risk and Return in Forward Foreign Exchange." *Journal of International Money and Finance* 3 (1984): 5–29.

Hogg, R., and Craig, A. T. *Introduction to Mathematical Statistics*. New York: Macmillan, 1970.

Horsefield, J. K. and Lovasy, G. "Evolution of the Fund's Policy on Drawings," in J. K. Horsefield (ed.) *The IMF 1946–65*, Vol. II. Washington, D.C.: International Monetary Fund, 1969.

Houthakker, H. S. "The Breakdown of Bretton Woods," in W. Sichel (ed.) *Economic Advice and Executive Policy*. New York: Praeger, 1978.

Howitt, P. "Optimal Disinflation in a Small Open Economy." University of

Western Ontario. Mimeo, 1987.

Hsieh, D. A. "International Risk Sharing and the Choice of Exchange Rate Regime." *Journal of International Money and Finance* 3 (1984): 141–151.

Huizinga, J. "An Empirical Investigation of the Long-Run Behavior of Real Exchange Rates." *Carnegie-Rochester Conference Series on Public Policy* 27 (1987): 149–214.

International Monetary Fund *World Economic Outlook*, 1987.

Ito, T. "Capital Controls and Uncovered Interest Parity." University of Minnesota. Mimeo 1985.

Jacquemin, A., and Sapir, A. "International Trade and Integration of the European Community: An Econometric Analysis." *Institute for International Economic Studies Discussion Paper No. 398*, University of Stockholm, 1987.

Johnson, H. G. *The World Economy at the Crossroads*. New York: Oxford University Press, 1965.

Johnson, H. G. "Political Economy Aspects of International Monetary Reform." *Journal of International Economics* 2 (1972): 401–423.

Johnson, H. G. "The Exchange-rate Question for a United Europe," in M. B. Krause (ed.) *The Economics of Integration*. London: George Allen & Unwin, 1973.

Johnson, R. B. "Some Aspects of the Determination of Euro-Currency Interest Rate." *Bank of England Quarterly Bulletin* I (1979): 35–46.

Josling, T. "The Agricultural Burden: A Reappraisal," in J. Pinder (ed.) *The Economics of Europe*. London: Charles Knight, 1971.

Katz, S.I. "The Case for the Par Value System." *Essays in International Finance* 92, International Finance Section, Princeton University, 1972.

Kaufman, H. M. "The Deutsche Mark Between the Dollar and the European Monetary System." *Kredit und Kapital* (1985)

Kenen, P. "Exchange Rates and Policy Coordination." Princeton University. Mimeo, 1987.

Kitzinger, U. *Diplomacy and Persuasion*. London: Thames and Hudson, 1973.

Kloten, N. "Germany's Monetary and Financial Policy and the European Economic Community," in W. L. Kohl and G. Basevi (eds.) *West Germany: A European and Global Power*. Lexington, Mass.: Lexington Books, 1978.

Kouri, P. J. K. "International Investment and Interest Rate Linkages Under Flexible Exchange Rates," in R. Z. Aliber (ed.) *The Political Economy of Monetary Reform*. New York: Macmillan, 1977.

Krugman, P. "A Model of Balance-of-Payments Crises." *Journal of Money, Credit and Banking* 11 (1979): 311– 325.

Krugman, P. "Rationale for Capital Controls." Paper presented at the Seminar on Exchange Controls in Bogota, 1987.

Krugman, P. "Target Zones and Exchange Rate Dynamics." *NBER Working Paper 2481*, 1988a.

Krugman, P. "Deindustrialization, Reindustrialization, and the Real Exchange Rate."*NBER Working Paper 2586*, 1988b.

Krugman, P. "EFTA and 1992." MIT. Mimeo, 1988.

Krugman, P. *Exchange Rate Instability*. Cambridge, Mass.: MIT Press, 1989.

Krugman, P., and Baldwin, R. "The Persistence of the U.S. Trade Deficit." *Brookings Papers on Economic Activity* II (1987): 1–55.

Kydland, F. E., and Prescott, E. C. "Rules Rather than Discretion: The Inconsistency of Optimal Plans." *Journal of Political Economy* 85 (1977): 473–491.

Lindberg, L. N. *The Political Dynamics of European Economic Integration*. Stanford: Stanford University Press, 1963.

Lucas, R. E., Jr. "Some International Evidence on Output-Inflation Tradeoffs." *American Economic Review* 63 (1973): 326–334.

Lucas, R. E., Jr. "Econometric Policy Evaluation: A Critique," in K. Brunner and A. Meltzer (eds.) *The Phillips Curve and Labor Markets*. Carnegie-Rochester Conference Series on Public Policy 1 (1976): 19–46.

Lucas, R. E., Jr. "Interest Rates and Currency Prices in a Two-Country World." *Journal of Monetary Economics* 10 (1982): 335–359.

Ludlow, P. *The Making of the European Monetary System: A Case Study of the Politics of the European Community*. London: Butterworth Scientific, 1982.

Maddala, G. S. *Econometrics*. New York: McGraw Hill, 1977.

Marston, R. C. "Cross Country Evidence of Sterilization, Reserve Currencies, and Foreign Exchange Intervention." *Journal of International Economics* 10 (1980): 63–78.

Marston, R. C. "Financial Disturbances and the Effects of an Exchange Rate Union," in J. P. Bhandari (ed.) *Exchange Rate Management Under Uncertainty*, Cambridge, Mass.: MIT Press, 1985.

Marston, R. C. "Exchange Rate Policy Reconsidered," in M. Feldstein (ed.) *International Economic Cooperation*. Chicago: University of Chicago Press, 1988.

Masera, R. S. "The First Two Years of the EMS: The Exchange Rate Experience." *Banca Nazionale del Lavoro Quarterly Review* 138 (1981): 271–296.

Masera, R. *L'Unificazione Monetaria e lo SME*. Bologna: Il Mulino, 1987.

Mastropasqua, C., Micossi, S., and Rinaldi, R. "Intervention, Sterilization, and Monetary Policy in EMS Countries (1979–1987)," in F. Giavazzi, S. Micossi, and M. Miller (eds.) *European Monetary System*. Cambridge (UK): Cambridge

University Press, 1988.

Mayes, D. G. "The Effects of Economic Integration on Trade." *Journal of Common Market Studies* XVII (1978): 125.

Mayshar, J. "On Divergence of Opinion and Imperfections in Capital Markets." *American Economic Review* 73 (1983): 114–128.

McKinnon, R. "Monetary and Exchange Rate Policies for International Financial Stability." *Journal of Economic Perspectives* 2, 1 (1988): 83–103.

Melitz, J. "The Welfare Case for the European Monetary System." *Journal of International Money and Finance* 4 (1985): 485–506.

Melitz, J. "Monetary Discipline, Germany, and the European Monetary System," in F. Giavazzi, S. Micossi, and M. Miller (eds.) *European Monetary System*. Cambridge (UK): Cambridge University Press, 1988.

Micossi, S. "The Intervention and Financing Mechanisms of the EMS and the Role of the ECU." *Banca Nazionale del Lavoro Quarterly Review* 155 (1985): 327–346.

Miller, M. and Williamson, J. "The International Monetary System: An Analysis of Alternative Regimes." *European Economic Review* 32 (1988): 1031–1054.

Modigliani, F., and La Malfa, G. "Inflation, Balance of Payments Deficit and their Cure through Monetary Policy: the Italian Example," *Banca Nazionale del Lavoro Quarterly Review*, n. 80 (1967): 3–47.

Morris, C. N. "The Common Agricultural Policy." *Fiscal Studies* 1 (1980): 1735.

Mundell, R. A. *International Economics*. New York: Macmillan, 1968.

Mundell, R. A. "Problems of the International Monetary System," in R. A. Mundell and A. K. Swoboda (eds.) *Monetary Problems of the International Economy*. Chicago: University of Chicago Press, 1969a.

Mundell, R. A. "The Crisis Problem," in R. A. Mundell and A. K. Swoboda (eds.) *Monetary Problems of the International Economy*. Chicago: University of Chicago Press, 1969b.

Mussa, M. "Empirical Regularities in the Behavior of Exchange Rates and Theories of the Foreign Exchange Market," in *Policies for Employment, Prices and Exchange Rates*. Carnegie-Rochester Conference Series on Public Policy 11 (1979): 9–58.

Mussa, M. "Nominal Exchange Rate Regimes and the Behavior of Real Exchange Rates: Evidence and Implications," in K. Brunner and A. H. Meltzer (eds.) *Carnegie Rochester Conference Series on Public Policy* 25. Amsterdam: North Holland, 1986.

Neme, C. "Les Possibilités d'Abolition du Control des Changes Francais." *Revue d'Economie Politique* 2(1986): 177– 94.

Neumann, M. J. "Intervention in the Mark/Dollar Market: The Authorities'

Reaction Function." *Journal of International Money and Finance* 3 (1984): 223–239.

Nurske, R. *International Currency Experience*. Geneva: League of Nations, 1944.

Obstfeld, M. "Sterilization and Offsetting Capital Movement: Evidence from West Germany, 1960–1970." *NBER Working Paper No. 494*, 1980.

Obstfeld, M. "Can We Sterilize? Theory and Evidence." *American Economic Review* 72 (1982a): 45–50.

Obstfeld, M. "Comments to Claassen and Wyplosz." *Annales de l'INSEE* 47/48 (1982b).

Obstfeld, M. "Exchange Rates, Inflation, and the Sterlization Problem." *European Economic Review* 21 (1983): 161–189.

Obstfeld, M. "Capital Controls, the Dual Exchange Rate and Devaluation." *NBER Working Paper 1324*, 1984.

Obstfeld, M. "Floating Exchange Rates: Experience and Prospects." *Brookings Papers on Economic Activity* 2 (1985): 369–464.

Obstfeld, M. "Rational and Self-Fulfilling Balance-of-Payments Crises." *American Economic Review* 76 (1986): 72–81.

Obstfeld, M. "Competitiveness, Realignment, and Speculation: The Role of Financial Markets." *NBER Working Paper 2539*, 1988.

Obstfeld, M., and Stockman, A. C. "Exchange-Rate Dynamics," in P. B. Kenen and R. W. Jones (eds.) *Handbook of International Economics* Vol. 2. Amsterdam: North Holland Publishing Company, 1985.

Padoa Schioppa, T. *Money, Economic Policy and Europe*. Luxembourg: Office for Official Publications of the European Community, 1985a.

Padoa Schioppa, T. "Policy Cooperation and the EMS Experience," in W. H. Buiter and R. C. Marstons (eds.) *International Economic Policy Coordination* Cambridge (UK): Cambridge University Press, 1985b.

Padoa-Schioppa, T. "The EMS; A Long-Term View," in F. Giavazzi, S. Micossi, and M. Miller (eds.) *The European Monetary System*. Cambridge (UK): Cambridge University Press, 1988.

Pagano, M. "Market Size and Asset Liquidity in Stock Exchange Economies." Unpublished Ph.D. dissertation, MIT, 1985.

Pippenger, J. "Bank of England Operations, 1893–1913," in M. D. Bordo and A. J. Schwarz (eds.) *A Retrospective on the Classical Gold Standard, 1891–1931*. Chicago: University of Chicago Press, 1984.

Rey, J.-J. "Some Comments on the Merits and Limits of the Indicator of Divergence in the European Monetary System."*Revue de la Banque*, 1 (1982): 3–15.

Rieke, W. "Comments," in R. Triffin (ed.) *EMS–The Emerging European Monetary System*. Offprint from the Bulletin of the National Bank of Belgium LIV,I

(1979).

Rogoff, K. "Can Exchange Rate Predictability be Achieved Without Monetary Convergence?" *European Economic Review* 28 (1985a): 93–115.

Rogoff, K. "Can International Monetary Policy Cooperation Be Counterproductive." *Journal of International Economics*, 18 (1985b): 199–217.

Rogoff, K. "The Optimal Degree of Commitment to an Intermediate Monetary Target." *Quarterly Journal of Economics* 100 (1985c): 1169–1190.

Roubini, N. "Sterilization Policies, Offsetting Capital Movements and Exchange Rate Intervention Policies in the EMS." Chapter 4 of unpublished Ph.D. dissertation. Harvard University, 1988.

Rueff, J. "The Rueff Approach," in R. Hinshaw (ed.) *Monetary Reform and the Price of Gold*. Baltimore: John Hopkins University Press, 1967.

Russo, M. "Cooperazione Monetaria Europea: Cinque Anni di Esperienza dello SME" EEC Commission. Mimeo, 1984.

Sachs, J. "The Bolivian Hyperinflation and Stabilization." *NBER Working Paper* 2073, 1986.

Sachs, J., and Wyplosz, C. "The Economic Consequences of President Mitterand." *Economic Policy* 2 (1986): 261–313.

Salop, J. "The Divergence Indicator: A Technical Note." *IMF Staff Papers* 28 (1981): 682–97.

Sargent, T. J. "The Observational Equivalence of Natural and Unnatural Rate Theories of Macroeconomics." *Journal of Political Economy* 84 (1976): 631–640.

Sargent, T. J., and Wallace, N. "Rational Expectations and the Theory of Economic Policy." *Journal of Monetary Economics* 2 (1976): 169–184.

Scholl, F. "Praktische Erfahrungen mit dem Europaischen Wahrungssystem," in W. Ehrlicher and R. Richter (eds.) *Probleme der Wahrungspolitik*. Berlin, 1981.

Sebastian, M. "Fixed Exchange Rates and Non-Cooperative Monetary Policies." Unpublished Ph.D. dissertation, University of Minnesota, 1985.

Sims, C. "Macroeconomics and Reality." *Econometrica* 48 (1980): 1–49.

Smith, M. A. M., and Venables, A. "Completing the Internal Market in the European Community: Some Industry Simulations." *CEPR Discussion Paper* 233, 1988.

Solomon, R. *The International Monetary System, 1945–1976. An Insider's View*. New York: Harper and Row, 1977.

Spaventa, L. "Algebraic Properties and Economic Improperties of the 'Indicator of Divergence' in the European Monetary System," in R. Cooper et al. (eds.) *The International Monetary System under Flexible Exchange Rates–Essays in Honor of Robert Triffin*. Cambridge, Mass.: Ballinger, 1982.

Stockman, A. C. "Real Exchange Rates under Alternative Nominal Exchange Rate Systems." *Journal of International Money and Finance* 2 (1983): 147–166.

Stockman, A. C. "Exchange Rate Systems and Relative Prices." *Journal of Policy Modeling* 9 (1987a): 245–256.

Stockman, A. C. "Real Exchange Rate Variability under Pegged and Floating Nominal Exchange Rate Systems: An Equilibrium Theory." University of Rochester. Mimeo, 1987b.

Stockman, A. C. "Sectoral and National Aggregate Disturbances to Industrial Output in Seven European Countries." *NBER Working Paper 2313*, 1987c.

Stockman, A. C. "Real Exchange Rate Variability under Pegged and Floating Exchange Rate Systems: An Equilibrium Theory." Unversity of Rochester. Mimeo, 1988

Stockman, A. C., and Hernandez, D. "Exchange Controls, Capital Controls, and International Financial Markets." *American Economic Review* 78 (1988): 362–374.

Stockman, A. C., and Svensson, L. E. O. "Capital Flows, Investment and Exchange Rates." *Journal of Monetary Economics*, 19 (1987): 171–202.

Stultz, R. M. "On the Effects of Barriers to International Investment." *Journal of Finance* 36 (1981): 923–936.

Svensson, L. E. O. "Currency Prices, Terms of Trade, and Interest Rates." *Journal of International Economics* 18 (1985): 17–41.

Thiel, E. "Macroeconomic Policy and Coordination: A View from Germany." Paper presented at the NBER Interdisciplinary Conference on the Political Economy of International Macroeconomic Policy Coordination, November 1987.

Thygesen, N. "The Emerging European Monetary System: Precursors, First Steps and Policy Options," in R. Triffin (ed.) *EMS–The Emerging European Monetary System.* Offprint from the Bulletin of the National Bank of Belgium LIV,I (1979).

Thygesen, N. "Are Monetary Policies and Performances Converging?" *Banca Nazionale del Lavoro Quarterly Review* 138 (1981): 297–326.

Thygesen, N. "Decentralization and Accountability within the Central Bank: Any Lessons from the U. S. Experience for the Potential Organization of a European Central Bank Institution." University of Copenhagen. Mimeo, 1987.

Tornell, A. "Capital Controls, Welfare and Reputation." MIT. Mimeo, 1986.

Triffin, R. "National Central Banking and the International Economy," in L.A. Metzler, R. Triffin and G. Haberler (eds.) *International Monetary Policies*, Washington: Board of Governors of the Federal Reserve System, 1947.

Triffin, R. *Gold and the Dollar Crisis.* New Haven: Yale University Press, 1960.

Tsoukalis, L. *The Politics and Economics of European Monetary Integration*. London: George Allen & Unwin, 1977.

Ungerer, H., Evans, O. and Young, P. "The European Monetary System: The Experience." *Occasional Paper 19*. Washington, D. C. : International Monetary Fund, 1983.

Ungerer, H., Evans, O., Mayer, T., and Young, P. "The European Monetary System: Recent Developments." *Occasional Paper No. 48*. Washington, D. C.: International Monetary Fund, 1986.

van Wijnbergen, S. "Capital Controls and the Real Exchange Rate." The World Bank. Mimeo, 1987.

van Ypersele, J. *The European Monetary System: Origins, Operation and Outlook*. Cambridge (UK): Woodhead-Faulkner, 1985.

Vickers, J. "Signalling in a Model of Monetary Policy with Incomplete Information." *Oxford Economic Papers* 38 (1987): 443–455.

Williamson, J. *The Failure of World Monetary Reform*. New York: New York University Press, 1977.

Williamson, J. *The Exchange Rate System*. Washington, D. C.: Institute for International Economics, 1985.

Winters, A. "Britain in Europe: A Survey of Quantitative Trade Studies." *CEPR Discussion Paper 110*, 1986.

Wyplosz, C. "The Swinging Dollar: Is Europe out of Step?" *INSEAD*. Mimeo 1988a.

Wyplosz, C. "Capital Movement Liberalization: A French Perspective." *European Economy* 36 (1988b).

Yaeger, L. E. *International Monetary Relations: Theory, History and Policy*. New York: Harper and Row, 1976.

Ypersele van, J. *The European Monetary System*. Cambridge, UK: Woodhead-Faulkner, 1985.

Index